Teach
Yourself
SQL

in 14 Days

Teach Yourself
SQL
in 14 Days

Bryan Morgan
Jeff Perkins

SAMS
PUBLISHING

201 West 103rd Street
Indianapolis, Indiana 46290

Publisher and President	*Richard K. Swadley*
Acquisitions Manager	*Greg Wiegand*
Development Manager	*Dean Miller*
Managing Editor	*Cindy Morrow*
Marketing Manager	*Gregg Bushyeager*

Acquisitions Editor
Rosemarie Graham

Development Editor
Todd Bumbalough

Production Editor
Mary Inderstrodt

Copy Editor
Angie Trzpacz

Technical Reviewers
Ricardo Birmele
Sunthar Rajan

Editorial Coordinator
Bill Whitmer

Technical Edit Coordinator
Lynette Quinn

Formatter
Frank Sinclair

Editorial Assistant
Sharon Cox

Cover Designer
Tim Amrhein

Book Designer
Alyssa Yesh

Production Team Supervisor
Brad Chinn

Production
Angela D. Bannan, Carol Bowers, Georgianna Briggs, Michael Brumitt, Louisa Klucznik, Nancy Price, Brian-Kent Proffitt, Bobbi Satterfield

Indexer
Greg Eldred

Overview

Contents

Acknowledgments

Special thanks to the following people: Jeff Perkins, David Blankenbeckler, Rosemarie Graham, Todd Bumbalough, Chris Denny, Shannon Little, Jr., Clint and Linda Morgan, and Shannon and Kaye Little.

This book is dedicated to my beautiful wife, Becky. I am truly appreciative to you for your support, encouragement, and love. Thanks for staying up with me during all of those late-night sessions. You are absolutely the best.

- Bryan Morgan

I would like to thank my wife Leslie for being the key to balancing work, writing, and home—and my parents, for creating and feeding my curiosity.

To all the hard-working programmers—especially the ones who design the hard parts that work so well they never get noticed. May you find an example in here that will save you days!

- Jeff Perkins

About the Authors

Bryan Morgan is a Software Engineer with Tybrin Corporation in Shalimar, Florida. He holds a Bachelor's of Science in Electrical Engineering from Clemson University. While working and designing with database products such as Oracle, Sybase, Informix, Access, and FoxPro, Bryan has developed numerous applications for the Windows and UNIX operating systems using a variety of tools. He coauthored *Teach Yourself ODBC In 21 Days* and was the Technical Editor for *Developing Client/Server Applications With Visual Basic* (both by Sams). In addition to this, Bryan has performed as a guest pianist with the New Orleans and Pensacola (FL) Symphony Orchestras. Bryan lives in Navarre, Florida, with his wife Becky.

Jeff Perkins is a Senior Software Engineer for Tybrin Corporation, currently serving as a Project Leader and Technical Lead. A graduate of the United States Air Force Academy (same class as Grady Booch), he is a veteran with more than 2,500 hours of flying time as a Navigator and Bombardier in the B-52. He has also been a programmer, team leader, and a program manager. His hobbies include micro-computers (currently owns five) and long-distance bicycling. He lives in Niceville, Florida, with his wife Leslie and two daughters, Laura and Kelly.

Introduction

Who Is This Book For?

Let us answer that question with a story that the person who needs this book will find all too familiar. Friday afternoon, your boss comes to your undersized cubicle and drops a new project onto your desk. This project looks just like what you have been working on except it includes ties to several databases. Recently your company decided to move away from homegrown, flat-file, data and is now using a relational database. You have seen terms like SQL, tables, records, queries, and RDBMS, but you don't remember exactly what they all mean. You notice the due date on the program is three—no, make that two—weeks away. (Apparently it had been on your boss's desk for a week.) As you begin looking for definitions and sample code to put those definitions into context, you discover this book.

The first 14 days of this book show how to use Structured Query Language (SQL) to incorporate the power of modern relational databases into your code. Day 15 leads you through the construction of both a C++ and Delphi program incorporating the use of SQL. This bonus day defines the terms *Relational Database* and *Structured Query Language* (SQL) and provides some historical context. By the end of the first week, you will be able to use basic SQL commands to retrieve selected data. At the end of the second week, you will be able to use the more advanced features of SQL, such as stored procedures and triggers, to make your programs more powerful. Throughout the book, the syntax of SQL is explained and then brought to life in examples using Personal Oracle7, Microsoft Query, and other database tools. You don't need access to any of these products to use this book; it will stand alone as an SQL syntax reference. However, if you are like us, using one of these platforms and walking though the examples will help put SQL into perspective. Perhaps one of the examples will be similar to what you need to finish the program your boss just dropped onto your desk.

How to Get the Most Out of This Book

This book is designed to teach you the many powerful capabilities of SQL. The target reader is the programmer or database designer who would like to study the advantages of using SQL and relational databases. If you are familiar with the basics and history of SQL, we suggest you skim the first week's chapters and begin in earnest with Day 8. Day 2 covers the query by outlining its structure and syntax. Special emphasis is placed upon the SELECT keyword. Day 3 covers operators, expressions, and conditions—things mostly used in the WHERE clause to focus on the required data. Day 4 covers various functions available to you, such as time and date. Day 5 covers different clauses, starting with WHERE. Day 6 covers joins, SQL's way of splicing data from different sources together. Day 7 covers subqueries. By the end of the first week, you should be familiar with all the concepts necessary to retrieve the data you want from a relational database.

The second week (beginning with Day 8) starts with everyone's favorite topic: data manipulation. On Day 9, you learn the secrets of creation. Day 10 has you creating indexes and views. Day 11 covers the important concepts of commit and rollback. Preventing unauthorized access to your data is the issue in Day 12. The concept of embedded SQL, where your queries are tightly bound to your programming platform, is presented in Day 13. Finally, Day 14 brings you the skills required to use stored procedures and triggers and to tune your database for optimum performance. By the end of the second week, your knowledge will be rivaled only by your workplace's database administrator. You will not only have increased your knowledge and worth to your company, but you will also be able to complete the program that led you here to begin with.

Let's Get Started

During this first week, SQL is introduced from a historical perspective. A brief history is given of databases and their usage today throughout the world. Following this, we introduce the SELECT statement. This statement retrieves data from the database based on a variety of options you give to the database system. Also, during the first week, you will study SQL functions, query joins, and SQL subqueries (a query within a query). Although these topics might sound foreign to you at the beginning, examples are given using a variety of methods. These examples are targeted to a wide audience to ensure this book's usefulness to a broad group of people. Examples are given using Oracle7, Sybase SQL Server, Microsoft Access, and Microsoft Query. Care is taken to delineate the differences and commonalties among this wide range of products.

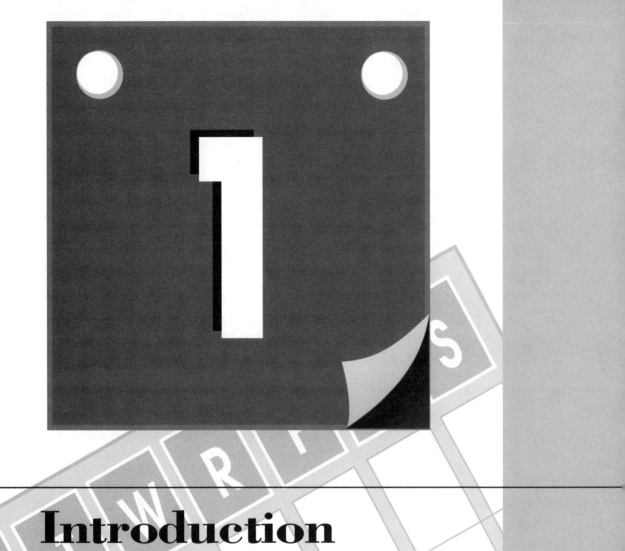

Introduction
to SQL

The history of SQL begins in an IBM Laboratory in San Jose, where SQL was developed in the late 1970s. The initials stand for Structured Query Language, and the language itself is often referred to as "sequel." It was originally developed for IBM's DB2 product (an RDBMS that can still be purchased today for a variety of platforms and environments). SQL differed from many of the procedural or 3GL languages that had been created up to that time. SQL is a nonprocedural language.

SQL is what makes a Relational Database Management System (RDBMS) possible. What differentiates a DBMS from an RDBMS is that the RDBMS provides a set-oriented database language. For most RDBMSs, this set-oriented database language is SQL.

 Note: Nonprocedural here means what rather than how. For example, SQL describes what data to retrieve, delete, or insert, rather than how that operation is to be done.

Time normally spent on designing file input/output can now be used to develop a proper database structure and overall project design. Two standards organizations, ANSI (the American National Standards Organization) and ISO (the International Standards Organization), currently promote SQL standards to industry. The ANSI-92 standard is the standard for the SQL used throughout this book. Although these standard-making bodies prepare standards for database system designers to follow, it should be noted here that all database products differ from the ANSI standard to some degree. In addition, most systems provide some proprietary extensions to SQL that extend the language into a true procedural language. One goal of this book is to prepare examples using different relational database systems to provide the programmer with some idea of what to expect from the common database systems.

To understand SQL it is important to understand a little about database theory and evolution.

A Brief History of Databases

Database systems are used to store information in every conceivable business environment today. From large tracking databases such as airline reservation systems to a child's baseball card collection, database systems are used to store and distribute the data that our lives have come to depend on. Until the last few years, large database systems could be run only on large mainframe-based computers. These machines have traditionally been expensive to design, purchase, and maintain. With the advent of powerful, inexpensive workstation-class computers, programmers now have the power to design software to maintain and distribute data quickly and inexpensively.

The most popular data storage model is the relational database. This new relational database model grew from the seminal paper entitled "A Relational Model of Data for Large Shared Data Banks" by Dr. E. F. Codd, written in 1970. It is important to understand the relational database model because SQL evolved to service its concepts. Dr. Codd defined 13 rules, oddly enough referred to as Codd's 12 rules, that define the relational model:

0. A relational DBMS must be able to manage databases entirely through its relational capabilities.

1. The Information Rule. All information in a relational database (including table and column names) is represented explicitly as values in tables.

2. Guaranteed Access. Every value in a relational database is guaranteed to be accessible by using a combination of the table name, primary key value, and column name.

3. Systematic Null Value Support. The DBMS provides systematic support for the treatment of null values (unknown or inapplicable data), distinct from default values, and independent of any domain.

4. Active, On-Line Relational Catalog. The description of the database and its contents is represented at the logical level as tables, and can therefore be queried using the database language.

5. Comprehensive Data Sublanguage. There must be at least one language supported that has a well-defined syntax and is comprehensive, in that it supports data definition, manipulation, integrity rules, authorization, and transactions.

6. View Updating Rule. All views that are theoretically updatable can be updated through the system.

7. Set-Level Insertion, Update, and Deletion. The DBMS supports not only set-level retrievals, but also set-level inserts, updates, and deletes.

8. Physical Data Independence. Application programs and ad hoc programs are logically unaffected when physical access methods or storage structures are altered.

9. Logical Data Independence. Application programs and ad hoc programs are logically unaffected, to the extent possible, when changes are made to the table structures.

10. Integrity Independence. The database language must be capable of defining integrity rules. They must be stored in the on-line catalog, and they cannot be bypassed.

11. Distribution Independence. Application programs and ad hoc requests are logically unaffected when data is first distributed, or when it is redistributed.

12. Nonsubversion. It must not be possible to bypass the integrity rules defined through the database language by using lower-level languages.

Databases have historically had a "parent/child" relationship. This means that a parent node would contain file pointers to its children. (See Figure 1.1.)

Figure 1.1.
Pre-relational database.

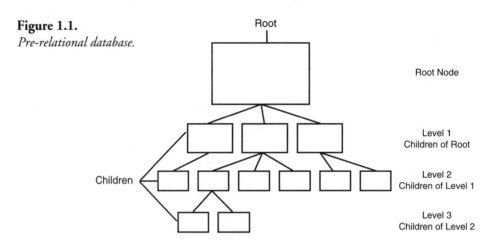

This method has several advantages and many disadvantages. In its favor, the physical structure of data on a disk becomes unimportant. The programmer simply stores pointers off to the next location, so data can be accessed in this manner. Also, data can be added and deleted easily. However, different groups of information could not be easily joined together to form new information. The format of the data on the disk could not be arbitrarily changed after the database was created. Doing this would require the creation of a new database structure.

Codd's idea for a Relational Database Management System (RDBMS) uses the mathematical concepts of relational algebra to break data down into sets and relate common subsets.

Because information can naturally be grouped into distinct sets, Dr. Codd organized his database system around this concept. Under the relational model, data is separated into sets that resemble a table structure. This table structure consists of individual data elements called columns or fields. A single set of a group of fields is known as a record or row. For instance, to create a relational database consisting of employee data, one might start with a table called EMPLOYEE. In this EMPLOYEE table, you might start with the following pieces of information: name, age, and occupation. These three pieces of data make up the fields in the EMPLOYEE table (Table 1.1).

Table 1.1. The EMPLOYEE table.

Name	Age	Occupation
Will Williams	25	Electrical Engineer
Dave Davidson	34	Museum Curator

Name	Age	Occupation
Jan Janis	42	Chef
Bill Jackson	19	Student
Don DeMarco	32	Game Programmer
Becky Boudreaux	25	Model

The six rows comprise the records for the EMPLOYEE table. If a user wanted to retrieve a specific record from this table, he would instruct the database management system to retrieve the records where the NAME field equaled, for instance, Dave Davidson. If the DBMS had been instructed to retrieve all the fields, the employee's name, age, and occupation would be returned to the user. SQL is the language used to instruct the database to retrieve this data. An example SQL statement that makes this query is

```
SELECT *
FROM EMPLOYEE
```

Remember that the exact syntax is not important at this point. We cover this topic in much greater detail beginning on Day 2.

Because the various data items can be grouped according to obvious relationships (such as the relationship of Employee Name to Employee Age), the relational database model gives the database designer a great deal of flexibility in describing the relationships between the data elements. Through the mathematical concepts of JOIN and UNION, relational databases can quickly retrieve pieces of data from different sets (tables) and return them to the user or program as one "joined" collection of data (see Figure 1.2). This enables the designer to store sets of information in separate tables to reduce repetition.

Figure 1.2.
A join.

Figure 1.3 shows the concept of a union. This would return only data common to both sources.

Figure 1.3.
A union.

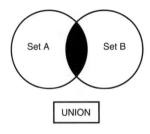

UNION

For instance, Table 1.2 is called RESPONSIBILITIES and contains two fields: NAME and DUTIES.

Table 1.2. The RESPONSIBILITIES table.

Name	Duties
Becky Boudreaux	Smile
Becky Boudreaux	Walk
Bill Jackson	Study
Bill Jackson	Interview for jobs

Note that it would be improper to duplicate the employee's AGE and OCCUPATION fields for each record. Over time this would also waste a great deal of hard disk space and increase access time for the RDBMS. However, if NAME and DUTIES were stored in a separate table named RESPONSIBILITIES, the user could join the RESPONSIBILITIES and EMPLOYEE tables together on the NAME field. Instructing the RDBMS to retrieve all fields from the RESPONSIBILITIES and EMPLOYEE tables where the NAME field equals "Becky Boudreaux" would return Table 1.3.

Table 1.3. Return values from retrieval, where name equals Becky Boudeaux.

Name	Age	Occupation	Duties
Becky Boudreaux	25	Model	Smile
Becky Boudreaux	25	Model	Walk

More detailed examples of joins are given beginning on Day 6.

Designing Database Structure

The most important decision for a database designer, after the hardware platform and the RDBMS have been chosen, is the structure of the tables. Decisions made at this stage of the design can affect performance and programming later during the development process. The process of separating data into distinct, unique sets is called *normalization*. In Codd's relational model, four levels of normalization are defined. Each of these levels reduces the amount of repetition within the database and also reduces the amount of complexity of the structure of the previous level.

Today's Database Landscape

Computing technology has made a permanent change in the ways businesses work around the world. Information that was at one time stored in warehouses full of filing cabinets can now be accessed instantaneously at the click of a mouse button. Orders placed by customers in foreign countries can now be instantly processed on the floor of a manufacturing facility. Although 20 years ago much of this information had been transported onto corporate mainframe databases, offices still operated in a batch-processing environment. If a query needed to be performed, the Management Information Systems (MIS) department was notified, and the appropriate data was delivered as soon as possible (though often not soon enough).

In addition to the development of the relational database model, two technologies led to the rapid growth of what are now called client/server database systems. The first important technology was the personal computer. Inexpensive, easy-to-use applications such as Lotus 1-2-3 and Word Perfect enabled employees (and home computer users) to create documents and manage data quickly and accurately. As sales of these products grew remarkably, technology advanced rapidly. Users became accustomed to continually upgrading systems because the rate of change was so rapid even as the price of the more advanced systems continued to fall.

The second important technology was the development of local area networks (LANs) and their integration into offices across the world. Although users were accustomed to terminal connections to a corporate mainframe, now word processing files could be stored locally within an office and accessed from any computer attached to the network. The advent of the Apple Macintosh introduced a friendly graphical user interface so that computers were inexpensive, powerful, and easy to use. In addition, they could be accessed from remote sites, and large amounts of data could be off-loaded to departmental data servers.

During this time of rapid change and advancement, a new type of system appeared. Called client/server development because processing is split between client computers and a database server, this new breed of application was a radical change from mainframe-based application programming. The many advantages to this type of architecture include the following:

☐ Reduced maintenance costs

☐ Reduction of network load (processing occurs on a database server or client computer)

☐ Multiple operating systems can interoperate as long as they share a common network protocol

☐ Improved data integrity due to centralized data location

In "Implementing Client/Server Computing," Bernard H. Boar defines client/server computing as the following:

> *Client/server computing* is a processing model in which a single application is partitioned between multiple processors (front-end and back-end) and the processors cooperate (transparent to the end user) to complete the processing as a single unified task. A client/server bond product ties the processors together to provide a single system image (illusion). Shareable resources are positioned as requestor clients that access authorized services. The architecture is endlessly recursive; in turn, servers can become clients and request services of other servers on the network, and so on and so on.

This type of application development has produced the need for an entirely different set of programming skills. User interface programming is now written for graphical user interfaces, whether it be MS Windows, IBM OS/2, Apple Macintosh, or the UNIX X Window system. Using SQL and a network connection, the application can interface to a database residing on a remote server. Due to the increased power of personal computer hardware, critical database information can be stored on a relatively inexpensive stand-alone server. It should also be noted that this server can be replaced at a later time with little or no change to the client applications.

The basic concepts introduced in this book can be applied in many situations, whether using Microsoft Access on a single-user Windows application or running SQL Server with 100 user connections. One of SQL's greatest benefits is that it is truly a cross-platform language. In addition, it is virtually a cross-platform, cross-product language. Because it is also what programmers refer to as a high-level or fourth-generation language (4GL), a large amount of work can be done in fewer lines of code.

Oracle Corporation released the first commercial RDBMS that used SQL. Although the original versions were developed for VAX/VMS systems, Oracle was one of the first vendors to release a DOS version of its RDBMS. Today, Oracle is available on more than 70 platforms and is also recognized for its performance and toolset. In the mid-1980s, Sybase released its RDBMS, SQL Server. With client libraries for database access, support for stored procedures

(discussed in Chapter 14), and interoperability with a variety of networks, SQL Server became a successful product, particularly in client/server environments. One of the strongest points for both of these powerful database systems is their scalability across platforms. C language code (combined with SQL) written for Oracle on a PC is virtually identical to that written for an Oracle database running on a VAX system.

The common thread that runs throughout client/server application development is the use of SQL and relational databases. Also, using this database technology in a single-user business application positions that application for future growth and scalability.

An Overview of SQL

From the start, the term SQL can be confusing. The S, for Structured, and the L, for Language, are straightforward enough, but the Q is a little misleading. Q stands, of course, for Query, which—if taken literally—would restrict you to asking the database questions. SQL does much more than that. With SQL you can also create tables, add data, delete data, splice data together, trigger actions based on changes to the database, and store your queries within your program or database. Unfortunately, there is no good word to replace Query with. It is certainly cumbersome to refer to it as the Structured Add Modify Delete Join Store Trigger and Query Language (SAMDJSTQL). In the interest of harmony we will stay with SQL. However, you now know that it is bigger than its name implies.

As you have already seen, Structured Query Language (SQL) is the de facto standard language used to manipulate and retrieve data from these relational databases. Through SQL, a programmer or database administrator can do the following:

- ☐ Modify a database's structure
- ☐ Change system security settings
- ☐ Add user permissions on databases or tables
- ☐ Query a database for information
- ☐ Update the contents of a database

The most commonly used statement in SQL is the SELECT statement (discussed on Day 2). This statement retrieves data from the database and returns this data to the user. The EMPLOYEE example illustrates a typical example of a SELECT statement situation. In addition to the SELECT statement, SQL provides statements for creating new databases, tables, fields, and indexes as well as statements for inserting and deleting records. ANSI SQL also recommends a core group of data manipulation functions. As you will find out, many database systems also provide tools for ensuring data integrity and enforcing security. The concept of a transaction is discussed on Day 11. This provides the programmer with the means to stop the execution of a group of commands if a certain condition occurs.

Examples Contained Within This Book

As we said earlier, this book will stand by itself as an SQL reference. However, we have also designed this book to give you practical software development examples. SQL is useful only where it solves your real-world problems, and that is inside your code. Microsoft Access is a PC-based database management system that is used to illustrate some of the examples within this text. Microsoft Query is a powerful querying tool that uses the ODBC standard to communicate with underlying databases. Personal Oracle7 represents a look into the larger corporate database world. This is important because the days of the stand-alone machine are drawing to an end, as are the days when knowing one database or one operating system was enough.

Personal Oracle7 is used to demonstrate command-line SQL and database management techniques. By command-line SQL, we mean that simple, stand-alone SQL statements are entered into Oracle's SQL*Plus tool. This tool then returns data to the screen for the user to see, or it performs the appropriate action on the database. These examples are directed toward the beginning programmer or first-time user of SQL. We begin with the simplest of SQL statements and advance to the topics of transaction management and stored procedure programming. The Oracle RDBMS is distributed with a full complement of development tools. It includes a C++ and Visual Basic language library (Oracle Objects for OLE) that can be used to link an application to a Personal Oracle database. It also comes with graphical tools for database, user, and object administration, as well as the SQL*Loader utility, which is used to import and export data to and from Oracle.

It should be noted that Personal Oracle7 is a scaled-down version of the full-blown Oracle7 server product. Personal Oracle7 allows only for single-user connections (as the name implies). However, the SQL syntax used on this product is identical to that used on the larger, more expensive versions of Oracle. In addition, the tools used have much in common with the Oracle7 product.

The Personal Oracle7 RDBMS was chosen for several reasons. It includes nearly all the tools needed to demonstrate the topics discussed in this book. It is available on virtually every platform in use today and is one of the most popular RDBMS products worldwide. In addition, a 90-day trial copy can be downloaded from Oracle Corporation's World Wide Web server (`http://www.oracle.com`). Keep in mind that nearly all the SQL code given in this book is portable to other database management systems. In cases where syntax differs greatly among different vendors' products, examples are given to illustrate these differences. Figure 1.4 shows SQL*Plus from this suite of tools.

Figure 1.4.
Oracle's SQL*Plus.

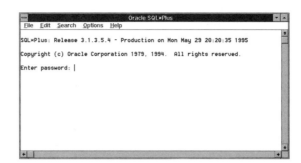

Shown in Figure 1.5, Microsoft Query is a useful querying tool that comes packaged with Microsoft's Windows development tools, Visual C++, and Visual Basic. It uses the ODBC standard to pass SQL statements to a driver, which processes the statements before passing them on to a database system.

Figure 1.5.
Microsoft Query.

ODBC is a functional library designed to provide a common Application Programming Interface (API) to underlying database systems. It communicates with the database through the use of a library driver, just as Windows communicates with a printer through the use of a printer driver. Depending on the database being used, a networking driver may be required to connect to a remote database. The architecture of ODBC is illustrated in Figure 1.6.

Figure 1.6.
ODBC structure.

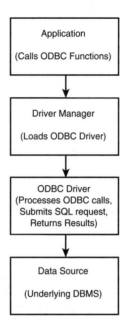

What is unique about ODBC (as compared to the Oracle or Sybase libraries) is that none of its functions are database-vendor specific. For instance, the same code written to perform queries against a Microsoft Access table can be used with little or no modification to query an Informix database. Once again, it should be noted that most vendors add some proprietary extensions to the SQL standard. There is even an ODBC SQL syntax that driver manufacturers are recommended to follow when implementing their drivers. Needless to say, documentation should always be consulted when beginning to work with a new data source. ODBC has developed into a standard adopted into many products, including Visual Basic, Visual C++, FoxPro, Borland Delphi, and PowerBuilder. As always, the application developer needs to weigh the benefit of using the emerging ODBC standard, which allows design independance of code from database, versus the speed gained by using a database specific function library. In other words, using ODBC will be more portable but slower than using the ORACLE7 or Sybase libraries.

Using SQL in Application Programming

Currently, there are two common methods of using SQL within an application program:

- ☐ Embedded SQL
- ☐ Call level interface for SQL

SQL was originally made an ANSI standard in 1986. The ANSI 1989 standard (often called SQL-89) defines three types of interfacing to SQL within an application program:

☐ **Module Language:** Uses procedures within programs. These procedures can be called by the application program and can return values to the program via parameter passing.

☐ **Embedded SQL:** Uses SQL statements embedded with actual program code. This often requires the use of a precompiler to process the SQL statements. The standard defines statements for Pascal, FORTRAN, COBOL, and PL/1.

☐ **Direct Invocation:** Left up to the implementor.

Embedded SQL was the most popular form of using SQL within a programming language for quite some time. It uses what is known as *static* SQL. This means that the SQL statement is compiled into the application and cannot be changed at runtime. The principle is much the same as a compiler versus an interpreter. The performance for this type of SQL is good; however, it is inflexible—particularly in today's changing business environments.

The ANSI 1992 standard (SQL-92) extended the language and became an international standard. It defines three levels of SQL compliance: entry, intermediate, and full. The new features introduced include the following:

☐ Connections to databases
☐ Scrollable cursors
☐ Dynamic SQL
☐ Outer joins

All of these extensions are addressed in this book, as well as some proprietary extensions used by relational database system vendors. Dynamic SQL allows for the preparation of the SQL statement at runtime. Although the performance for this type of SQL is not as good as that of embedded SQL, it provides the application developer (and user) with a great degree of flexibility. A call level interface, such as ODBC or Sybase's DB-Library, is an example of using Dynamic SQL.

Call level interfaces should not be a new concept to application programmers. When using ODBC, for instance, you simply fill a variable with your SQL statement and call the function to send the SQL statement to the database. Errors or results can be returned to the program through the use of other function calls designed for those purposes. Results are returned through what is known as the "binding" of variables.

Summary

Today started off with a quick glimpse ahead to topics that will be covered during the next two weeks. We then covered some of the history and structure behind SQL. Because SQL and relational databases are so closely linked, we also performed a quick review of the history and function of relational databases. Tomorrow you learn the first and most important SQL component: the query.

Q&A

Q Why should I be concerned about SQL?

A Until recently, if you weren't working on a large database system, you probably had only a passing knowledge of SQL. With the advent of client/server development tools (such as Visual Basic, Visual C++, ODBC, Borland's Delphi, and Powersoft's PowerBuilder), and the movement of several large databases (Oracle and Sybase) to the PC platform, the majority of business applications being developed today require a working knowledge of SQL.

Q Why do I need to know anything about relational database theory to use SQL?

A SQL was developed to service relational databases. Without a minimal understanding of relational database theory you will not be able to use SQL effectively except in the most trivial of cases.

Workshop

The workshop provides quiz questions to help solidify your understanding of the material covered, as well as exercises to provide you with experience in using what you have learned. Try to answer the quiz and exercise questions before checking the answers in Appendix F, and make sure you understand the answers before continuing to the next chapter.

Quiz

1. What makes SOL a nonprocedural language?
2. How can you tell if a database is truly relational?
3. What can you do with SQL?

Exercise

1. Compare the database you use at work or at home to see if it is truly relational.

Introduction
to the Query

Objectives

Welcome to Day 2! By the end of today, you will be able to do the following:

- [ ] Understand what a query is and how it is used.
- [ ] Understand the syntax and use of SELECT and FROM.
- [ ] Select and list all rows and columns from a table.
- [ ] Select and list selected columns from a table.
- [ ] Select and list columns from multiple tables.

Background

To fully utilize the power of a relational database, described briefly on Day 1, you need to communicate with it. The ultimate communication would be to turn to your computer and say, in a clear, distinct voice, "Show me all the left-handed, brown-eyed, bean counters who have worked for this company for at least 10 years." A few of you may already be doing this (talking to your computer, not listing bean counters). The rest of us need a more conventional way of getting what we need from the database. We gain this vital link through SQL's middle name, Query.

As mentioned on Day 1, Query is really a misnomer. An SQL query is not necessarily a question to the database. It can be a command to do one of the following:

- [ ] Build or delete a table
- [ ] Insert, modify, or delete rows or fields
- [ ] Search several tables for specific information and return the results in a specific order
- [ ] Modify security information

It can also be a simple question to the database. To use this powerful tool, you need to learn how to make an SQL query.

General Rules of Syntax

Take a look at a common query:

```
SELECT NAME, STARTTERM, ENDTERM
FROM PRESIDENTS
WHERE NAME = 'LINCOLN';
```

In this example everything is capitalized. Does it have to be? The answer is no. The preceding example would work just as well if it were written like this:

```
select name, startterm, endterm
from presidents
where name = 'LINCOLN';
```

> **Note:** Not all implementations of SQL are case-insensitive. So Select or select might cause an error. Check your implementation.

Notice LINCOLN was left in caps. Don't worry about it for now; Day 3 covers conditional statements tomorrow. As for the rest of the line, it would work the same way.

Is there something magical in the spacing? Again the answer is no. The following would work as well:

```
select name, startterm, endterm from presidents where name = 'LINCOLN';
```

However, some regard for spacing and capitalization makes your statements much easier to read. It also makes your statements much easier to maintain once they become a part of your project.

It is also important to note the semicolon at the end of the expression. This tells the command line SQL program your query is complete.

If the magic isn't in the capitalization or the format, then where is it? It's in the key words! In the previous example those words are as follows:

- ☐ SELECT
- ☐ FROM
- ☐ WHERE

A quick glance at the Table of Contents of this book will show you which keywords are covered and in what chapters. If you look hard enough you will find them all listed by name except for SELECT and FROM. Let's cover those two now.

The Building Blocks of Data Retrieval: SELECT and FROM

As your experience with SQL grows, you will notice that you are typing the words SELECT and FROM more than any other words in the SQL vocabulary. They aren't as glamorous as CREATE or as ruthless as DROP, but they are indispensable to any conversation you hope to have with the computer concerning data retrieval. Isn't data retrieval why you took all that time to enter mountains of information into your very expensive database in the first place? How does this work?

Let's start with SELECT, because most of your statements will also start with SELECT:

```
SELECT <COLUMN NAMES>
```

It couldn't be simpler. However, it does not work alone. If you typed SELECT into your system by itself, this might happen:

```
SQL> SELECT;
```

```
SELECT
      *
ERROR at line 1:
ORA-00936: missing expression
```

> **Note:** This is the first error message we have encountered. Each implementation of SQL has a different way of indicating errors. Microsoft Query says it can't show the Query, leaving you to find the problem. Borland's Interbase pops up a dialog box with the error. Personal Oracle7, the engine used in the preceding example, gives you an error number (so you can look up the detailed explanation in your manuals) and a short version of the problem.

Note that the asterisk below the offending line indicates where Oracle7 thinks the offense occurred.

It says there is something missing. That something is the FROM clause:

```
FROM <TABLE>
```

Together these two statements begin to unlock the power behind your database.

Examples

Before going any further, look at the example database we will use for the next several examples. We use this database to illustrate the basic functions of SELECT and FROM. In the real world you would use the techniques described on Day 8 to build this database, but for the purpose of describing how to use SELECT and FROM, assume it already exists.

Sample database: The CHECKS Table

```
CHECK# PAYEE               AMOUNT REMARKS
-------- ----------------- --------- -----------------
       1 Ma Bell              150 Have sons next time
       2 Reading R.R.      245.34 Train to Chicago
       3 Ma Bell           200.32 Cellular Phone
       4 Local Utilities       98 Gas
       5 Joes Stale $ Dent    150 Groceries
       6 Cash                  25 Wild Night Out
       7 Joans Gas           25.1 Gas
```

Your First Query

```
SQL> select * from checks;
```

```
CHECK#   PAYEE                AMOUNT REMARKS
-------- ------------------ -------- -------------------
1        Ma Bell                 150 Have sons next time
2        Reading R.R.         245.34 Train to Chicago
3        Ma Bell              200.32 Cellular Phone
4        Local Utilities          98 Gas
5        Joes Stale $ Dent       150 Groceries
6        Cash                     25 Wild Night Out
7        Joans Gas              25.1 Gas

7 rows selected.
```

 This looks just like the code in the example database. How did this happen? Let's look at this simple statement in some detail.

```
select *
```

The asterisk (*) tells the database to return all the columns associated with the given table described in the FROM clause. They are returned in an order determined by the database.

How You Know When It Is Over: The Terminator

The semicolon at the end of the statement lets the interpreter know you are finished writing the query. Some implementations of SQL do not use the semicolon as a terminator. For example, Microsoft Query and Borland's ISQL don't require a semicolon because your query is typed in an edit box and executed when you push a button. Oracle's SQL*PLUS, on the other hand, won't execute the query until it finds a semicolon.

Changing the Order of the Columns

If you wanted the columns to be in a different order, you could type

```
SQL> SELECT payee, remarks, amount, check# from checks;
```

You would get an output that looks like this:

```
          PAYEE                REMARKS               AMOUNT   CHECK#
          -------------------  -------------------  --------  --------
          Ma Bell              Have sons next time  150       1
          Reading R.R.         Train to Chicago     245.34    2
          Ma Bell              Cellular Phone       200.32    3
          Local Utilities      Gas                  98        4
          Joes Stale $ Dent    Groceries            150       5
          Cash                 Wild Night Out       25        6
          Joans Gas            Gas                  25.1      7
```

7 rows selected.

Notice the use of the comma. Column names are separated by a comma, with a space after the last column name and the next clause (in this case, FROM). This is commonplace in SQL. The statement could also have been written like this:

```
SELECT payee, remarks, amount, check#
FROM checks;
```

Then the output would look like this:

```
          PAYEE                REMARKS               AMOUNT   CHECK#
          -------------------  -------------------  --------  --------
          Ma Bell              Have sons next time      150   1
          Reading R.R.         Train to Chicago      245.34   2
          Ma Bell              Cellular Phone        200.32   3
          Local Utilities      Gas                       98   4
          Joes Stale $ Dent    Groceries                150   5
          Cash                 Wild Night Out            25   6
          Joans Gas            Gas                     25.1   7
```

7 rows selected.

Notice the output is identical. Now that you have established control over the order of the columns, let's change which columns you see.

Selecting Individual Columns

Suppose you were interested in only a couple of columns. You had just used SELECT * to find out what was available, and now you find your interest riveted on check# and amount. You type

```
SQL> SELECT CHECK#, amount from checks;
```

which returns

```
          CHECK#    AMOUNT
          --------  --------
               1       150
               2    245.34
               3    200.32
               4        98
               5       150
               6        25
               7      25.1
     7 rows selected.
```

Now you have the columns you were interested in. Notice the use of upper- and lowercase in the query. It did not have an effect on the result.

What if you need information from a different table?

Selecting Different Tables

Suppose you had a table called DEPOSITS with this structure:

```
DEPOSIT# WHOPAID                  AMOUNT REMARKS
-------- --------------------     ------ ------------------
       1 Rich Uncle                  200 Take off Xmas list
       2 Employer                   1000 15 June Payday
       3 Credit Union                500 Loan
```

You would simply change the FROM clause to the desired table and type

```
SQL> select * from deposits
```

which would result in

```
DEPOSIT# WHOPAID                  AMOUNT REMARKS
-------- --------------------     ------ ------------------
       1 Rich Uncle                  200 Take off Xmas list
       2 Employer                   1000 15 June Payday
       3 Credit Union                500 Loan
```

With a single change you have a new data source.

Queries with Distinction

If you look at the original table, CHECKS, you see that some of th data repeats. For example, if you looked at the AMOUNT column using

```
SQL> select amount from checks;
```

you would see

```
   AMOUNT
   -------
      150
   245.34
   200.32
       98
      150
       25
     25.1
```

Notice the amount 150 is repeated. What if you wanted to see how may different amounts were in this column? Try this:

```
SQL> select DISTINCT amount from checks;
```

The result would be

```
AMOUNT
--------
      25
    25.1
      98
     150
  200.32
  245.34

6 rows selected.
```

 Notice there are only six rows selected. Because you specified DISTINCT, only one instance of the duplicated data is shown, and one less row is returned. ALL is a keyword that is implied in the basic SELECT statement. You almost never see ALL because SELECT <Table> and SELECT ALL <Table> have the same result.

Try this now for the first and hopefully only time in your SQL career:

```
SQL> SELECT ALL AMOUNT
  2  FROM CHECKS;

AMOUNT
--------
     150
  245.34
  200.32
      98
     150
      25
    25.1

7 rows selected.
```

 It is the same as a SELECT <Column>. Who needs the extra keystrokes?

Summary

You have learned that an SQL query is an incredibly simple thing with powers of creation, change, and destruction over the database. It also has the power of data retrieval through the use of the keywords SELECT and FROM. You can make a broad statement and include all tables with a SELECT * statement, or you can rearrange or retrieve specific tables. You also saw how the keyword DISTINCT, used in front of SELECT, causes you to see only unique values in a column. Tomorrow you learn how to be even more selective.

Q&A

Q Where did this data come from and how do I connect to it?

A As mentioned, the data was created using the methods described in Day 8. The database connection depends on how you are using SQL. The method shown is the traditional command-line method used on commercial quality databases. These have traditionally been the domain of the mainframe or the workstation, but recently there has been a migration of these databases to the PC.

Q OK, but if I don't use one of these databases how will I use SQL?

A SQL is also used from within a programming language. Embedded SQL is normally a language extension, most commonly seen in COBOL, where SQL is written inside of and compiled with the program. Microsoft has created an entire Application Programming Interface (API) that enables the programmer to use SQL from inside Visual Basic, C, or C++. Libraries available from Sybase and Oracle also provide a way of putting SQL in your program. Borland has encapsulated SQL into database objects in Delphi. The concepts in this book apply in all these places.

Workshop

The workshop provides quiz questions to help solidify your understanding of the material covered, as well as exercises to provide you with experience in using what you have learned. Try to answer the quiz and exercise questions before checking the answers in Appendix F, and make sure you understand the answers before continuing to the next chapter.

Quiz

1. Is there a difference between what `SELECT * FROM CHECKS;` and `select * from checks;` return?

2. None of the following queries work. Why?

    A. `Select *`

    B. `Select * from checks`

    C. `Select amount name FROM checks;`

Exercises

1. Using the CHECKS table from the beginning of the chapter, write a query to return just the check numbers and the remarks.

2. Using the CHECKS table, write a query to return all the unique remarks.

Expressions, Conditions, and Operators

Objectives

Today you learn the rest of the basic query. On Day 2 you used SELECT and FROM to manipulate data in interesting (and hopefully useful) ways. Today we add some new terms to go with query, table, and row, as well as a new clause and a bunch of handy items called operators. When the sun sets on Day 3 you will have reached the following goals:

☐ Know what an expression is and how to use it

☐ Know what a condition is and how to use it

☐ Be familiar with the basic uses of the WHERE clause

☐ Be able to use arithmetic, comparison, character, logical, and set operators

☐ Have a working knowledge of some miscellaneous operators

This chapter also extends what you have learned about SELECT and FROM, making them more useful.

Expressions

The definition of an expression is simple: it returns a value. It is also very broad, covering different types like string, numeric, and Boolean. In fact, almost anything following a clause (SELECT or FROM, for example) is an expression. You have already used expressions on Day 2. In the statement

```
SELECT (FIRSTNAME + ' ' + LASTNAME)
FROM ADDRESSBOOK;
```

the phrase (FIRSTNAME + ' ' + LASTNAME) is an expression, returning the complete name from ADDRESSBOOK. A useful addition to this query would be

```
WHERE NAME = 'BROWN'
```

which is more interesting. It contains the condition NAME = 'BROWN', which is an example of a Boolean expression (NAME = 'BROWN' will be either true or false depending upon the condition =).

Conditions

If you ever want to find a particular item or group of items in your database, you need one or more conditions (you also need a WHERE clause—we cover that in a few moments). In the preceding example the condition is

```
NAME = 'BROWN'
```

If your problem was to find everyone in your organization who worked more than 100 hours last month, you could type

```
NUMBEROFHOURS > 100
```

Conditions make selective queries possible. In their most common form they are composed of a variable, a constant, and a comparison operator. In the first example the variable is NAME, the constant is 'BROWN', and the comparison operator is =. In the second example the variable is NUMBEROFHOURS, the constant is 100, and the comparison operator is >. Now you're cooking! You need only two more things before you can start making conditional queries: an understanding of the operators, and the WHERE clause.

> **Note:** The concept of selective queries in SQL is based on the idea of subsets. A selective query returns a subset of the data.

The WHERE Clause

The syntax of the WHERE clause is

```
WHERE <SEARCH CONDITION>
```

Along with SELECT and FROM, WHERE is the most frequently used clause in SQLdom. It simply causes your queries to be more selective. Without the WHERE clause, the most useful thing you could do with a query is display the database. For example, using SELECT and FROM you type

```
SQL> SELECT * FROM BIKES;
```

which lists the database

```
NAME            FRAMESIZE COMPOSITION     MILESRIDDEN TYPE
--------------- --------- --------------- ----------- --------
TREK 2300         22.5    CARBON FIBER        3500    RACING
BURLEY            22      STEEL               2000    TANDEM
GIANT             19      STEEL               1500    COMMUTER
FUJI              20      STEEL                500    TOURING
SPECIALIZED       16      STEEL                100    MOUNTAIN
CANNONDALE        22.5    ALUMINUM            3000    RACING

6 rows selected.
```

If you wanted a particular bike you could type

```
SQL> SELECT *
     FROM BIKES
     WHERE NAME = 'BURLEY';
```

which would yield only one record:

```
NAME            FRAMESIZE COMPOSITION   MILESRIDDEN TYPE
--------------- --------- -------------- ----------- ------
BURLEY                 22 STEEL                 2000 TANDEM
```

This is getting interesting, or at least more useful. This example uses only one operator. There are over a dozen.

Operators

Operators are what you use inside the condition of an expression to articulate exactly what you want out of the database. Operators fall into roughly six groups: arithmetic, comparison, character, logical, set, and miscellaneous.

Arithmetic Operators

The arithmetic operators are plus (+), minus (–), divide (/), multiply (*), and modulo (%). The first four are self-explanatory. The last one, modulo, returns the integer remainder of a division. For example:

```
5 % 2 = 1
6 % 2 = 0
```

The modulo operator does not work with data types that have decimals, like real or number.

If you place several of these arithmetic operators in an expression without any parentheses, they are resolved in this order: multiplication, division, modulo, addition, then subtraction. For example, the expression

```
2*6+9/3
```

would equal

```
12 + 3 = 15
```

However, the expression

```
2 * (6 + 9) / 3
```

would equal

```
2 * 15 / 3 = 10
```

Watch where you put those parentheses, because sometimes the expression does exactly what you told it to rather than what you wanted it to.

Let's look at each arithmetic operator in some detail and write some queries.

Plus (+)

The plus sign can be used a couple of different ways. Type

```
SQL> SELECT * FROM PRICE;
```

to display the PRICE table:

```
ITEM           WHOLESALE
-----------    ---------
TOMATOES             .34
POTATOES            .51
BANANAS             .67
TURNIPS             .45
CHEESE              .89
APPLES              .23

6 rows selected.
```

Now type

```
SQL> SELECT ITEM, WHOLESALE, WHOLESALE + 0.15
         FROM PRICE;
```

This adds 15 cents to each price to produce the following:

```
ITEM            WHOLESALE WHOLESALE+0.15
--------------- --------- --------------
TOMATOES             .34            .49
POTATOES             .51            .66
BANANAS              .67            .82
TURNIPS              .45            .60
CHEESE               .89           1.04
APPLES               .23            .38

6 rows selected.
```

What is this last column? It's not in the original table. (Remember, you used the * in the SELECT clause, which causes all the columns to be shown.) What is this unattractive title WHOLESALE+0.15? SQL allows you to create a virtual or derived column by combining or modifying existing columns.

Retyping

```
SQL> SELECT * FROM PRICE;
```

results in the following:

```
ITEM            WHOLESALE
----------      ----------
TOMATOES              .34
POTATOES             .51
BANANAS             .67
TURNIPS             .45
CHEESE              .89
APPLES              .23

6 rows selected.
```

This confirms that the original data has not been changed and WHOLESALE+0.15 is not a permanent part of it. WHOLESALE+0.15 is such an unattractive column heading; let's do something about it.

Type

```
SQL> SELECT ITEM, WHOLESALE, (WHOLESALE + 0.15) RETAIL
        FROM PRICE;
```

to get

```
ITEM              WHOLESALE    RETAIL
----------------  ----------   ----------
TOMATOES                .34       .49
POTATOES               .51       .66
BANANAS               .67       .82
TURNIPS               .45       .60
CHEESE                .89      1.04
APPLES                .23       .38

6 rows selected.
```

This is wonderful! Not only can you create new columns, you can rename them on the fly. You can rename any of the columns using the syntax column_name alias (note the space between the column_name and alias).

For example, the query

```
SQL> SELECT ITEM PRODUCE, WHOLESALE, WHOLESALE + 0.25 RETAIL
     FROM PRICE;
```

causes the columns to be renamed as follows:

```
PRODUCE          WHOLESALE     RETAIL
- - - - - - - - - - -   - - - - - - - - -   - - - - - - - - -
TOMATOES              .34        .59
POTATOES              .51        .76
BANANAS               .67        .92
TURNIPS               .45        .70
CHEESE                .89       1.14
APPLES                .23        .48
```

3

> **Note:** Some implementations of SQL use the syntax <column name = alias>.
> The preceding example would be written as follows:
> ```
> SQL> SELECT ITEM = PRODUCE,
>      WHOLESALE,
>      WHOLESALE + 0.25 = RETAIL,
>      FROM PRICE;
> ```
> Isn't diversity interesting? Check your implementation.

You might be wondering what use aliasing is if you are not using command-line SQL. Fair enough. Have you ever wondered how report builders work? Someday, when you are asked to write a report generator, you will remember this and not spend weeks reinventing what Dr. Codd and IBM have wrought.

In some implementations of SQL the plus sign does double duty as a character operator. You see that side of plus in a few pages.

Minus (–)

Minus also has two uses. It can be used to change the sign of a number. For example, starting with the table HILOW

```
SQL> SELECT * FROM HILOW;
```

```
STATE        HIGHTEMP   LOWTEMP
-----------  ---------- -------
CA                 -50      120
FL                  20      110
LA                  15       99
ND                 -70      101
NE                 -60      100
```

You can manipulate the data using

```
SQL> SELECT STATE, -HIGHTEMP LOWS, -LOWTEMP HIGHS
         FROM HILOW;
```

```
STATE           LOWS      HIGHS
-----------  --------  ---------
CA                50       -120
FL               -20       -110
LA               -15        -99
ND                70       -101
NE                60       -100
```

Notice the use of aliases to correct my mis-entered data. This technique is handy (how would you like to reenter thousand of records?), but you learn better tricks in Chapter 8.

The other obvious use of the minus is to subtract one column from another. For example

```
SQL> SELECT STATE,
  2  HIGHTEMP LOWS,
  3  LOWTEMP HIGHS,
  4  (LOWTEMP - HIGHTEMP) DIFFERENCE
  5  FROM HILOW;
```

```
STATE           LOWS     HIGHS  DIFFERENCE
-----------  --------  --------- -----------
CA               -50       120        170
FL                20       110         90
LA                15        99         84
ND               -70       101        171
NE               -60       100        160
```

Note: Where did these line numbers come from? They were added by the SQL engine. I typed in the following code.

```
SQL> SELECT STATE,
   HIGHTEMP LOWS,
   LOWTEMP HIGHS,
   (LOWTEMP - HIGHTEMP) DIFFERENCE
   FROM HILOW;
```

> **Note:** And the SQL engine (in this case, Oracle7) added the line numbers to the output. Notice the output includes the original query. Not all implementation of SQL do this. In later chapters, you will see examples from Borland's ISQL tool that do not include line numbers.

This query not only fixed (at least visually) my mis-entered data but it created a new column with the difference between the highs and lows of each state.

If you accidentally use minus on a character field, you get something like this:

```
SQL> SELECT -STATE FROM HILOW;
```

```
ERROR:
ORA-01722: invalid number

no rows selected
```

Your error message varies with implementation, but the result is the same.

Divide (/)

The divide has only one obvious meaning. Using the table PRICE from a few pages ago, type

```
SQL> SELECT * FROM PRICE;
```

```
ITEM          WHOLESALE
------------- ----------
TOMATOES            .34
POTATOES           .51
BANANAS            .67
TURNIPS            .45
CHEESE             .89
APPLES             .23

6 rows selected.
```

You can show the effects of a two-for-one sale by typing

```
SQL> SELECT ITEM, WHOLESALE, (WHOLESALE/2) SALEPRICE
  2  FROM PRICE;
```

```
ITEM              WHOLESALE SALEPRICE
----------------  --------- ---------
TOMATOES               .34       .17
POTATOES               .51      .255
BANANAS                .67      .335
TURNIPS                .45      .225
CHEESE                 .89      .445
APPLES                 .23      .115

6 rows selected.
```

This is pretty straightforward, except that coming up with half pennies can be tough.

Multiply (*)

The multiplication operator is also straightforward. Using the PRICE table, type

```
SQL> SELECT * FROM PRICE;
```

```
ITEM              WHOLESALE
----------------  ---------
TOMATOES               .34
POTATOES               .51
BANANAS                .67
TURNIPS                .45
CHEESE                 .89
APPLES                 .23

6 rows selected.
```

This query changes the table to reflect an across-the-board 10 percent discount:

```
SQL> SELECT ITEM, WHOLESALE, WHOLESALE * 0.9 NEWPRICE
     FROM PRICE;
```

```
ITEM              WHOLESALE NEWPRICE
----------------  --------- --------
TOMATOES               .34     .306
POTATOES               .51     .459
BANANAS                .67     .603
TURNIPS                .45     .405
CHEESE                 .89     .801
APPLES                 .23     .207

6 rows selected.
```

This is easy, but powerful.

Modulo (%)

This operator returns the integer remainder of the division operation. Using the table REMAINS, type

```
SQL> SELECT * FROM REMAINS;
```

```
NUMERATOR  DENOMINATOR
---------  -----------
       10            5
        8            3
       23            9
       40           17
     1024           16
       85           34
```

6 rows selected.

Let's create a new column, REMAINDER, to hold the values of NUMERATOR % DENOMINATOR:

```
SQL> SELECT NUMERATOR,
            DENOMINATOR,
            NUMERATOR%DENOMINATOR REMAINDER
     FROM REMAINS;
```

```
NUMERATOR DENOMINATOR REMAINDER
--------- ----------- ---------
       10           5         0
        8           3         2
       23           9         5
       40          17         6
     1024          16         0
       85          34        17
```

6 rows selected.

Some implementations of SQL implement modulo as a function, MOD (covered in Day 4). The statement

```
SQL> SELECT NUMERATOR,
            DENOMINATOR,
            MOD(NUMERATOR,DENOMONATOR) REMAINDER
     FROM REMAINS;
```

would produce an identical result.

Precedence

We talked about precedence at the top of this section. You now know enough to create a meaningful example.

Using the database PRECEDENCE, type

```
SQL> SELECT * FROM PRECEDENCE;
```

```
         N1          N2          N3          N4
----------  ----------  ----------  ----------
          1           2           3           4
         13          24          35          46
          9           3          23           5
         63           2          45           3
          7           2           1           4
```

Let's test this precedence:

```
SQL> SELECT
  2  N1+N2*N3/N4,
  3  (N1+N2)*N3/N4,
  4  N1+(N2*N3)/N4
  5  FROM PRECEDENCE;
```

```
N1+N2*N3/N4  (N1+N2)*N3/N4 N1+(N2*N3)/N4
-----------  ------------- -------------
        2.5           2.25           2.5
   31.26087      28.152174      31.26087
       22.8           55.2          22.8
         93            975            93
        7.5           2.25           7.5
```

Notice the first and last columns are identical. If you added N1+N2*(N3/N4), it would also be identical.

Comparison Operators

True to their name, comparison operators compare expressions and return one of three values: TRUE, FALSE, or Unknown. Wait a minute! Unknown? TRUE and FALSE are self-explanatory, but what is this Unknown?

To understand how you could get an Unknown, we need to talk a little about the concept of NULL. In database terms, NULL is the absence of data in a field. It does not mean a

column has a zero or a blank in it. A zero or a blank is a value. NULL means nothing is in that field. If you make a comparison like Field = 9, and Field is NULL, the comparison will come back Unknown. Because this is an uncomfortable condition, most flavors of SQL change Unknown to FALSE and provide a special operator IS NULL to test for a NULL condition. Someday, if you have been chasing a logic bug for what seems like forever, make sure you are not trying to compare a NULL value and getting back the default value of FALSE.

The PRICE table has been modified to have a NULL in the WHOLESALE field for the item ORANGES (someone in the data entry department was asleep at the switch). The table looks like this:

```
SQL> SELECT * FROM PRICE;
```

```
ITEM              WHOLESALE
--------------    ---------
TOMATOES               .34
POTATOES               .51
BANANAS                .67
TURNIPS                .45
CHEESE                 .89
APPLES                 .23
ORANGES
```

Notice there is nothing printed out in the NULL field position. It is noticeable in this case because it is in a numeric column. If the NULL were in the ITEM column it would be impossible to tell the difference between NULL and a blank.

Let's try to find the NULL:

```
SQL> SELECT *
  2  FROM PRICE
  3  WHERE WHOLESALE IS NULL;
```

```
ITEM              WHOLESALE
--------------    ---------
ORANGES
```

That worked! Now could you use the equal sign instead?

```
SQL> SELECT *
     FROM PRICE
     WHERE WHOLESALE = NULL;
```

```
no rows selected
```

You didn't find anything because the comparison WHOLESALE = NULL returned a FALSE because the result was unknown. This would be a good place to use an IS NULL, changing the WHERE statement to WHERE WHOLESALE IS NULL. In this case you would get all the rows where a NULL existed.

The example you just did also illustrates both the use of the most common comparison operator, =, and the playground of all comparison operators, the WHERE clause. We have already reviewed the WHERE clause, so let's look briefly at the =.

Equal (=)

You have already seen one possible use of the equal sign. Earlier in this chapter you saw how some implementations of SQL use it in the SELECT clause to assign an alias. In the WHERE clause it is the most commonly used comparison operator. Used alone, it is a very convenient way of selecting one value out of many. Try this:

```
SQL> SELECT * FROM FRIENDS;
```

```
LASTNAME        FIRSTNAME        AREACODE PHONE     ST ZIP
-----------     -----------      -------- --------  -- -----
BUNDY           AL                    100 555-1111  IL 22333
MEZA            AL                    200 555-2222  UK
MERRICK         BUD                   300 555-6666  CO 80212
MAST            JD                    381 555-6767  LA 23456
BULHER          FERRIS                345 555-3223  IL 23332
```

Let's find JD's row. (On this short list, this appears trivial; but you may have more friends than this—or you may have a list with thousands of records.)

```
SQL> SELECT *
     FROM FRIENDS
     WHERE FIRSTNAME = 'JD';
```

```
LASTNAME        FIRSTNAME        AREACODE PHONE     ST ZIP
-----------     -----------      -------- --------  -- -----
MAST            JD                    381 555-6767  LA 23456
```

This is what we expected. Try this:

```
SQL> SELECT *
     FROM FRIENDS
     WHERE FIRSTNAME = 'AL';
```

```
LASTNAME          FIRSTNAME          AREACODE PHONE     ST ZIP
----------------  ----------------   -------- --------  -- -----
BUNDY             AL                      100 555-1111  IL 22333
MEZA              AL                      200 555-2222  UK
```

Note: Here you see that = is capable of pulling in multiple records. Notice that ZIP is blank on the second record. ZIP is a character field (you learn how to create and populate tables in Chapter 8), and in this particular record we entered a NULL to demonstrate what we were discussing earlier—that a NULL in a character field is impossible to differentiate from a blank field.

Greater Than (>) and Greater Than or Equal To (>=)

The greater than operator (>) works like this:

```
SQL> SELECT *
     FROM FRIENDS
     WHERE AREACODE > 300;
```

```
LASTNAME          FIRSTNAME          AREACODE PHONE     ST ZIP
----------------  ----------------   -------- --------  -- -----
MAST              JD                      381 555-6767  LA 23456
BULHER            FERRIS                  345 555-3223  IL 23332
```

Here you found all the area codes greater than (but not including) 300. To include 300, write

```
SQL> SELECT *
  2  FROM FRIENDS
  3  WHERE AREACODE >= 300;
```

```
LASTNAME         FIRSTNAME        AREACODE PHONE     ST ZIP
---------------  ---------------  -------- --------  -- -----
MERRICK          BUD                   300 555-6666  CO 80212
MAST             JD                    381 555-6767  LA 23456
BULHER           FERRIS                345 555-3223  IL 23332
```

With this change you get area codes starting at 300 and going up.

Less Than (<) and Less Than or Equal To (<=)

As you might expect, these comparison operators work the same way, only in reverse:

```
SQL> SELECT *
  2  FROM FRIENDS
  3  WHERE STATE < 'LA';
```

```
LASTNAME         FIRSTNAME        AREACODE PHONE     ST ZIP
---------------  ---------------  -------- --------  -- -----
BUNDY            AL                    100 555-1111  IL 22333
MERRICK          BUD                   300 555-6666  CO 80212
BULHER           FERRIS                345 555-3223  IL 23332
```

Note: How did STATE get changed to ST? Because the column is only two characters long, the column name is shortened to two characters in the returned rows. If the column name had been COWS, it would come out CO. AREACODE and PHONE both have widths wider than their column names so they are not truncated.

Wait a minute. Did you just use < on a character field? Of course you did. You can use any of these operators on any data type. The result varies by data type. For example, substitute lowercase in the state search:

```
SQL> SELECT *
  2  FROM FRIENDS
  3  WHERE STATE < 'la';
```

```
LASTNAME         FIRSTNAME        AREACODE PHONE     ST ZIP
---------------  ---------------  -------- --------  -- -----
BUNDY            AL                    100 555-1111  IL 22333
MEZA             AL                    200 555-2222  UK
MERRICK          BUD                   300 555-6666  CO 80212
MAST             JD                    381 555-6767  LA 23456
BULHER           FERRIS                345 555-3223  IL 23332
```

Analysis The results are a little different from what we expected (we thought lowercase would fall below uppercase and therefore the table would be empty). Again, to be safe, check your implementation.

> **Note:** To be sure of how these operators will behave, check your language tables. Most PC implementations use the ASCII tables. Some other platforms use EBCDIC.

To include the state of Louisiana in the original search, type

```
SQL> SELECT *
  2  FROM FRIENDS
  3  WHERE STATE <= 'LA';
```

3

```
LASTNAME          FIRSTNAME          AREACODE PHONE      ST ZIP
---------------   ---------------    -------- --------   -- -----
BUNDY             AL                      100 555-1111   IL 22333
MERRICK           BUD                     300 555-6666   CO 80212
MAST              JD                      381 555-6767   LA 23456
BULHER            FERRIS                  345 555-3223   IL 23332
```

Inequalities (< > or !=)

Sometimes you need to find everything but certain data. For this you use the inequality symbol, which can be either <> or !=, depending on your SQL implementation. To find everyone who is not Al, type

```
SQL> SELECT *
  2  FROM FRIENDS
  3  WHERE FIRSTNAME <> 'AL';
```

```
LASTNAME          FIRSTNAME          AREACODE PHONE      ST ZIP
---------------   ---------------    -------- --------   -- -----
MERRICK           BUD                     300 555-6666   CO 80212
MAST              JD                      381 555-6767   LA 23456
BULHER            FERRIS                  345 555-3223   IL 23332
```

To find everyone not living in California, type

```
SQL> SELECT *
  2  FROM FRIENDS
  3  WHERE STATE != 'CA';
```

```
LASTNAME         FIRSTNAME      AREACODE PHONE     ST ZIP
---------------  -------------- -------- --------  -- -----
BUNDY            AL                  100 555-1111  IL 22333
MEZA             AL                  200 555-2222  UK
MERRICK          BUD                 300 555-6666  CO 80212
MAST             JD                  381 555-6767  LA 23456
BULHER           FERRIS              345 555-3223  IL 23332
```

Note: Notice that we used both symbols, <> and !=, with the same effect.

Character Operators

I Want to Be Like LIKE

What if you wanted to select parts of a database that fit a pattern but weren't quite exact matches? You could use the equal sign and run through all the possible cases, but that would be boring and time-consuming. Instead, you could use LIKE. Consider the following:

```
SQL> SELECT * FROM PARTS;
```

```
NAME             LOCATION         PARTNUMBER
---------------  ---------------  ----------
APPENDIX         MID-STOMACH               1
ADAMS APPLE      THROAT                    2
HEART            CHEST                     3
SPINE            BACK                      4
ANVIL            EAR                       5
KIDNEY           MID-BACK                  6
```

How can you find all the parts located in the back? A quick visual inspection of this simple table shows two, but unfortunately the locations have slightly different names. Try this:

```
SQL> SELECT *
  2  FROM PARTS
  3  WHERE LOCATION LIKE '%BACK%';
```

```
NAME             LOCATION         PARTNUMBER
---------------  ---------------  ----------
SPINE            BACK                      4
KIDNEY           MID-BACK                  6
```

You can see that pesky modulo symbol in the statement after LIKE. What is it doing there? When used inside a LIKE expression, % is a wildcard. What you asked for was any occurrence of BACK in the column location. If you queried

```
SQL> SELECT *
     FROM PARTS
     WHERE LOCATION LIKE 'BACK%';
```

you would get any occurrence that started with BACK:

```
NAME             LOCATION          PARTNUMBER
---------------  ---------------   ----------
SPINE            BACK                       4
```

If you ask

```
SQL> SELECT *
     FROM PARTS
     WHERE NAME LIKE 'A%';
```

you get back any name that starts with A:

```
NAME             LOCATION          PARTNUMBER
---------------  ---------------   ----------
APPENDIX         MID-STOMACH                1
ADAMS APPLE      THROAT                     2
ANVIL            EAR                        5
```

Is LIKE case-sensitive? Try the next query and find out.

```
SQL> SELECT *
     FROM PARTS
     WHERE NAME LIKE 'a%';
```

```
no rows selected
```

The answer is yes. This makes sense because not all the data you store is in uppercase.

What if you want to find data that matches all but one character in a certain pattern? You need a different kind of wildcard.

Underscore (_)

The underscore is the single-character wildcard. Using a modified version of the table FRIENDS, type

```
SQL> SELECT * FROM FRIENDS;
```

```
LASTNAME          FIRSTNAME         AREACODE PHONE      ST ZIP
--------------    ----------------  -------- --------   -- -----
BUNDY             AL                     100 555-1111   IL 22333
MEZA              AL                     200 555-2222   UK
MERRICK           BUD                    300 555-6666   CO 80212
MAST              JD                     381 555-6767   LA 23456
BULHER            FERRIS                 345 555-3223   IL 23332
PERKINS           ALTON                  911 555-3116   CA 95633
BOSS              SIR                    204 555-2345   CT 95633
```

To find all the records where STATE starts with C, write

```
SQL> SELECT *
  2  FROM FRIENDS
  3  WHERE STATE LIKE 'C_';
```

```
LASTNAME          FIRSTNAME         AREACODE PHONE      ST ZIP
--------------    ----------------  --------- --------  -- -----
MERRICK           BUD                    300 555-6666   CO 80212
PERKINS           ALTON                  911 555-3116   CA 95633
BOSS              SIR                    204 555-2345   CT 95633
```

You can use several underscores in a statement:

```
SQL> SELECT *
  2  FROM FRIENDS
  3  WHERE PHONE LIKE'555-6 6 ';
```

```
LASTNAME          FIRSTNAME         AREACODE PHONE      ST ZIP
--------------    ----------------  --------- --------  -- -----
MERRICK           BUD                    300 555-6666   CO 80212
MAST              JD                     381 555-6767   LA 23456
```

This could also be written as follows:

```
SQL> SELECT *
  2  FROM FRIENDS
  3  WHERE PHONE LIKE '555-6%';
```

```
LASTNAME          FIRSTNAME         AREACODE PHONE      ST ZIP
--------------    ----------------  --------- --------  -- -----
MERRICK           BUD                    300 555-6666   CO 80212
MAST              JD                     381 555-6767   LA 23456
```

Notice the results are identical. These two wildcards can be combined. Look at this:

```
SQL> SELECT *
  2  FROM FRIENDS
  3  WHERE FIRSTNAME LIKE '_L%';
```

LASTNAME	FIRSTNAME	AREACODE	PHONE	ST	ZIP
BUNDY	AL	100	555-1111	IL	22333
MEZA	AL	200	555-2222	UK	
PERKINS	ALTON	911	555-3116	CA	95633

This finds all records with L as the second character.

Concatonation (| |)

The || symbol concatonates two strings. Try this:

```
SQL> SELECT FIRSTNAME ¦¦ LASTNAME ENTIRENAME
  2  FROM FRIENDS;
```

```
ENTIRENAME
------------------------------
AL        BUNDY
AL        MEZA
BUD       MERRICK
JD        MAST
FERRIS    BULHER
ALTON     PERKINS
SIR       BOSS

7 rows selected.
```

Notice || is used instead of +. If you use the + to try to concatonate the strings, the SQL interpreter used for this example (Personal Oracle7) returns the following:

```
SQL> SELECT FIRSTNAME + LASTNAME ENTIRENAME
     FROM FRIENDS;
```

```
ERROR:
ORA-01722: invalid number
```

It is looking for two numbers to add and throws the error invalid number when it doesn't find any.

Note: Some implementations of SQL use the plus sign (+) to concatonate strings. Check your implementation.

So far you have done the comparisons one at a time. That's fine for some problems, but what if you need to find all the people at work with last names that start with P who have less than three days of vacation time?

Logical Operators

Vacation time is always a hot topic around the workplace. Say you designed this for the accounting department:

```
SQL> SELECT * FROM VACATION;
```

```
LASTNAME        EMPLOYEENUM    YEARS LEAVETAKEN
--------------- -----------  --------- ----------
ABLE                    101        2          4
BAKER                   104        5         23
BLEDSOE                 107        8         45
BOLIVAR                 233        4         80
BOLD                    210       15        100
COSTALES                211       10         78

6 rows selected.
```

Suppose your company gives each employee 12 days of leave each year. Using what you have learned and a logical operator, find all the employees whose name starts with B who have more than 50 days of leave coming.

```
SQL> SELECT LASTNAME,
  2  YEARS * 12 - LEAVETAKEN REMAINING
  3  FROM VACATION
  4  WHERE LASTNAME LIKE 'B%'
  5  AND
  6  YEARS * 12 - LEAVETAKEN > 50;
```

```
LASTNAME        REMAINING
--------------- ---------
BLEDSOE                51
BOLD                   80
```

Because this is the most complicated query you have done to date, let's examine it.

The SELECT clause (lines 1 and 2) uses some of your new-found arithmetic operators to determine how many days of leave each employee has remaining. We let the normal precedence compute YEARS * 12 - LEAVETAKEN. It would be safer and clearer to type (YEARS * 12) - LEAVETAKEN.

LIKE is used in line 4 with the wildcard % to find all the B names. Line 6 uses the > to find all occurrences bigger than 50.

The new element is on line 5. You used the logical operator AND to ensure that you found records that met the criteria in lines 4 *and* 6.

AND

AND means that both expressions it connects must be true to return TRUE. If either one is FALSE, AND returns FALSE. For example, if you wanted to know who had been with the company for 5 years or more and had taken less than 50 percent of their leave, you would try this:

```
SQL> SELECT LASTNAME WORKAHOLICS
  2  FROM VACATION
  3  WHERE YEARS >= 5
  4  AND
  5  ((YEARS *12)-LEAVETAKEN)/(YEARS * 12) >= 0.50;
```

```
WORKAHOLICS
--------------
BAKER
BLEDSOE
```

Check these people for burnout. Also check out how we used the AND to combine these two conditions.

OR

OR is also used to sum up a series of conditions. If any of the comparisons are TRUE, OR returns TRUE. To illustrate the difference, run the last query with OR instead of AND:

```
SQL> SELECT LASTNAME WORKAHOLICS
  2  FROM VACATION
  3  WHERE YEARS >= 5
  4  OR
  5  ((YEARS *12)-LEAVETAKEN)/(YEARS * 12) >= 0.50;
```

```
WORKAHOLICS
--------------
ABLE
BAKER
BLEDSOE
BOLD
COSTALES
```

The original names are still in the list, but you have three more who were not here before (and who would probably resent being called workaholics). They made the list because they satisfied one of the conditions. That is the essence of OR.

NOT

NOT means just that. If the condition it applies to evaluates to TRUE, NOT makes it FALSE. If the condition after the NOT is FALSE, it becomes TRUE. For example, typing this

```
SQL> SELECT *
  2  FROM VACATION
  3  WHERE LASTNAME NOT LIKE 'B%';
```

```
LASTNAME        EMPLOYEENUM     YEARS LEAVETAKEN
-------------   -----------  -------- ----------
ABLE                    101         2          4
COSTALES                211        10         78
```

returns the only two non-B names in the table.

NOT can also be used with the operator IS when applied to NULL. Recall the PRICES table where we put a NULL value in the WHOLESALE column opposite the item ORANGES.

```
SQL> SELECT * FROM PRICE;
```

```
ITEM            WHOLESALE
-------------   ---------
TOMATOES             .34
POTATOES             .51
BANANAS              .67
TURNIPS              .45
CHEESE               .89
APPLES               .23
ORANGES

7 rows selected.
```

To find the non-NULL items, type

```
SQL> SELECT *
  2  FROM PRICE
  3  WHERE WHOLESALE IS NOT NULL;
```

```
ITEM            WHOLESALE
-------------   ---------
TOMATOES             .34
POTATOES             .51
BANANAS              .67
TURNIPS              .45
CHEESE               .89
APPLES               .23

6 rows selected.
```

> **Note:** I recommend not mixing NOTs with ORs. Just thinking about it is
> confusing. A good rule of thumb is, if you don't understand logic tables, don't
> use NOT and OR.

Set Operators

Day 1 discussed the fact that SQL is based on the theory of sets. To support this foundation, there is a set of set operators.

UNION and UNION ALL

UNION returns the results of two queries minus the duplicate rows. The following two tables represent the rosters of teams:

```
SQL> SELECT * FROM FOOTBALL;

NAME
- - - - - - - - - - - - - -
ABLE
BRAVO
CHARLIE
DECON
EXITOR
FUBAR
GOOBER

7 rows selected.
```

```
SQL> SELECT * FROM SOFTBALL;

NAME
- - - - - - - - - - - - - - - - - - -
ABLE
BAKER
CHARLIE
DEAN
EXITOR
FALCONER
GOOBER

7 rows selected.
```

Who's on first? Wait. How many separate people play on one team or another?

```
SQL> SELECT NAME FROM SOFTBALL
  2  UNION
  3  SELECT NAME FROM FOOTBALL;
```

```
NAME
-------------------
ABLE
BAKER
BRAVO
CHARLIE
DEAN
DECON
EXITOR
FALCONER
FUBAR
GOOBER

10 rows selected.
```

UNION returned 10 distinct names from the two lists. How many names are on both lists (including duplicates)?

```
SQL> SELECT NAME FROM SOFTBALL
  2  UNION ALL
  3  SELECT NAME FROM FOOTBALL;
```

```
NAME
-------------------
ABLE
BAKER
CHARLIE
DEAN
EXITOR
FALCONER
GOOBER
ABLE
BRAVO
CHARLIE
DECON
EXITOR
FUBAR
GOOBER

14 rows selected.
```

There are 14 names on the combined list. This comes courtesy of the UNION ALL statement. UNION ALL works just like UNION except it does not eliminate duplicates. Now show me a list of players who are on both teams. You can't do that with UNION—you need to learn INTERSECT.

INTERSECT

INTERSECT returns only the rows found by both queries. To show the list of players who play on both teams, you type

```
SQL> SELECT * FROM FOOTBALL
  2  INTERSECT
  3  SELECT * FROM SOFTBALL;
```

```
NAME
--------------------
ABLE
CHARLIE
EXITOR
GOOBER
```

This finds the short list of players who are on both teams.

Minus (Difference)

Minus return the rows from the first query that were not present in the second. Using the example

```
SQL> SELECT * FROM FOOTBALL
  2  MINUS
  3  SELECT * FROM SOFTBALL;
```

```
NAME
----------------
BRAVO
DECON
FUBAR
```

This shows the three football players not on the softball team. If you reverse the order

```
SQL> SELECT * FROM SOFTBALL
  2  MINUS
  3  SELECT * FROM FOOTBALL;
```

```
NAME
----------------
BAKER
DEAN
FALCONER
```

you get the three softball players who aren't on the football team.

Miscellaneous Operators, IN and BETWEEN

The two operators IN and BETWEEN provide a shorthand for functions you already know how to do. If you wanted to find friends in Colorado, California, and Louisiana, you could type

```
SQL> SELECT *
  2  FROM FRIENDS
  3  WHERE STATE= 'CA'
  4  OR
  5  STATE ='CO'
  6  OR
  7  STATE = 'LA';
```

```
LASTNAME         FIRSTNAME        AREACODE PHONE     ST ZIP
---------------  ---------------- -------- --------  -- -----
MERRICK          BUD                   300 555-6666  CO 80212
MAST             JD                    381 555-6767  LA 23456
PERKINS          ALTON                 911 555-3116  CA 95633
```

or you could type

```
SQL> SELECT *
  2  FROM FRIENDS
  3  WHERE STATE IN('CA','CO','LA');
```

```
LASTNAME         FIRSTNAME        AREACODE PHONE     ST ZIP
---------------  ---------------- -------- --------  -- -----
MERRICK          BUD                   300 555-6666  CO 80212
MAST             JD                    381 555-6767  LA 23456
PERKINS          ALTON                 911 555-3116  CA 95633
```

This is not only shorter—it is more readable. You never know when you might have to go back and work on something you wrote months ago. IN also works with numbers. Consider the following, where the column AREACODE is a number:

```
SQL> SELECT *
  2  FROM FRIENDS
  3  WHERE AREACODE IN(100,381,204);
```

```
LASTNAME         FIRSTNAME        AREACODE PHONE     ST ZIP
---------------  ---------------- -------- --------  -- -----
BUNDY            AL                    100 555-1111  IL 22333
MAST             JD                    381 555-6767  LA 23456
BOSS             SIR                   204 555-2345  CT 95633
```

BETWEEN

If you needed a range of things from the PRICES table you could write

```
SQL>  SELECT *
  2   FROM PRICE
  3   WHERE WHOLESALE > 0.25
  4   AND
  5   WHOLESALE < 0.75;
```

```
ITEM              WHOLESALE
--------------    ---------
TOMATOES              .34
POTATOES             .51
BANANAS              .67
TURNIPS              .45
```

Using BETWEEN, you would write

```
SQL> SELECT *
  2   FROM PRICE
  3   WHERE WHOLESALE BETWEEN 0.25 AND 0.75;
```

```
ITEM              WHOLESALE
--------------    ---------
TOMATOES              .34
POTATOES             .51
BANANAS              .67
TURNIPS              .45
```

Again, this is a cleaner, more readable solution.

Summary

You entered today knowing only how to use the basic SELECT and FROM clauses. To this foundation you have added a host of operators, allowing you to more finely tune your requests to the database. You learned how to use arithmetic, comparison, character, logical, and set operators. In combination this powerful set of tools provides the cornerstone of your SQL knowledge. You aren't a database guru yet, but you have made a good start.

Q&A

Q How does all of this apply to me if I am not using SQL from the command line as depicted in the examples?

A Whether you use SQL in COBOL as Embedded SQL or in Microsoft's Open Database Connectivity (ODBC), you use the same basic constructions. What you have learned in this chapter and the one before it you will use over and over again in your journey through SQL.

Q **Why are you constantly telling me to check my implementation? I thought there was a standard!**

A There is an ANSI standard (the most recent version is 1992); however, most vendors modify it somewhat to suit their databases. The basics are similar if not identical, and each instance has extensions that other vendors copy and improve. We have chosen to use ANSI as a starting point but point out the differences as we go along.

Workshop

The workshop provides quiz questions to help solidify your understanding of the material covered, as well as exercises to provide you with experience in using what you have learned. Try to answer the quiz and exercise questions before checking the answers in Appendix F, and make sure you understand the answers before continuing to the next chapter.

Quiz

Use the FRIENDS table to answer the following questions:

```
LASTNAME         FIRSTNAME        AREACODE PHONE      ST ZIP
---------------- ---------------- -------- --------   -- -----
BUNDY            AL                    100 555-1111   IL 22333
MEZA             AL                    200 555-2222   UK
MERRICK          BUD                   300 555-6666   CO 80212
MAST             JD                    381 555-6767   LA 23456
BULHER           FERRIS                345 555-3223   IL 23332
PERKINS          ALTON                 911 555-3116   CA 95633
BOSS             SIR                   204 555-2345   CT 95633
```

1. Write a query that returns everyone in the database whose last name begins with M.

2. Write a query that returns everyone who lives in Illinois with a first name of Al.

3. Given two tables (PART1 and PART2) containing columns named PARTNO, how would you find out which part numbers are in both tables? How would you write the query?

4. What shorthand could you use instead of WHERE a > 10 AND a < 30?

Exercise

1. Using the FRIENDS table, write a query that returns the following:

```
NAME               ST
------------------ --
AL                 FROM IL
```

Functions

Objectives

Today we talk about functions. Functions in SQL enable you to perform feats such as determining the sum of a column or converting all the characters of a string to uppercase. By the end of the day you will understand and be able to use all of the following:

- [ ] Aggregate functions
- [ ] Date and time functions
- [ ] Arithmetic functions
- [ ] Character functions
- [ ] Conversion functions
- [ ] Miscellaneous functions

These functions greatly increase your ability to manipulate the information you retrieved using the basic functions of SQL you have learned during the first three days of this week. The first five functions, COUNT, SUM, AVG, MAX, and MIN, covered in the first section, aggregate functions, are defined in the ANSI standard. Most implementations of SQL have extended these to cover the rest of the functions you will learn in this chapter. The implementation you use may use different names.

Aggregate Functions

These are also referred to as group functions. They return a value based on the values in a column. This makes sense when you think about it. What would the average of a single field be? What about the average of a row with several different field types? For this section, we use the following table, TEAMSTATS:

```
SQL> SELECT * FROM TEAMSTATS;
```

NAME	POS	AB	HITS	WALKS	SINGLES	DOUBLES	TRIPLES	HR	SO
JONES	1B	145	45	34	31	8	1	5	10
DONKNOW	3B	175	65	23	50	10	1	4	15
WORLEY	LF	157	49	15	35	8	3	3	16
DAVID	OF	187	70	24	48	4	0	17	42
HAMHOCKER	3B	50	12	10	10	2	0	0	13
CASEY	DH	1	0	0	0	0	0	0	1

```
6 rows selected.
```

COUNT

The function COUNT returns the number of rows that satisfy the condition in the WHERE clause. Say you wanted to know how many ball players were hitting under 350. You would type

```
SQL> SELECT COUNT(*)
  2  FROM TEAMSTATS
  3  WHERE HITS/AB < .35;
```

```
  COUNT(*)
---------
        4
```

To make it more readable, try an alias:

```
SQL> SELECT COUNT(*) NUM_BELOW_350
  2  FROM TEAMSTATS
  3  WHERE HITS/AB < .35;
```

```
NUM_BELOW_350
-------------
            4
```

Would it make any difference if you tried a column name instead of the asterisk? Try this:

```
SQL> SELECT COUNT(NAME) NUM_BELOW_350
  2  FROM TEAMSTATS
  3  WHERE HITS/AB < .35;
```

```
NUM_BELOW_350
-------------
            4
```

The answer is no. The column you selected, NAME, was not involved in the WHERE statement. If you use COUNT without a WHERE clause

```
SQL> SELECT COUNT(*)
  2  FROM TEAMSTATS;
```

```
  COUNT(*)
---------
        6
```

it returns the number of records in the table.

SUM

SUM does just that. It returns the sum of all values in a column. To find out how many singles have been hit, type

```
SQL> SELECT SUM(SINGLES) TOTAL_SINGLES
  2  FROM TEAMSTATS;
```

```
TOTAL_SINGLES
-------------
          174
```

To get several SUMs, use

4

```
SQL> SELECT SUM(SINGLES) TOTAL_SINGLES, SUM(DOUBLES) TOTAL_DOUBLES,
SUM(TRIPLES) TOTAL_TRIPLES, SUM(HR) TOTAL_HR
  2  FROM TEAMSTATS;
```

```
TOTAL_SINGLES TOTAL_DOUBLES TOTAL_TRIPLES  TOTAL_HR
------------- ------------- -------------  --------
          174            32             5        29
```

To collect similar information on all 300 or better players, type

```
SQL> SELECT SUM(SINGLES) TOTAL_SINGLES, SUM(DOUBLES) TOTAL_DOUBLES,
SUM(TRIPLES) TOTAL_TRIPLES, SUM(HR) TOTAL_HR
  2  FROM TEAMSTATS
  3  WHERE HITS/AB >= .300;
```

```
TOTAL_SINGLES TOTAL_DOUBLES TOTAL_TRIPLES  TOTAL_HR
------------- ------------- -------------  --------
          164            30             5        29
```

To compute a team batting average, type

```
SQL> SELECT SUM(HITS)/SUM(AB) TEAM_AVERAGE
  2  FROM TEAMSTATS;
```

```
TEAM_AVERAGE
------------
  .33706294
```

SUM works with numbers only. If you try it on a non-numerical field you get

```
SQL> SELECT SUM(NAME)
  2  FROM TEAMSTATS;
```

```
ERROR:
ORA-01722: invalid number
no rows selected
```

This is logical, because the sum of a group of names makes no sense.

AVG

This function, AVG, computes the average of a column. To find the average number of strike outs, use this:

```
SQL> SELECT AVG(SO) AVE_STRIKE_OUTS
  2  FROM TEAMSTATS;
```

```
AVE_STRIKE_OUTS
---------------
      16.166667
```

Let's see if you get the same team batting average you got in the section on SUM:

```
SQL> SELECT AVG(HITS/AB) TEAM_AVERAGE
  2  FROM TEAMSTATS;
```

```
TEAM_AVERAGE
------------
  .26803448
```

The team was batting over 300 in the previous example! What happened? Sometimes you have to be careful what you ask for. AVG computed the average of the combined column hits divided by at bats, whereas the example in SUM divided the total number of hits by the number of at bats. For example, Player A gets 50 hits in 100 at bats for a .500 average. Player B gets 0 hits in 1 at bat for a 0.0 average. The average of 0.0 and 0.5 is .250. If you compute the combined average of 50 hits in 101 at bats, the answer is a respectable .495. The statement:

```
SQL> SELECT AVG(HITS)/AVG(AB) TEAM_AVERAGE
  2  FROM TEAMSTATS;
```

```
TEAM_AVERAGE
------------
  .33706294
```

returns the correct batting average. AVG also works with numbers only.

MAX

If you want to find the largest value in a column, use MAX. For example, what is the highest number of hits?

```
SQL> SELECT MAX(HITS)
  2  FROM TEAMSTATS;
```

```
MAX(HITS)
---------
       70
```

Can you find who has the most hits?

```
SQL> SELECT NAME
  2  FROM TEAMSTATS
  3  WHERE HITS = MAX(HITS);
```

```
ERROR at line 3:
ORA-00934: group function is not allowed here
```

Unfortunately not. The error message reminds us that this group function (remember we said that aggregate functions are also called group functions) does not work in the WHERE clause. Don't despair, Chapter 7 covers the concept of subqueries and provides a way to find who has the MAX hits.

What happens if you try a non-numeric column?

```
SQL> SELECT MAX(NAME)
  2  FROM TEAMSTATS;
```

```
MAX(NAME)
- - - - - - - - - - - - -
WORLEY
```

Here's something new. MAX returns the highest (closest to Z) string. Finally, a function that works with both characters and numbers.

MIN

MIN does the expected thing and works like MAX, except it returns the lowest member of a column. If you needed to know what the fewest at bats was, you would type

```
SQL> SELECT MIN(AB)
  2  FROM TEAMSTATS;
```

```
   MIN(AB)
- - - - - - - - -
         1
```

The statement

```
SQL> SELECT MIN(NAME)
  2  FROM TEAMSTATS;
```

```
MIN(NAME)
- - - - - - - - - - - - -
CASEY
```

returns the name closest to the beginning of the alphabet. This function can be combined with MAX to give a range of values. For example

```
SQL> SELECT MIN(AB), MAX(AB)
  2  FROM TEAMSTATS;
```

```
   MIN(AB)    MAX(AB)
- - - - - - - - -  - - - - - - - - -
         1        187
```

This sort of information can be useful when using statistical functions.

Note: As we mentioned in the introduction, the five previous functions are described in the ANSI standard. From here on we explore functions that have become de facto standards, present in all important implementations of SQL.

We use the Oracle7 names for these functions. Other implementations may use different names.

VARIANCE

This function produces the square of the standard deviation, a number vital to many statistical calculations. It works like this:

```
SQL> SELECT VARIANCE(HITS)
  2  FROM TEAMSTATS;
```

```
VARIANCE(HITS)
--------------
   802.96667
```

If you try a string

```
SQL> SELECT VARIANCE(NAME)
  2  FROM TEAMSTATS;
```

```
ERROR:
ORA-01722: invalid number
no rows selected
```

you find that VARIANCE is another function that works exclusively with numbers.

STDDEV

The final group function, STDDEV, finds the standard deviation of a column of numbers, as demonstrated by this example:

```
SQL> SELECT STDDEV(HITS)
  2  FROM TEAMSTATS;
```

```
STDDEV(HITS)
------------
   28.336666
```

It also returns an error when confronted by a string:

```
SQL> SELECT STDDEV(NAME)
  2  FROM TEAMSTATS;
```

```
ERROR:
ORA-01722: invalid number
no rows selected
```

These aggregate functions can be used in conjunction with each other:

```
SQL> SELECT COUNT(AB),
  2  AVG(AB),
  3  MIN(AB),
  4  MAX(AB),
  5  STDDEV(AB),
  6  VARIANCE(AB),
  7  SUM(AB)
  8  FROM TEAMSTATS;
```

```
COUNT(AB) AVG(AB) MIN(AB) MAX(AB) STDDEV(AB) VARIANCE(AB) SUM(AB)
--------- ------- ------- ------- ---------- ------------ -------
6         119.167 1       187     75.589     5712.97      715
```

Next time you hear a sportscaster use statistics to fill the time between plays, you will know that at some level SQL is at work.

Date and Time Functions

Unfortunately, we live in a civilization governed by times and dates. Fortunately, most major implementations of SQL have functions to cope with these concepts. In this section we use the table PROJECT to demonstrate how they work.

```
SQL> SELECT * FROM PROJECT;
```

```
TASK            STARTDATE ENDDATE
--------------- --------- ---------
KICKOFF MTG     01-APR-95 01-APR-95
TECH SURVEY     02-APR-95 01-MAY-95
USER MTGS       15-MAY-95 30-MAY-95
DESIGN WIDGET   01-JUN-95 30-JUN-95
CODE WIDGET     01-JUL-95 02-SEP-95
TESTING         03-SEP-95 17-JAN-96

6 rows selected.
```

Note: This table used the DATE data type. Most implementations of SQL have a DATE data type, but again its exact syntax may vary.

ADD_MONTHS

This function adds a number of months to a specified date. For example, say something extraordinary happened, and the preceding project slipped to the right by two months. You could make a new schedule by typing

```
SQL> SELECT TASK,
  2  STARTDATE,
  3  ENDDATE ORIGINAL_END,
  4  ADD_MONTHS(ENDDATE,2)
  5  FROM PROJECT;
```

```
TASK            STARTDATE  ORIGINAL_  ADD_MONTH
--------------  ---------  ---------  ---------
KICKOFF MTG     01-APR-95  01-APR-95  01-JUN-95
TECH SURVEY     02-APR-95  01-MAY-95  01-JUL-95
USER MTGS       15-MAY-95  30-MAY-95  30-JUL-95
DESIGN WIDGET   01-JUN-95  30-JUN-95  31-AUG-95
CODE WIDGET     01-JUL-95  02-SEP-95  02-NOV-95
TESTING         03-SEP-95  17-JAN-96  17-MAR-96

6 rows selected.
```

Not that a slip like this is possible, but it's nice to have a function that makes it so easy. ADD_MONTHS also works outside the SELECT clause. Typing

```
SQL> SELECT TASK TASKS_SHORTER_THAN_ONE_MONTH
  2  FROM PROJECT
  3  WHERE ADD_MONTHS(STARTDATE,1) > ENDDATE;
```

produces the following result:

```
TASKS_SHORTER_THAN_ONE_MONTH
----------------------------
KICKOFF MTG
TECH SURVEY
USER MTGS
DESIGN WIDGET
```

At last a function that works in more than one place. You will find that is the case with all the functions in this section. This function does not work with other data types like characters or numbers without a couple of helper functions, TO_CHAR and TO_DATE, which are discussed a few sections down when we get to character functions.

LAST_DAY

This returns the last day of a specified month. It is for those of us who haven't mastered the "Thirty days has September..." rhyme—or at least those of us who have not yet taught it to our computers. If, for example, you need to know what the last day of the month is in the column ENDDATE, you would type

```
SQL> SELECT ENDDATE, LAST_DAY(ENDDATE)
  2  FROM PROJECT;
```

to receive this result:

```
ENDDATE    LAST_DAY(ENDDATE)
---------  -----------------
01-APR-95  30-APR-95
01-MAY-95  31-MAY-95
```

```
30-MAY-95 31-MAY-95
30-JUN-95 30-JUN-95
02-SEP-95 30-SEP-95
17-JAN-96 31-JAN-96

6 rows selected.
```

How does it handle leap years?

```
SQL> SELECT LAST_DAY('1-FEB-95') NON_LEAP,
  2  LAST_DAY('1-FEB-96') LEAP
  3  FROM PROJECT;
```

```
NON_LEAP  LEAP
--------- ---------
28-FEB-95 29-FEB-96
28-FEB-95 29-FEB-96
28-FEB-95 29-FEB-96
28-FEB-95 29-FEB-96
28-FEB-95 29-FEB-96
28-FEB-95 29-FEB-96

6 rows selected.
```

You got the right result, but why so many? Because you didn't specify an existing column or any conditions, the SQL engine applied this to each existing row. Let's get something less redundant by using the following:

```
SQL> SELECT DISTINCT LAST_DAY('1-FEB-95') NON_LEAP,
  2  LAST_DAY('1-FEB-96') LEAP
  3  FROM PROJECT;
```

This uses the word DISTINCT (remember Day 2) to produce the singular result

```
NON_LEAP  LEAP
--------- ---------
28-FEB-95 29-FEB-96
```

Unlike me, this function knows which years are leap years. But before you trust your own or your company's financial future to this or any other function, check your implementation!

MONTHS_BETWEEN

If you need to know how many months there are between month x and month y, use MONTHS_BETWEEN like this:

```
SQL> SELECT TASK, STARTDATE, ENDDATE, MONTHS_BETWEEN(STARTDATE,ENDDATE)
        DURATION
  2  FROM PROJECT;
```

TASK	STARTDATE	ENDDATE	DURATION
KICKOFF MTG	01-APR-95	01-APR-95	0
TECH SURVEY	02-APR-95	01-MAY-95	-.9677419
USER MTGS	15-MAY-95	30-MAY-95	-.483871
DESIGN WIDGET	01-JUN-95	30-JUN-95	-.9354839

画像

```
CODE WIDGET     01-JUL-95 02-SEP-95 -2.032258
TESTING         03-SEP-95 17-JAN-96 -4.451613

6 rows selected.
```

Wait a minute—that doesn't look right. Try this:

```
SQL> SELECT TASK, STARTDATE, ENDDATE,
  2  MONTHS_BETWEEN(ENDDATE,STARTDATE) DURATION
  3  FROM PROJECT;
```

```
TASK             STARTDATE ENDDATE    DURATION
---------------- --------- --------- ---------
KICKOFF MTG      01-APR-95 01-APR-95         0
TECH SURVEY      02-APR-95 01-MAY-95 .96774194
USER MTGS        15-MAY-95 30-MAY-95 .48387097
DESIGN WIDGET    01-JUN-95 30-JUN-95 .93548387
CODE WIDGET      01-JUL-95 02-SEP-95 2.0322581
TESTING          03-SEP-95 17-JAN-96 4.4516129

6 rows selected.
```

That's better. You see that this function is sensitive to the way you order the months. Negative months might not be bad. For example, you could use a negative result to determine if one date happened before another, like this:

```
SQL> SELECT *
  2  FROM PROJECT
  3  WHERE MONTHS_BETWEEN('19 MAY 95', STARTDATE) > 0;
```

This shows all the tasks that started before May 19, 1995.

```
TASK             STARTDATE ENDDATE
---------------- --------- ---------
KICKOFF MTG      01-APR-95 01-APR-95
TECH SURVEY      02-APR-95 01-MAY-95
USER MTGS        15-MAY-95 30-MAY-95
```

NEW_TIME

If you need to adjust the time according to the time zone you are in, this is your function. These are the time zones you can use with this function:

Abbreviation	Time Zone
AST or ADT	Atlantic Standard or Daylight Time
BST or BDT	Bering Standard or Daylight Time
CST or CDT	Central Standard or Daylight Time
EST or EDT	Eastern Standard or Daylight Time
GMT	Greenwich Mean Time
HST or HDT	Alaska-Hawaii Standard or Daylight Time

continues

Abbreviation	Time Zone
MST or MDT	Mountain Standard or Daylight Time
NST	Newfoundland Standard Time
PST or PDT	Pacific Standard or Daylight Time
YST or YDT	Yukon Standard or Daylight Time

You can adjust your time like this:

```
SQL> SELECT ENDDATE EDT,
  2  NEW_TIME(ENDDATE, 'EDT','PDT')
  3  FROM PROJECT;
```

```
EDT                NEW_TIME(ENDDATE
----------------   ----------------
01-APR-95 1200AM   31-MAR-95 0900PM
01-MAY-95 1200AM   30-APR-95 0900PM
30-MAY-95 1200AM   29-MAY-95 0900PM
30-JUN-95 1200AM   29-JUN-95 0900PM
02-SEP-95 1200AM   01-SEP-95 0900PM
17-JAN-96 1200AM   16-JAN-96 0900PM

6 rows selected.
```

Like magic, all the times are in the new time zone and the dates are adjusted.

NEXT_DAY

NEXT_DAY finds the name of the first day of the week that is equal to or later than another specified date. It's easier to do an example than spend more time explaining. Suppose you needed to send a report on the Friday following the first day of each event. You would type

```
SQL> SELECT STARTDATE,
  2  NEXT_DAY(STARTDATE, 'FRIDAY')
  3  FROM PROJECT;
```

which would return

```
STARTDATE NEXT_DAY(
--------- ---------
01-APR-95 07-APR-95
02-APR-95 07-APR-95
15-MAY-95 19-MAY-95
01-JUN-95 02-JUN-95
01-JUL-95 07-JUL-95
03-SEP-95 08-SEP-95

6 rows selected.
```

This gives you the date of the first Friday that occurs after your STARTDATE.

SYSDATE

SYSDATE returns the system time and date:

```
SQL> SELECT DISTINCT SYSDATE
  2  FROM PROJECT;
```

```
SYSDATE
---------------
18-JUN-95 1020PM
```

If you wanted to see where you stood today in a certain project you could type

```
SQL> SELECT *
  2  FROM PROJECT
  3  WHERE STARTDATE > SYSDATE;
```

```
TASK            STARTDATE ENDDATE
--------------- --------- ---------
CODE WIDGET     01-JUL-95 02-SEP-95
TESTING         03-SEP-95 17-JAN-96
```

Now you can see what parts of the project start after today.

Arithmetic Functions

Many of the uses you have for the data you retrieve involve mathematics. Most implementations of SQL provide arithmetic functions similar to the ones we explore in this section. We use the NUMBERS table for our examples:

```
SQL> SELECT *
  2  FROM NUMBERS;
```

```
         A         B
--------- ---------
   3.1415         4
     -45      .707
       5         9
 -57.667        42
      15        55
    -7.2       5.3

6 rows selected.
```

ABS

The ABS function returns the absolute value of the number you point to, as in the following:

```
SQL> SELECT ABS(A) ABSOLUTE_VALUE
  2  FROM NUMBERS;
```

```
ABSOLUTE_VALUE
- - - - - - - - - - - - - -
       3.1415
          45
           5
      57.667
          15
         7.2
```

6 rows selected.

This changes all the negative numbers to positive and leaves positive numbers alone.

CEIL and FLOOR

The first of these functions, CEIL, returns the smallest integer greater than or equal to its argument. The latter, FLOOR, does just the reverse, returning the largest integer equal to or less than its argument. For example

```
SQL> SELECT B, CEIL(B) CEILING
  2  FROM NUMBERS;
```

```
        B   CEILING
- - - - - - - - -  - - - - - - - - -
        4         4
     .707         1
        9         9
       42        42
       55        55
      5.3         6
```

6 rows selected.

And

```
SQL> SELECT A, FLOOR(A) FLOOR
  2  FROM NUMBERS;
```

```
        A     FLOOR
- - - - - - - - -  - - - - - - - - -
    3.1415         3
       -45       -45
         5         5
   -57.667       -58
        15        15
      -7.2        -8
```

6 rows selected.

COS, COSH, SIN, SINH, TAN, and TANH

The COS, SIN, and TAN functions provide support for various trigonometric concepts. The COSH, SINH, and TANH functions return the hyperbolic values of their arguments. They all work on the assumption that **A** is in radians. For example

```
SQL> SELECT A, COS(A)
  2  FROM NUMBERS;
```

```
        A    COS(A)
--------- ---------
   3.1415        -1
     -45 .52532199
       5 .28366219
 -57.667   .437183
      15 -.7596879
    -7.2 .60835131
```

returns some unexpected values if you don't realize COS expects A to be in radians. You would expect the COS of 45 degrees to be in the neighborhood of .707, not .525. To make this work the way you would expect it to in a degree-oriented world, you need to convert degrees to radians. (When is the last time you heard a news broadcast saying some politician had done a π radian turn? You hear about a 180 degree turn.) Because 360 degrees = 2π radians, you can write

```
SQL> SELECT A, COS(A* 0.01745329251994)
  2  FROM NUMBERS;
```

```
        A COS(A*0.01745329251994)
--------- -----------------------
   3.1415              .99849724
     -45               .70710678
       5                .9961947
 -57.667                .5348391
      15               .96592583
    -7.2                .9921147
```

Note that the number 0.01745329251994 is radians divided by degrees. The trigonometric functions work as follows:

```
SQL> SELECT A, COS(A*0.017453), COSH(A*0.017453)
  2  FROM NUMBERS;
```

```
        A COS(A*0.017453) COSH(A*0.017453)
--------- --------------- ----------------
   3.1415       .99849729        1.0015035
     -45        .70711609        1.3245977
       5        .99619483         1.00381
 -57.667        .53485335        1.5507072
      15        .96592696        1.0344645
    -7.2        .99211497        1.0079058
```

```
6 rows selected.
```

And

```
SQL> SELECT A, SIN(A*0.017453), SINH(A*0.017453)
  2  FROM NUMBERS;
```

```
        A SIN(A*0.017453) SINH(A*0.017453)
--------- --------------- ----------------
   3.1415       .05480113        .05485607
     -45        -.7070975        -.8686535
       5        .08715429         .0873758
 -57.667        -.8449449        -1.185197
      15        .25881481        .26479569
    -7.2        -.1253311        -.1259926
```

6 rows selected.

And

```
SQL> SELECT A, TAN(A*0.017453), TANH(A*0.017453)
  2  FROM NUMBERS;
```

```
        A TAN(A*0.017453) TANH(A*0.017453)
--------- --------------- ----------------
   3.1415       .05488361        .05477372
     -45        -.9999737        -.6557867
       5        .08748719        .08704416
 -57.667       -1.579769        -.7642948
      15        .26794449        .25597369
    -7.2        -.1263272        -.1250043
```

6 rows selected.

EXP

If you need to raise e (e is a mathematical constant used in various formulas) to a power, this is your function. Typing

```
SQL> SELECT A, EXP(A)
  2  FROM NUMBERS;
```

```
        A       EXP(A)
--------- ----------
   3.1415   23.138549
     -45    2.863E-20
       5    148.41316
 -57.667    9.027E-26
      15    3269017.4
    -7.2     .00074659
```

6 rows selected.

raises e by the values in column A.

LN and LOG

These two functions center on logarithms. The first, LN, returns the natural logarithm of its argument. Type

```
SQL> SELECT A, LN(A)
  2  FROM NUMBERS;
```

```
ERROR:
ORA-01428: argument '-45' is out of range
```

Did we neglect to mention that the argument had to be positive? Write

```
SQL> SELECT A, LN(ABS(A))
  2  FROM NUMBERS;
```

```
        A LN(ABS(A))
--------- ----------
   3.1415  1.1447004
      -45  3.8066625
        5  1.6094379
  -57.667  4.0546851
       15  2.7080502
     -7.2   1.974081

6 rows selected.
```

Notice how we embedded the function ABS inside the LN call. The other logarithmic function, LOG, takes two arguments, returning the logarithm of the first argument in the base of the second. The following table

```
SQL> SELECT B, LOG(B, 10)
  2  FROM NUMBERS;
```

```
        B LOG(B,10)
--------- ---------
        4  1.660964
     .707 -6.640962
        9 1.0479516
       42 .61604832
       55 .57459287
      5.3 1.3806894

6 rows selected.
```

returns the logarithms of column B in base 10.

MOD

You have encountered MOD before. In Day 3 you saw that the ANSI standard for the modulo operator, %, is sometimes implemented as the function MOD. The query

```
SQL> SELECT A, B, MOD(A,B)
  2  FROM NUMBERS;
```

```
         A          B   MOD(A,B)
--------- ---------- ---------
    3.1415          4     3.1415
       -45       .707      -.459
         5          9          5
   -57.667         42    -15.667
        15         55         15
      -7.2        5.3       -1.9

6 rows selected.
```

returns a table showing the remainder of A divided by B.

POWER

To raise one number to the power of another, use POWER. In this function the first argument is raised to the power of the second:

```
SQL> SELECT A, B, POWER(A,B)
  2  FROM NUMBERS;
```

```
ERROR:
ORA-01428: argument '-45' is out of range
```

At first glance this indicates that the first argument can't be negative. But that can't be true because we know that a number like –4 can be raised to a power. It turns out that in this function if the first number is negative the second must be an integer. You can fix this by using CEIL (or FLOOR) like this:

```
SQL> SELECT A, CEIL(B), POWER(A,CEIL(B))
  2  FROM NUMBERS;
```

```
         A    CEIL(B)  POWER(A,CEIL(B))
--------- ---------- ----------------
    3.1415          4           97.3976
       -45          1               -45
         5          9           1953125
   -57.667         42         9.098E+73
        15         55         4.842E+64
      -7.2          6         139314.07

6 rows selected.
```

That's better!

SIGN

SIGN returns –1 if its argument is less than 0, 0 if its argument is equal to 0, and 1 if its argument is greater than 0, as shown by the following:

```
SQL> SELECT A, SIGN(A)
  2  FROM NUMBERS;
```

```
         A   SIGN(A)
--------- ---------
    3.1415         1
      -45        -1
        5         1
  -57.667        -1
       15         1
     -7.2        -1
        0         0
```

```
7 rows selected.
```

You could also use SIGN in a SELECT WHERE clause like this:

```
SQL> SELECT A
  2  FROM NUMBERS
  3  WHERE SIGN(A) = 1;
```

```
         A
---------
    3.1415
        5
       15
```

4

SQRT

The square root of an argument is returned by the function SQRT. Because the square root of a negative number is undefined, you cannot use this function on negative numbers:

```
SQL> SELECT A, SQRT(A)
  2  FROM NUMBERS;
```

```
ERROR:
ORA-01428: argument '-45' is out of range
```

Fixing this problem with ABS, you get

```
SQL> SELECT ABS(A), SQRT(ABS(A))
  2  FROM NUMBERS;
```

```
    ABS(A)  SQRT(ABS(A))
--------- ------------
    3.1415    1.7724277
       45    6.7082039
        5     2.236068
```

```
          57.667   7.5938791
              15   3.8729833
             7.2   2.6832816
               0           0
```

7 rows selected.

Character Functions

Many implementations of SQL provide functions to manipulate characters and strings of characters. The following are representative of the most common character functions. We use the table CHARACTERS for our examples.

```
SQL> SELECT * FROM CHARACTERS;
```

```
LASTNAME          FIRSTNAME        M    CODE
---------------   --------------   --   --------
PURVIS            KELLY            A      32
TAYLOR            CHUCK            J      67
CHRISTINE         LAURA            C      65
ADAMS             FESTER           M      87
COSTALES          ARMANDO          A      77
KONG              MAJOR            G      52
```

6 rows selected.

CHR

CHR returns the character equivalent of the number it uses as an argument. The character it returns depends on the character set of the database. For our example the database is set to ASCII. The column CODE includes numbers.

```
SQL> SELECT CODE, CHR(CODE)
  2  FROM CHARACTERS;
```

```
      CODE CH
---------- --
        32
        67 C
        65 A
        87 W
        77 M
        52 4
```

6 rows selected.

Where did the space come from opposite the 32? It turns out that 32 is a space in the ASCII character set.

CONCAT

You used the equivalent of this function back on Day 3, when we discussed operators. The || symbol splices two strings together, as does CONCAT. It works like this:

```
SQL> SELECT CONCAT(FIRSTNAME, LASTNAME) "FIRST AND LAST NAMES"
  2  FROM CHARACTERS;
```

```
FIRST AND LAST NAMES
------------------------------
KELLY          PURVIS
CHUCK          TAYLOR
LAURA          CHRISTINE
FESTER         ADAMS
ARMANDO        COSTALES
MAJOR          KONG

6 rows selected.
```

There are two things to note here. First, we used quotation marks to surround the multiword alias "FIRST AND LAST NAMES". Again, it is safest to check your implementation to see if it allows this. Second, even though the table looks like two separate columns, what you are seeing is one column. The first value we concatenated, FIRSTNAME, is 15 characters wide. This operation retained all the characters in the field.

INITCAP

This useful function capitalizes the first letter of a word and makes all other characters lowercase.

```
SQL> SELECT FIRSTNAME BEFORE, INITCAP(FIRSTNAME) AFTER
  2  FROM CHARACTERS;
```

```
BEFORE          AFTER
--------------  --------------
KELLY           Kelly
CHUCK           Chuck
LAURA           Laura
FESTER          Fester
ARMANDO         Armando
MAJOR           Major

6 rows selected.
```

LOWER and UPPER

As you might expect, LOWER changes all the characters to lowercase and UPPER does just the reverse. Look at the following example.

First you do a little magic with the UPDATE function (you learn this during the second week) to change one of the values to lowercase:

```
SQL> UPDATE CHARACTERS
  2  SET FIRSTNAME = 'kelly'
  3  WHERE FIRSTNAME = 'KELLY';
```

```
1 row updated.
```

```
SQL> SELECT FIRSTNAME
  2  FROM CHARACTERS;
```

```
FIRSTNAME
---------------
kelly
CHUCK
LAURA
FESTER
ARMANDO
MAJOR

6 rows selected.
```

Then you write

```
SQL> SELECT FIRSTNAME, UPPER(FIRSTNAME), LOWER(FIRSTNAME)
  2  FROM CHARACTERS;
```

```
FIRSTNAME       UPPER(FIRSTNAME LOWER(FIRSTNAME
--------------- --------------- ---------------
kelly           KELLY           kelly
CHUCK           CHUCK           chuck
LAURA           LAURA           laura
FESTER          FESTER          fester
ARMANDO         ARMANDO         armando
MAJOR           MAJOR           major

6 rows selected.
```

Now you see the desired behavior.

LPAD and RPAD

These two functions, LPAD and RPAD, take a minimum of two and a maximum of three arguments. The first argument is the charter string to be operated on. The second is the number of characters to pad it with, and the optional third argument is the character to pad it with. The third argument defaults to a blank, or it can be a single character or a character string. If you type

```
SQL> SELECT LASTNAME, LPAD(LASTNAME,20,'*')
  2  FROM CHARACTERS;
```

```
LASTNAME          LPAD(LASTNAME,20,'*'
--------------    --------------------
PURVIS            *****PURVIS
TAYLOR            *****TAYLOR
CHRISTINE         *****CHRISTINE
ADAMS             *****ADAMS
COSTALES          *****COSTALES
KONG              *****KONG

6 rows selected.
```

you find that only five pad characters are put in. Why? Remember that the LASTNAME column is 15 characters wide and that LASTNAME includes the blanks to the right of the characters that make up the name. Try the right side:

```
SQL> SELECT LASTNAME, RPAD(LASTNAME,20,'*')
  2  FROM CHARACTERS;
```

```
LASTNAME          RPAD(LASTNAME,20,'*'
--------------    --------------------
PURVIS            PURVIS          *****
TAYLOR            TAYLOR          *****
CHRISTINE         CHRISTINE       *****
ADAMS             ADAMS           *****
COSTALES          COSTALES        *****
KONG              KONG            *****

6 rows selected.
```

Here you see graphic proof that the blanks are considered part of the field name for these operations. That's where the next functions come in handy.

LTRIM and RTRIM

These functions take at least one and at most two arguments. The first argument, like LPAD and RPAD, is a character string. The second, optional, element is a character or character string or defaults to a blank. If you use a second argument that is not a blank, these trim functions will trim that character the same way they trim the blanks in the following examples. Type

```
SQL> SELECT LASTNAME, RTRIM(LASTNAME)
  2  FROM CHARACTERS;
```

```
LASTNAME          RTRIM(LASTNAME)
--------------    --------------
PURVIS            PURVIS
TAYLOR            TAYLOR
CHRISTINE         CHRISTINE
ADAMS             ADAMS
COSTALES          COSTALES
KONG              KONG

6 rows selected.
```

79

Wait a minute! How do you know the characters have been trimmed? Use this:

```
SQL> SELECT LASTNAME, RPAD(RTRIM(LASTNAME),20,'*')
  2  FROM CHARACTERS;
```

```
LASTNAME          RPAD(RTRIM(LASTNAME)
--------------    --------------------
PURVIS            PURVIS**************
TAYLOR            TAYLOR**************
CHRISTINE         CHRISTINE***********
ADAMS             ADAMS***************
COSTALES          COSTALES************
KONG              KONG****************

6 rows selected.
```

This is proof-positive that trim is working. Now try LTRIM:

```
SQL> SELECT LASTNAME, LTRIM(LASTNAME, 'C')
  2  FROM CHARACTERS;
```

```
LASTNAME          LTRIM(LASTNAME,
--------------    --------------
PURVIS            PURVIS
TAYLOR            TAYLOR
CHRISTINE         HRISTINE
ADAMS             ADAMS
COSTALES          OSTALES
KONG              KONG

6 rows selected.
```

Note the missing Cs in the third and fifth rows.

REPLACE

REPLACE does just that. Of its three arguments, the first is the string to be searched. The second is the search key. The last is the optional replacement string. If the third argument is left out or NULL, each occurrence of the search key on the string to be searched is removed and is not replaced with anything.

```
SQL> SELECT LASTNAME, REPLACE(LASTNAME, 'ST') REPLACEMENT
  2  FROM CHARACTERS;
```

```
LASTNAME          REPLACEMENT
--------------    --------------
PURVIS            PURVIS
TAYLOR            TAYLOR
CHRISTINE         CHRIINE
ADAMS             ADAMS
COSTALES          COALES
KONG              KONG
```

```
6 rows selected.
```

If there is a third argument, it is substituted for each occurrence of the search key in the target string. For example

```
SQL> SELECT LASTNAME, REPLACE(LASTNAME, 'ST','**') REPLACEMENT
  2  FROM CHARACTERS;
```

```
LASTNAME         REPLACEMENT
--------------   -----------
PURVIS           PURVIS
TAYLOR           TAYLOR
CHRISTINE        CHRI**INE
ADAMS            ADAMS
COSTALES         CO**ALES
KONG             KONG

6 rows selected.
```

If the second argument is NULL, the target string is returned with no changes.

```
SQL> SELECT LASTNAME, REPLACE(LASTNAME, NULL) REPLACEMENT
  2  FROM CHARACTERS;
```

```
LASTNAME         REPLACEMENT
--------------   --------------
PURVIS           PURVIS
TAYLOR           TAYLOR
CHRISTINE        CHRISTINE
ADAMS            ADAMS
COSTALES         COSTALES
KONG             KONG

6 rows selected.
```

SUBSTR

This three-argument function enables you to take a piece out of a target string. The first argument is the target string. The second argument is the position of the first character to be output. The third argument is the number of characters to show.

```
SQL> SELECT FIRSTNAME, SUBSTR(FIRSTNAME,2,3)
  2  FROM CHARACTERS;
```

```
FIRSTNAME        SUB
--------------   ---
kelly            ell
CHUCK            HUC
LAURA            AUR
FESTER           EST
ARMANDO          RMA
MAJOR            AJO

6 rows selected.
```

4

If you use a negative number as the second argument, the starting point is determined by counting backwards from the end, like this:

```
SQL> SELECT FIRSTNAME, SUBSTR(FIRSTNAME,-13,2)
  2  FROM CHARACTERS;
```

```
FIRSTNAME       SU
--------------  ---
kelly           ll
CHUCK           UC
LAURA           UR
FESTER          ST
ARMANDO         MA
MAJOR           JO

6 rows selected.
```

Remember the character field FIRSTNAME in this example is 15 characters long. That is why you used a –13 to start at the third character. Remember, counting back from 15 leaves you at the start of the third character not the start of the second. If there is no third argument, use

```
SQL> SELECT FIRSTNAME, SUBSTR(FIRSTNAME,3)
  2  FROM CHARACTERS;
```

```
FIRSTNAME       SUBSTR(FIRSTN
--------------  -------------
kelly           lly
CHUCK           UCK
LAURA           URA
FESTER          STER
ARMANDO         MANDO
MAJOR           JOR

6 rows selected.
```

The rest of the target string is returned.

TRANSLATE

The function TRANSLATE takes three arguments. The first is the target string. Then there is the FROM string, followed by the TO string. Elements of the target string that occur in the FROM string are translated to the corresponding element in the TO string.

```
SQL> SELECT FIRSTNAME, TRANSLATE(FIRSTNAME
  2  '0123456789ABCDEFGHIJKLMNOPQRSTUVWXYZ
  3  'NNNNNNNNNNAAAAAAAAAAAAAAAAAAAAAAAAAAA)
  4  FROM CHARACTERS;
```

```
FIRSTNAME        TRANSLATE(FIRST
--------------   --------------
kelly            kelly
CHUCK            AAAAA
LAURA            AAAAA
FESTER           AAAAAA
ARMANDO          AAAAAAA
MAJOR            AAAAA

6 rows selected.
```

Notice that the function is case-sensitive.

INSTR

To find out where in a string a particular pattern occurs, use INSTR. Its first argument is the target string. The second argument is the pattern to match. The third and fourth are numbers representing where to start looking and which match to report. This example

```
SQL> SELECT LASTNAME, INSTR(LASTNAME, 'O', 2, 1)
  2  FROM CHARACTERS;
```

```
LASTNAME         INSTR(LASTNAME,'O',2,1)
--------------   -----------------------
PURVIS                                 0
TAYLOR                                 5
CHRISTINE                              0
ADAMS                                  0
COSTALES                               2
KONG                                   2

6 rows selected.
```

returns a number representing the first occurrence of O starting with the second character. The third and fourth arguments, if you don't specify them, default to 1. If the third argument is negative, the search starts at a position determined from the end of the string instead of the beginning.

LENGTH

LENGTH returns the length of its lone character argument. For example

```
SQL> SELECT FIRSTNAME, LENGTH(RTRIM(FIRSTNAME))
  2  FROM CHARACTERS;
```

```
FIRSTNAME        LENGTH(RTRIM(FIRSTNAME))
--------------   ------------------------
kelly                                   5
CHUCK                                   5
LAURA                                   5
FESTER                                  6
```

```
      ARMANDO                                      7
      MAJOR                                        5

   6 rows selected.
```

Note the use of the RTRIM function. Otherwise LENGTH would return 15 for every value.

Conversion Functions

These three conversion functions provide a handy way of converting one type of data to another. To demonstrate them we use the table CONVERSIONS.

```
SQL> SELECT * FROM CONVERSIONS;
```

```
NAME              TESTNUM
--------------    ---------
40                     95
13                     23
74                     68
```

The NAME column is a character string 15 characters wide, and TESTNUM is a number.

TO_CHAR

The primary use of this function is to convert a number into a character. Different implementations may also use it to convert other data types, like DATE, into a character, or to include different formatting arguments. This primary purpose gets the focus:

```
SQL> SELECT TESTNUM, TO_CHAR(TESTNUM)
   2 FROM CONVERT;
```

```
TESTNUM   TO_CHAR(TESTNUM)
--------  ----------------
     95                 95
     23                 23
     68                 68
```

Not very exciting, or convincing. Try this

```
SQL> SELECT TESTNUM, LENGTH(TO_CHAR(TESTNUM))
   2 FROM CONVERT;
```

```
TESTNUM LENGTH(TO_CHAR(TESTNUM))
-------- ------------------------
     95                        2
     23                        2
     68                        2
```

to verify the function returned a character string. LENGTH of a number would have returned an error. Notice the difference between this and the CHR function discussed earlier.

CHR would have turned this number into a character or a symbol, depending on which character set you are working with.

TO_NUMBER

This is the companion function to TO_CHAR, and of course it takes a string and converts it into a number. For example, type

```
SQL> SELECT NAME, TESTNUM, TESTNUM*TO_NUMBER(NAME)
  2  FROM CONVERT;
```

```
NAME            TESTNUM TESTNUM*TO_NUMBER(NAME)
--------------- --------- -----------------------
40                   95                    3800
13                   23                     299
74                   68                    5032
```

This would have returned an error if TO_NUMBER had returned a character.

Miscellaneous Functions

Here are three miscellaneous functions you may find useful.

GREATEST and LEAST

These functions find the GREATEST or the LEAST member from a series of expressions. For example

```
SQL> SELECT GREATEST('ALPHA', 'BRAVO','FOXTROT', 'DELTA')
  2  FROM CONVERT;
```

```
GREATEST
------
FOXTROT
FOXTROT
FOXTROT
```

Notice GREATEST found the word closest to the end of the alphabet. Notice also a seemingly unnecessary FROM and three occurrences of FOXTROT. Without the FROM there is an error. If you write a SELECT, you must use a FROM. The particular table used in the FROM has three rows, so the function in the SELECT clause is performed for each of them.

```
SQL> SELECT LEAST(34, 567, 3, 45, 1090)
  2  FROM CONVERT;
```

```
LEAST(34,567,3,45,1090)
-----------------------
                      3
                      3
                      3
```

This shows that these functions also work with numbers.

USER

This function returns information about the system. USER returns the character name of the current user of the database.

```
SQL> SELECT USER FROM CONVERT;
```

```
USER
------------------------------
PERKINS
PERKINS
PERKINS
```

There really is only one of me. Again, there is an echo because of the number of rows.

Summary

It has been a long day. We covered 47 different functions over very diverse areas, from aggregates to conversions. All of this is adding to your foundation knowledge of SQL. You don't have to remember every one of these functions—just knowing the general types (aggregate functions, date and time functions, arithmetic functions, character functions, conversion functions, and miscellaneous functions) is enough to point you in the right direction when you build a query that requires a function.

Q&A

Q Why are there so few functions defined in the ANSI standard and so many defined by the individual implementations?

A ANSI standards are broad strokes and are not meant to drive companies into bankruptcy by forcing all implementations to have dozens of functions. On the other hand, when company X adds a statistical package to its SQL and it sells well, you can bet company Y and Z will follow suit.

Workshop

The workshop provides quiz questions to help solidify your understanding of the material covered, as well as exercises to provide you with experience in using what you have learned. Try to answer the quiz and exercise questions before checking the answers in Appendix F and make sure you understand the answers before continuing to the next chapter.

Quiz

1. What function capitalizes the first letter of a character string and makes the rest lowercase?
2. What functions are also known by the name group functions?

Exercise

1. Using the TEAMSTATS table in the section on aggregate functions, write a query to determine who is batting under .25. (For the baseball-challenged, batting average is hits/ab.)

5

Clauses

Introduction

Today we talk about clauses. Not the kind that distribute presents during the holidays, but the ones you use with a SELECT statement. By the end of the day you will understand and be able to use the following clauses:

☐ WHERE

☐ STARTING WITH

☐ ORDER BY

☐ GROUP BY

☐ HAVING

To get a feel for where these functions fit in, let's look at the general syntax for a SELECT statement:

```
SELECT [DISTINCT ¦ ALL] { *
                    ¦ { [schema.]{table ¦ view ¦ snapshot}.*
                    ¦ expr } [ [AS] c_alias ]
                    [, { [schema.]{table ¦ view ¦ snapshot}.*
                    ¦ expr } [ [AS] c_alias ]  ] ... }
FROM [schema.]{table ¦ view ¦ snapshot}[@dblink] [t_alias]
[, [schema.]{table ¦ view ¦ snapshot}[@dblink] [t_alias] ] ...
    [WHERE condition ]
    [GROUP BY expr [, expr] ... [HAVING condition] ]
    [{UNION ¦ UNION ALL ¦ INTERSECT ¦ MINUS} SELECT command ]
    [ORDER BY {expr¦position} [ASC ¦ DESC]
         [, {expr¦position} [ASC ¦ DESC]] ...]
```

Note: In my experience with SQL, the ANSI standard is really more of an ANSI *suggestion*. The preceding syntax will generally work with any SQL engine, but there can be some slight variations.

Up until now we have avoided this type of complicated syntax diagram. Many people find them more puzzling than illuminating when learning something new, so we have looked for examples to illustrate a particular point. You are at the point in your SQL knowledge where this diagram serves to tie several of the concepts we have already covered to the concepts we will cover today. Don't worry about the exact syntax—it varies slightly from implementation to implementation anyway. Instead, focus on the relationships. At the top of this statement is SELECT, which you have used hundreds of times in previous examples. SELECT is followed by FROM, used with every SELECT statement you have typed (you learn a new use for FROM in the next chapter). WHERE, GROUP BY, HAVING, and ORDER BY all follow (UNION, UNION ALL, INTERSECT, and MINUS were covered in Day 3 in the section "Set Operators"). Each of these clauses plays an important part in selecting and manipulating data.

The WHERE Clause

Using just SELECT and FROM, you are limited to returning every row in a table. For example, using these two key words on the CHECKS table, you get all seven rows:

```
SQL> SELECT *
  2  FROM CHECKS;

   CHECK# PAYEE                     AMOUNT REMARKS
-------- -------------------- --------- -------------------
       1 Ma Bell                      150 Have sons next time
       2 Reading R.R.              245.34 Train to Chicago
       3 Ma Bell                   200.32 Cellular Phone
       4 Local Utilities               98 Gas
       5 Joes Stale $ Dent            150 Groceries
      16 Cash                          25 Wild Night Out
      17 Joans Gas                   25.1 Gas

7 rows selected.
```

With WHERE in your vocabulary, you can be more selective. To find all the checks you wrote with a value of more than $100, write this:

```
SQL> SELECT *
  2  FROM CHECKS
  3  WHERE AMOUNT > 100;
```

This returns the four instances in the table that meet the requirement:

```
   CHECK# PAYEE                     AMOUNT REMARKS
-------- -------------------- --------- -------------------
       1 Ma Bell                      150 Have sons next time
       2 Reading R.R.              245.34 Train to Chicago
       3 Ma Bell                   200.32 Cellular Phone
       5 Joes Stale $ Dent            150 Groceries
```

WHERE can also be used to solve other popular puzzles. Given the following table of names and locations

```
SQL> SELECT *
  2  FROM PUZZLE;

NAME            LOCATION
--------------- ---------------
TYLER           BACKYARD
MAJOR           KITCHEN
SPEEDY          LIVING ROOM
WALDO           GARAGE
LADDIE          UTILITY CLOSET
ARNOLD          TV ROOM

6 rows selected.
```

you can ask that popular question, "Where's Waldo?"

```
SQL> SELECT LOCATION AS "WHERE'S WALDO?"
  2  FROM PUZZLE
  3  WHERE NAME = 'WALDO';
```

Output

```
WHERE'S WALDO?
- - - - - - - - - - - - - -
GARAGE
```

Analysis

Sorry, we couldn't resist. We promise no more corny queries (we'll save those for that SQL bathroom humor book everyone's been wanting). Corniness aside, this query shows that the column used in the condition of the WHERE statement does not have to be mentioned in the SELECT clause. In this example you selected the location column but used WHERE on the name. This is perfectly legal. Also notice the AS on the SELECT line. This is an optional assignment operator, assigning the alias WHERE'S WALDO? to LOCATION. You might never see this again because it involves extra typing. In most implementations of SQL you can type

Input

```
SQL> SELECT LOCATION "WHERE'S WALDO?"
   2  FROM PUZZLE
   3  WHERE NAME ='WALDO';
```

with the same result:

Output

```
WHERE'S WALDO?
- - - - - - - - - - - - - -
GARAGE
```

Next to SELECT and FROM, WHERE will be your most frequently used SQL term.

The STARTING WITH Clause

STARTING WITH is an addition to the WHERE clause that works exactly like LIKE(<exp>%). Compare this

Input

```
SELECT PAYEE, AMOUNT, REMARKS
FROM CHECKS
WHERE PAYEE LIKE('Ca%');
```

Output

```
PAYEE                       AMOUNT REMARKS
==================== =============== ====================

Cash                            25 Wild Night Out
Cash                            60 Trip to Boston
Cash                            34 Trip to Dayton
```

with the results from this query:

Input

```
SELECT PAYEE, AMOUNT, REMARKS
FROM CHECKS
WHERE PAYEE STARTING WITH('Ca');
```

```
PAYEE                   AMOUNT REMARKS
==================== =============== ====================

Cash                        25 Wild Night Out
Cash                        60 Trip to Boston
Cash                        34 Trip to Dayton
```

The results are identical. You can even use them together, as shown by this:

```
SELECT PAYEE, AMOUNT, REMARKS
FROM CHECKS
WHERE PAYEE STARTING WITH('Ca')
OR
REMARKS LIKE 'G%';
```

```
PAYEE                   AMOUNT REMARKS
==================== =============== ====================

Local Utilities             98 Gas
Joes Stale $ Dent          150 Groceries
Cash                        25 Wild Night Out
Joans Gas                 25.1 Gas
Cash                        60 Trip to Boston
Cash                        34 Trip to Dayton
Joans Gas                15.75 Gas
```

Note: STARTING WITH is a common feature of most implementations of SQL. Check your implementation before you grow fond of it.

Order from Chaos:
The ORDER BY Clause

From time to time it is imperative that the results of your query be presented in some kind of order. SELECT FROM gives you a listing, and unless you have defined a primary key (discussed in Day 10, "Creating Views and Indexes"), your query comes out in the order the rows were entered. Consider a beefed-up CHECKS table:

```
SQL> SELECT * FROM CHECKS;
```

```
CHECK# PAYEE                  AMOUNT REMARKS
--------- -------------------- --------- ----------------
      1 Ma Bell                  150 Have sons next time
      2 Reading R.R.          245.34 Train to Chicago
      3 Ma Bell               200.32 Cellular Phone
      4 Local Utilities          98 Gas
      5 Joes Stale $ Dent        150 Groceries
     16 Cash                      25 Wild Night Out
```

```
         17 Joans Gas                 25.1 Gas
          9 Abes Cleaners            24.35 X-Tra Starch
         20 Abes Cleaners            10.5 All Dry Clean
          8 Cash                        60 Trip to Boston
         21 Cash                        34 Trip to Dayton

11 rows selected.
```

You're going to have to trust me on this one, but this is exactly the order in which we entered the data. After you read Day 8, where you learn how to use INSERT to create tables, you can try this on your own.

The ORDER BY clause gives you a way of ordering your results. For example, if you wanted the preceding listing ordered by check number, you would type this:

```
SQL> SELECT *
  2   FROM CHECKS
  3   ORDER BY CHECK#;
```

```
    CHECK# PAYEE                      AMOUNT REMARKS
    ------ -------------------- --------- --------------------
          1 Ma Bell                        150 Have sons next time
          2 Reading R.R.                245.34 Train to Chicago
          3 Ma Bell                     200.32 Cellular Phone
          4 Local Utilities               98 Gas
          5 Joes Stale $ Dent            150 Groceries
          8 Cash                          60 Trip to Boston
          9 Abes Cleaners              24.35 X-Tra Starch
         16 Cash                          25 Wild Night Out
         17 Joans Gas                  25.1 Gas
         20 Abes Cleaners              10.5 All Dry Clean
         21 Cash                          34 Trip to Dayton

11 rows selected.
```

Now you have the data ordered the way you want it, not the way it was entered.

In your journey through SQL, you have seen several key words that were optional. For example, in this chapter you saw that AS could be used to assign an alias, but it wasn't really needed. Is BY such a term? Try this:

```
SQL> SELECT * FROM CHECKS ORDER CHECK#;
```

```
SELECT * FROM CHECKS ORDER CHECK#
                           *
ERROR at line 1:
ORA-00924: missing BY keyword
```

The answer is no. ORDER requires BY; it is not optional.

What if you needed the data listed in reverse, with the highest number or letter first? You're in luck! For instance, to list the PAYEEs starting at the end of the alphabet, you query like this:

```
SQL> SELECT *
  2  FROM CHECKS
  3  ORDER BY PAYEE DESC;
```

```
       CHECK# PAYEE                     AMOUNT REMARKS
    --------- --------------------    --------- --------------------
            2 Reading R.R.             245.34 Train to Chicago
            1 Ma Bell                     150 Have sons next time
            3 Ma Bell                  200.32 Cellular Phone
            4 Local Utilities             98 Gas
            5 Joes Stale $ Dent          150 Groceries
           17 Joans Gas                 25.1 Gas
           16 Cash                        25 Wild Night Out
            8 Cash                        60 Trip to Boston
           21 Cash                        34 Trip to Dayton
            9 Abes Cleaners            24.35 X-Tra Starch
           20 Abes Cleaners             10.5 All Dry Clean

11 rows selected.
```

The new bit is the DESC at the end of the ORDER BY clause. This causes the list to be ordered in descending order instead of the default ascending order. Here you find another optional, and almost never-used keyword, ASC:

```
SQL> SELECT PAYEE, AMOUNT
  2  FROM CHECKS
  3  ORDER BY CHECK# ASC;
```

```
PAYEE                     AMOUNT
--------------------    ---------
Ma Bell                     150
Reading R.R.             245.34
Ma Bell                  200.32
Local Utilities             98
Joes Stale $ Dent          150
Cash                        60
Abes Cleaners            24.35
Cash                        25
Joans Gas                 25.1
Abes Cleaners             10.5
Cash                        34

11 rows selected.
```

5

There are a couple of things evident here. First, if you compare this list with the one you did at the beginning of the section when the ORDER BY clause was not followed by ASC, you will see that the ordering is identical. This is because ASC is the default. The other notable thing about this query is that it shows that the expression used after the ORDER BY clause does not have to be in the SELECT statement. In this example you selected only PAYEE and AMOUNT and were still able to successfully order by CHECK#.

Sometimes it might be useful to use ORDER BY on more than one field. To order CHECKS by PAYEE and REMARKS, you would query as follows:

```
SQL> SELECT *
  2  FROM CHECKS
  3  ORDER BY PAYEE, REMARKS;
```

```
CHECK# PAYEE                AMOUNT REMARKS
--------- ------------------ --------- ------------------
       20 Abes Cleaners        10.5 All Dry Clean
        9 Abes Cleaners       24.35 X-Tra Starch
        8 Cash                   60 Trip to Boston
       21 Cash                   34 Trip to Dayton
       16 Cash                   25 Wild Night Out
       17 Joans Gas            25.1 Gas
        5 Joes Stale $ Dent     150 Groceries
        4 Local Utilities        98 Gas
        3 Ma Bell            200.32 Cellular Phone
        1 Ma Bell               150 Have sons next time
        2 Reading R.R.       245.34 Train to Chicago
```

Notice the entries for Cash under the PAYEE Column. In the previous ORDER BY the CHECK#s were in the order of 16, 21, 8. Now, with the addition of the second field, REMARKS, into the ORDER BY clause, they are ordered alphabetically according to REMARKS. Does the order of multiple columns in the ORDER BY clause make a difference? Let's do the same query and simply reverse PAYEE and REMARKS:

```
SQL> SELECT *
  2  FROM CHECKS
  3  ORDER BY REMARKS, PAYEE;
```

```
CHECK# PAYEE                AMOUNT REMARKS
--------- ------------------ --------- ------------------
       20 Abes Cleaners        10.5 All Dry Clean
        3 Ma Bell            200.32 Cellular Phone
       17 Joans Gas            25.1 Gas
        4 Local Utilities        98 Gas
        5 Joes Stale $ Dent     150 Groceries
        1 Ma Bell               150 Have sons next time
        2 Reading R.R.       245.34 Train to Chicago
        8 Cash                   60 Trip to Boston
       21 Cash                   34 Trip to Dayton
       16 Cash                   25 Wild Night Out
        9 Abes Cleaners       24.35 X-Tra Starch
```

```
11 rows selected.
```

As you might have guessed, the results are completely different. Suppose you needed the results from one column ordered alphabetically and the second column in reverse alphabetical order. Try this:

```
SQL> SELECT *
  2  FROM CHECKS
  3  ORDER BY PAYEE ASC, REMARKS DESC;
```

```
CHECK# PAYEE                AMOUNT REMARKS
--------- ------------------ --------- ------------------
        9 Abes Cleaners       24.35 X-Tra Starch
       20 Abes Cleaners        10.5 All Dry Clean
       16 Cash                   25 Wild Night Out
```

```
           21  Cash                        34  Trip to Dayton
            8  Cash                        60  Trip to Boston
           17  Joans Gas                 25.1  Gas
            5  Joes Stale $ Dent          150  Groceries
            4  Local Utilities             98  Gas
            1  Ma Bell                    150  Have sons next time
            3  Ma Bell                 200.32  Cellular Phone
            2  Reading R.R.            245.34  Train to Chicago

11 rows selected.
```

In this example, PAYEE is sorted alphabetically and REMARKS is in descending order. Note how the remarks in the three checks with a PAYEE of Cash are sorted.

There is another way to specify the column you wish to order. If you know that CHECK# column is the first column (which you would know because it appears first when you type **SELECT ***, which lists columns in order) you could type this:

```
SQL> SELECT *
  2  FROM CHECKS
  3  ORDER BY 1;
```

```
CHECK# PAYEE                      AMOUNT REMARKS
-------- -------------------- ---------- -------------------
       1 Ma Bell                     150 Have sons next time
       2 Reading R.R.             245.34 Train to Chicago
       3 Ma Bell                  200.32 Cellular Phone
       4 Local Utilities              98 Gas
       5 Joes Stale $ Dent           150 Groceries
       8 Cash                         60 Trip to Boston
       9 Abes Cleaners             24.35 X-Tra Starch
      16 Cash                         25 Wild Night Out
      17 Joans Gas                  25.1 Gas
      20 Abes Cleaners              10.5 All Dry Clean
      21 Cash                         34 Trip to Dayton

11 rows selected.
```

As you can see upon comparing this with the first ORDER BY query you did, this is identical to the result produced by this:

```
SELECT * FROM CHECKS ORDER BY CHECK#;
```

The GROUP BY Clause

On Day 3 you learned how to use aggregate functions (COUNT, SUM, AVG, MIN, and MAX). If you wanted to find out the total amount of money spent from the slightly changed CHECKS table, you would type

```
SELECT *
FROM CHECKS;
```

to see the modified table:

```
CHECKNUM PAYEE            AMOUNT          REMARKS
======= ============= =============== =====================

      1 Ma Bell                   150 Have sons next time
      2 Reading R.R.           245.34  Train to Chicago
      3 Ma Bell                200.33 Cellular Phone
      4 Local Utilities            98 Gas
      5 Joes Stale $ Dent         150 Groceries
     16 Cash                       25 Wild Night Out
     17 Joans Gas                25.1 Gas
      9 Abes Cleaners           24.35 X-Tra Starch
     20 Abes Cleaners            10.5 All Dry Clean
      8 Cash                       60 Trip to Boston
     21 Cash                       34 Trip to Dayton
     30 Local Utilities          87.5 Water
     31 Local Utilities            34 Sewer
     25 Joans Gas               15.75 Gas
```

Then you would type

```
SELECT SUM(AMOUNT)
FROM CHECKS;
```

```
            SUM
===============

        1159.87
```

This, of course, returns the sum of the column AMOUNT. What if you wanted to find out how much you have spent on each PAYEE? SQL helps you with the GROUP BY clause. To find out who you have paid and how much, you would query like this:

```
SELECT PAYEE, SUM(AMOUNT)
FROM CHECKS
GROUP BY PAYEE;
```

```
PAYEE                         SUM
==================== ===============

Abes Cleaners          34.849998
Cash                         119
Joans Gas              40.849998
Joes Stale $ Dent            150
Local Utilities            219.5
Ma Bell                350.33002
Reading R.R.              245.34
```

Let's examine this statement more closely. In the SELECT clause you have a normal column selection, PAYEE, followed by the aggregate function SUM(AMOUNT). If you had tried this with only the FROM CHECKS that follows, you would see this:

```
SELECT PAYEE, SUM(AMOUNT)
FROM CHECKS;
```

SQL is complaining about the combination of the normal column and the aggregate function. This is where the GROUP BY comes in. GROUP BY runs the aggregate function described in the SELECT statement for each grouping of the column that follows the GROUP BY clause. The table CHECKS returned 14 rows when queried with SELECT * FROM CHECKS. The query on the same table, SELECT PAYEE, SUM(AMOUNT) FROM CHECKS GROUP BY PAYEE, took the 14 rows in the table and made seven groupings, returning the SUM of each grouping.

Can you use more than one aggregate function? Suppose you wanted to know how much you gave to whom with how many checks. Let's query:

```
SELECT PAYEE, SUM(AMOUNT), COUNT(PAYEE)
FROM CHECKS
GROUP BY PAYEE;
```

PAYEE	SUM	COUNT
====================	===============	===========
Abes Cleaners	34.849998	2
Cash	119	3
Joans Gas	40.849998	2
Joes Stale $ Dent	150	1
Local Utilities	219.5	3
Ma Bell	350.33002	2
Reading R.R.	245.34	1

This SQL is becoming more and more useful! What would happen if you tried to group by more than one column? Try this:

```
SELECT PAYEE, SUM(AMOUNT), COUNT(PAYEE)
FROM CHECKS
GROUP BY PAYEE, REMARKS;
```

PAYEE	SUM	COUNT
====================	===============	===========
Abes Cleaners	10.5	1
Abes Cleaners	24.35	1
Cash	60	1
Cash	34	1
Cash	25	1
Joans Gas	40.849998	2
Joes Stale $ Dent	150	1
Local Utilities	98	1
Local Utilities	34	1
Local Utilities	87.5	1
Ma Bell	200.33	1
Ma Bell	150	1
Reading R.R.	245.34	1

5

This is interesting. You have gone from 7 groupings of 14 rows to 13 groupings. What is different about the one grouping with more than one check associated with it? Look at the entries for Joans Gas:

```
SELECT PAYEE, REMARKS
FROM CHECKS
WHERE PAYEE = 'Joans Gas';
```

```
PAYEE                   REMARKS
==================== ====================

Joans Gas               Gas
Joans Gas               Gas
```

You see that the combination of PAYEE and REMARKS creates identical entities, which SQL groups together into one line with the GROUP BY clause. The other rows produce unique combinations of PAYEE and REMARKS and are assigned their own unique groupings.

If you wanted to find the largest and smallest amounts, grouped by REMARKS, you would type this:

```
SELECT MIN(AMOUNT), MAX(AMOUNT)
FROM CHECKS
GROUP BY REMARKS;
```

```
            MIN              MAX
=============== ===============

         245.34           245.34
           10.5             10.5
         200.33           200.33
          15.75               98
            150              150
            150              150
             34               34
             60               60
             34               34
           87.5             87.5
             25               25
          24.35            24.35
```

If you try to include a column in the select statement that has several different values within the group formed by GROUP BY, this will happen:

```
SELECT PAYEE, MAX(AMOUNT), MIN(AMOUNT)
FROM CHECKS
GROUP BY REMARKS;
```

```
Dynamic SQL Error
-SQL error code = -104
-invalid column reference
```

Using our table, this query tries to group checks by remark. When it finds two records with the same remark but different PAYEEs, like the rows that have gas as a remark but have PAYEEs of Local Utilities and Joans Gas, it throws out an error.

OK, so the rule is don't SELECT columns that have multiple values for the column used in the GROUP BY clause. The reverse is not true. You can use GROUP BY on columns not mentioned in the SELECT statement. For example:

```
SELECT PAYEE, COUNT(AMOUNT)
FROM CHECKS
GROUP BY PAYEE, AMOUNT;
```

```
PAYEE                        COUNT
==================== ===========

Abes Cleaners                    1
Abes Cleaners                    1
Cash                             1
Cash                             1
Cash                             1
Joans Gas                        1
Joans Gas                        1
Joes Stale $ Dent                1
Local Utilities                  1
Local Utilities                  1
Local Utilities                  1
Ma Bell                          1
Ma Bell                          1
Reading R.R.                     1
```

This is a silly query unless you need to show how many checks you had written for identical amounts to the same PAYEE. However, it shows that AMOUNT can be used in the GROUP BY clause, even though it is not mentioned in the SELECT clause. Try moving AMOUNT out of the GROUP BY clause and into the SELECT clause, like this:

```
SELECT PAYEE, AMOUNT, COUNT(AMOUNT)
FROM CHECKS
GROUP BY PAYEE;
```

```
Dynamic SQL Error
-SQL error code = -104
-invalid column reference
```

You find that SQL cannot run the query. This makes sense if you play the part of SQL for a moment. Say you had the following lines you had to group:

```
SELECT PAYEE, AMOUNT, REMARKS
FROM CHECKS
WHERE PAYEE ='Cash';
```

```
PAYEE                        AMOUNT REMARKS
==================== =============== ====================

Cash                             25 Wild Night Out
Cash                             60 Trip to Boston
Cash                             34 Trip to Dayton
```

If the user asked you to output all three columns and group by PAYEE only, where would you put the unique remarks? Remember you have only one row per group when you use GROUP BY. SQL can't do two things at once, so it complains (much as I do

5

at work to no avail—maybe I should try handing my boss a note with "Error #31: Can't do two things at once" written on it).

The HAVING Clause

How can you qualify the data used in your GROUP BY clause? Using the table ORGCHART, try this:

```
SELECT * FROM ORGCHART;
```

NAME	TEAM	SALARY	SICKLEAVE	ANNUALLEAVE
======	======	========	===========	=============
ADAMS	RESEARCH	34000.00	34	12
WILKES	MARKETING	31000.00	40	9
STOKES	MARKETING	36000.00	20	19
MEZA	COLLECTIONS	40000.00	30	27
MERRICK	RESEARCH	45000.00	20	17
RICHARDSON	MARKETING	42000.00	25	18
FURY	COLLECTIONS	35000.00	22	14
PRECOURT	PR	37500.00	24	24

If you wanted to group this into divisions and show the average salary in each division, you would type this:

```
SELECT TEAM, AVG(SALARY)
FROM ORGCHART
GROUP BY TEAM;
```

TEAM	AVG
======	=====
COLLECTIONS	37500.00
MARKETING	36333.33
PR	37500.00
RESEARCH	39500.00

If you wanted to qualify this query to return only those departments with average salaries under $38,000, you might try this:

```
SELECT TEAM, AVG(SALARY)
FROM ORGCHART
WHERE AVG(SALARY) < 38000
GROUP BY TEAM;
```

```
Dynamic SQL Error
-SQL error code = -104
-Invalid aggregate reference
```

This error occurred because WHERE does not work with aggregate functions. To make this query, you need something new. You need the HAVING clause. If you type

```
SELECT TEAM, AVG(SALARY)
FROM ORGCHART
GROUP BY TEAM
HAVING AVG(SALARY) < 38000;
```

```
TEAM                AVG
=============== ===========

COLLECTIONS       37500.00
MARKETING         36333.33
PR                37500.00
```

 you get what you asked for. HAVING enables you to use aggregate functions in a comparison statement, providing for aggregate functions what WHERE provides for individual rows. Does HAVING work with non-aggregate expressions? Try this:

```
SELECT TEAM, AVG(SALARY)
FROM ORGCHART
GROUP BY TEAM
HAVING SALARY < 38000;
```

```
TEAM                AVG
=============== ===========

PR                37500.00
```

 This is interesting. Why is this different from the last query? The HAVING AVG(SALARY) < 38000 clause evaluated each grouping and returned only those with an average salary of under $38,000, just what you expected. HAVING SALARY < 38000, on the other hand, had a different outcome. Let's play SQL engine again. If the user asks you to evaluate and return groups of divisions where SALARY < 38000, you would examine each group and reject those where an individual SALARY is greater than 38000. In each division, except PR, you would find at least one salary over 38000:

```
SELECT NAME, TEAM, SALARY
FROM ORGCHART
ORDER BY TEAM;
```

```
NAME            TEAM             SALARY
=============== ================ ===========

FURY            COLLECTIONS      35000.00
MEZA            COLLECTIONS      40000.00
WILKES          MARKETING        31000.00
STOKES          MARKETING        36000.00
RICHARDSON      MARKETING        42000.00
PRECOURT        PR               37500.00
ADAMS           RESEARCH         34000.00
MERRICK         RESEARCH         45000.00
```

Therefore, you would reject all other groups except PR. What you really asked was "Select all groups where no individual makes more than $38,000." Don't you just hate it when the computer does exactly what you tell it to?

Note: Some implementations of SQL return an error if you use anything other than an aggregate function in a HAVING clause. Don't bet the farm on using the previous example until you check the implementation of the particular SQL you use.

Can you use more than one condition in your HAVING clause? Try this:

```
SELECT TEAM, AVG(SICKLEAVE),AVG(ANNUALLEAVE)
FROM ORGCHART
GROUP BY TEAM
HAVING AVG(SICKLEAVE)>25 AND
AVG(ANNUALLEAVE)<20;
```

This produces a table grouped by team, showing all the teams with SICKLEAVE averages above 25 days and ANNUALLEAVE averages below 20 days, and looks like:

```
TEAM                AVG           AVG
===============  ===========  ===========

MARKETING            28            15
RESEARCH             27            15
```

You can also use an aggregate function in the HAVING clause that was not in the SELECT statement. For example:

```
SELECT TEAM, AVG(SICKLEAVE),AVG(ANNUALLEAVE)
FROM ORGCHART
GROUP BY TEAM
HAVING COUNT(TEAM) > 1;
```

```
TEAM                AVG           AVG
===============  ===========  ===========

COLLECTIONS          26            21
MARKETING            28            15
RESEARCH             27            15
```

This query returns the number of teams with more than one member. COUNT(TEAM) is not used in the SELECT statement but still functions as expected in the HAVING clause.

The other logical operators all work well within the HAVING clause. Consider this:

```
SELECT TEAM,MIN(SALARY),MAX(SALARY)
FROM ORGCHART
GROUP BY TEAM
HAVING AVG(SALARY) > 37000
OR
MIN(SALARY) > 32000;
```

```
TEAM                    MIN         MAX
=============== =========== ===========

COLLECTIONS        35000.00    40000.00
PR                 37500.00    37500.00
RESEARCH           34000.00    45000.00
```

The operator IN also works in a HAVING clause, as demonstrated by this:

```
SELECT TEAM,AVG(SALARY)
FROM ORGCHART
GROUP BY TEAM
HAVING TEAM IN ('PR','RESEARCH');
```

```
TEAM                    AVG
=============== ===========

PR                 37500.00
RESEARCH           39500.00
```

Combinations of Clauses

Nothing exists in a vacuum, so let's see how you can make combinations of these clauses perform together. This section takes you through some composite exercises.

Exercise 5.1

Find all the checks written for Cash and Gas in the CHECKS table and order them by REMARKS.

```
SELECT PAYEE, REMARKS
FROM CHECKS
WHERE PAYEE = 'Cash'
OR REMARKS LIKE 'Ga%'
ORDER BY REMARKS;
```

```
PAYEE                REMARKS
==================== ====================

Joans Gas            Gas
Joans Gas            Gas
Local Utilities      Gas
Cash                 Trip to Boston
Cash                 Trip to Dayton
Cash                 Wild Night Out
```

Note the use of LIKE to find the remarks that started with Ga. You were lucky in this small table, but this could have led to a match with any word that started with Ga. Be careful what you ask for.

Could you ask for the same information and group it by PAYEE? The query would look something like this:

```
SELECT PAYEE, REMARKS
FROM CHECKS
WHERE PAYEE = 'Cash'
OR REMARKS LIKE'Ga%'
ORDER BY REMARKS
GROUP BY PAYEE;
```

This would not work because the SQL engine would not know what to do with the remarks. Remember that whatever columns you put in the SELECT clause must also be in the GROUP BY clause—unless you don't specify any columns in the SELECT clause.

Exercise 5.2

Using the table ORGCHART, find the salary of everyone with less than 25 days of sick leave. Order the results by NAME.

```
SELECT NAME, SALARY
FROM ORGCHART
WHERE SICKLEAVE < 25
ORDER BY NAME;
```

NAME	SALARY
===============	===========
FURY	35000.00
MERRICK	45000.00
PRECOURT	37500.00
STOKES	36000.00

This is pretty straightforward using your new-found skills with WHERE and ORDER BY.

Exercise 5.3

Again, using ORGCHART, display TEAM, AVG(SALARY), AVG(SICKLEAVE), and AVG(ANNUALLEAVE) on each team:

```
SELECT TEAM,
AVG(SALARY),
AVG(SICKLEAVE),
AVG(ANNUALLEAVE)
FROM ORGCHART
GROUP BY TEAM;
```

TEAM	AVG	AVG	AVG
===============	===========	===========	===========
COLLECTIONS	37500.00	26	21
MARKETING	36333.33	28	15
PR	37500.00	24	24
RESEARCH	39500.00	26	15

Here's an interesting variation on this query. See if you can figure out what happened:

```
SELECT TEAM,
AVG(SALARY),
AVG(SICKLEAVE),
AVG(ANNUALLEAVE)
FROM ORGCHART
GROUP BY TEAM
ORDER BY NAME;
```

```
TEAM                     AVG          AVG          AVG
================ =========== =========== ===========

RESEARCH            39500.00          27           15
COLLECTIONS         37500.00          26           21
PR                  37500.00          24           24
MARKETING           36333.33          28           15
```

A simpler query using ORDER BY might shed some light on this:

```
SELECT NAME, TEAM
FROM ORGCHART
ORDER BY NAME, TEAM;
```

```
NAME             TEAM
=============== ===============

ADAMS            RESEARCH
FURY             COLLECTIONS
MERRICK          RESEARCH
MEZA             COLLECTIONS
PRECOURT         PR
RICHARDSON       MARKETING
STOKES           MARKETING
WILKES           MARKETING
```

 When the SQL engine got around to ordering the results of the query, it used the NAME column (remember, it is perfectly legal to use a column not specified in the SELECT statement), ignored duplicate TEAM entries, and came up with the order RESEARCH, COLLECTIONS, PR, and MARKETING. Including TEAM in the ORDER BY clause is unnecessary, because you have unique values in the NAME column. You can get the same result by typing this:

```
SELECT NAME, TEAM
FROM ORGCHART
ORDER BY NAME;
```

```
NAME             TEAM
=============== ===============

ADAMS            RESEARCH
FURY             COLLECTIONS
MERRICK          RESEARCH
MEZA             COLLECTIONS
PRECOURT         PR
RICHARDSON       MARKETING
STOKES           MARKETING
WILKES           MARKETING
```

While you are looking at variations, don't forget you can reverse the order with this:

```
SELECT NAME, TEAM
FROM ORGCHART
ORDER BY NAME DESC;
```

```
NAME             TEAM
===============  ================

WILKES           MARKETING
STOKES           MARKETING
RICHARDSON       MARKETING
PRECOURT         PR
MEZA             COLLECTIONS
MERRICK          RESEARCH
FURY             COLLECTIONS
ADAMS            RESEARCH
```

Exercise 5.4

Is it possible to use all of what you have learned in one query? It is, but the results will be convoluted because in many ways you are working with apples and oranges—or aggregates and non-aggregates, if you prefer. For example, WHERE and ORDER BY are usually found in queries that act on single rows, such as this:

```
SELECT *
FROM ORGCHART
ORDER BY NAME DESC;
```

```
NAME             TEAM         SALARY    SICKLEAVE  ANNUALLEAVE
===============  ========  ===========  =========  ===========

WILKES           MARKETING    31000.00        40            9
STOKES           MARKETING    36000.00        20           19
RICHARDSON       MARKETING    42000.00        25           18
PRECOURT         PR           37500.00        24           24
MEZA             COLLECTIONS  40000.00        30           27
MERRICK          RESEARCH     45000.00        20           17
FURY             COLLECTIONS  35000.00        22           14
ADAMS            RESEARCH     34000.00        34           12
```

GROUP BY and HAVING are normally seen in the company of aggregates:

```
SELECT PAYEE,
SUM(AMOUNT) TOTAL,
COUNT(PAYEE) NUMBER_WRITTEN
FROM CHECKS
GROUP BY PAYEE
HAVING SUM(AMOUNT) > 50;
```

```
PAYEE                         TOTAL  NUMBER_WRITTEN
====================  =============  ==============

Cash                            119               3
Joes Stale $ Dent               150               1
```

```
Local Utilities                 219.5              3
Ma Bell                     350.33002              2
Reading R.R.                   245.34              1
```

You have seen that combining these two groups of clauses can have unexpected results, including the following:

```
SELECT PAYEE,
SUM(AMOUNT) TOTAL,
COUNT(PAYEE) NUMBER_WRITTEN
FROM CHECKS
WHERE AMOUNT >= 100
GROUP BY PAYEE
HAVING SUM(AMOUNT) > 50;
```

```
PAYEE                             TOTAL NUMBER_WRITTEN
==================== =============== ==============

Joes Stale $ Dent                   150              1
Ma Bell                       350.33002              2
Reading R.R.                     245.34              1
```

Compare these two result sets to each other and look at the raw data:

```
SELECT PAYEE, AMOUNT
FROM CHECKS
ORDER BY PAYEE;
```

```
PAYEE                            AMOUNT
==================== ===============

Abes Cleaners                      10.5
Abes Cleaners                     24.35
Cash                                 25
Cash                                 34
Cash                                 60
Joans Gas                         15.75
Joans Gas                          25.1
Joes Stale $ Dent                   150
Local Utilities                      34
Local Utilities                    87.5
Local Utilities                      98
Ma Bell                             150
Ma Bell                          200.33
Reading R.R.                     245.34
```

You see how the WHERE clause filtered out all the checks less than $100 before GROUP BY did its thing? We are not trying to tell you not to mix these groups—you may have a requirement that this sort of construction will meet. However, you should not casually mix aggregate and non-aggregate functions. The previous examples have been tables with only a handful of rows (otherwise you would need a cart to carry this book). In the real world you will be working with thousands and thousands (or billions and billions) of rows, and the subtle changes brought about by mixing these clauses might not be so apparent.

Summary

Today you learned all the clauses you need to exploit the power of a SELECT statement. Remember to be careful what you ask for, because you just might get it. This chapter completes your basic education. With what you know now you can work effectively with single tables. In the next chapter we extend our reach to include multiple tables.

Q&A

Q I thought we covered some of these functions in previous chapters. If so, why are we covering them again?

A We did indeed cover WHERE on Day 3. You needed a knowledge of WHERE to understand how certain operators worked. In this chapter we included WHERE again because it is a clause and this is the chapter on clauses. When you use this book as a reference, you don't want to have to search all over to find a clause, which you would expect to find in the chapter on clauses.

Workshop

The workshop provides quiz questions to help solidify your understanding of the material covered, as well as exercises to provide you with experience in using what you have learned. Try to answer the quiz and exercise questions before checking the answers in Appendix F, and make sure you understand the answers before continuing to the next chapter.

Quiz

1. Which clause works just like LIKE(<exp>%)?
2. Why won't the SQL engine let me select several columns to display when I am using only a few of them in the GROUP BY clause?

Exercise

1. Using the ORGCHART table used in many of the preceding examples, find out how many people on each team have 30 or more days of sick leave.

6

Joins

Objectives

Today you will learn about joins. What you learn today will enable you to gather and manipulate data across several tables. By the end of the day you will understand and be able to do the following:

- ☐ Perform an outer join
- ☐ Perform a left join
- ☐ Perform a right join
- ☐ Perform an equi-join
- ☐ Perform a non-equi-join
- ☐ Join a table to itself

Introduction

One of the most powerful features of SQL is its capability to gather and manipulate data from across several tables. If you couldn't do this, you would have to store all the data elements necessary for each application in one table. Without common tables you would need to store the same data in several tables. Imagine having to redesign, rebuild, and repopulate your tables and databases every time your user needed a query with a new piece of information. With the JOIN feature of SQL, you can design smaller, more specific, tables that are easier to maintain.

Like Dorothy in the "Wizard of OZ," you have had the power to join tables since Day 2, when you learned about SELECT and FROM. Unlike Dorothy, you don't have to click your heels together three times to perform a join. Use the following two tables, named, cleverly enough, TABLE1 and TABLE2:

> **Note:** The queries in the next two chapters were produced using Borlands ISQL tool. You will notice some differences from the previous queries. For example, there is no SQL prompt. Another difference is the lack of a semicolon at the end of the statement. ISQL will accept a semicolon but does not require one. The SQL basics, however, are still the same.

```
SELECT *
FROM TABLE1
```

```
ROW          REMARK
==========   ==========

row 1        Table 1
row 2        Table 1
```

```
row 3      Table 1
row 4      Table 1
row 5      Table 1
row 6      Table 1
```

```
SELECT *
FROM TABLE2
```

```
ROW          REMARKS
==========  ==========

row 1        table 2
row 2        table 2
row 3        table 2
row 4        table 2
row 5        table 2
row 6        table 2
```

To join these two tables, type this:

```
SELECT *
FROM TABLE1,TABLE2
```

```
ROW          REMARK       ROW          REMARKS
==========  ==========  ==========  ==========

row 1        Table 1      row 1        table 2
row 1        Table 1      row 2        table 2
row 1        Table 1      row 3        table 2
row 1        Table 1      row 4        table 2
row 1        Table 1      row 5        table 2
row 1        Table 1      row 6        table 2
row 2        Table 1      row 1        table 2
row 2        Table 1      row 2        table 2
row 2        Table 1      row 3        table 2
row 2        Table 1      row 4        table 2
row 2        Table 1      row 5        table 2
row 2        Table 1      row 6        table 2
row 3        Table 1      row 1        table 2
row 3        Table 1      row 2        table 2
row 3        Table 1      row 3        table 2
row 3        Table 1      row 4        table 2
row 3        Table 1      row 5        table 2
row 3        Table 1      row 6        table 2
row 4        Table 1      row 1        table 2
row 4        Table 1      row 2        table 2
row 4        Table 1      row 3        table 2
row 4        Table 1      row 4        table 2
row 4        Table 1      row 5        table 2
row 4        Table 1      row 6        table 2
row 5        Table 1      row 1        table 2
row 5        Table 1      row 2        table 2
row 5        Table 1      row 3        table 2
row 5        Table 1      row 4        table 2
row 5        Table 1      row 5        table 2
row 5        Table 1      row 6        table 2
```

6

```
row 6       Table 1     row 1       table 2
row 6       Table 1     row 2       table 2
row 6       Table 1     row 3       table 2
row 6       Table 1     row 4       table 2
row 6       Table 1     row 5       table 2
row 6       Table 1     row 6       table 2
```

Thirty-six rows! Where did all this come from? And what kind of join is this?

A close examination of the result of your first JOIN shows that each row from TABLE1 was added to each row from TABLE2. An extract from this JOIN illustrates this:

```
ROW         REMARK      ROW         REMARKS
==========  ==========  ==========  ==========

row 1       Table 1     row 1       table 2
row 1       Table 1     row 2       table 2
row 1       Table 1     row 3       table 2
row 1       Table 1     row 4       table 2
row 1       Table 1     row 5       table 2
row 1       Table 1     row 6       table 2
```

Notice how each row in TABLE2 was combined with row 1 in TABLE1. Congratulations! You have performed your first JOIN. But what kind of join? An inner, an outer, or what? Well, actually this is what's called a CROSS join. A Cross join is not normally as useful as the other joins we will cover in this chapter. But it does serve to illustrate the basic combinatory property of all joins. The basic rule is that joins bring tables together. How can we be more selective?

If we were more selective we could perform some useful work; let's try a real-world example.

Suppose you sold parts to bike shops for a living. When you designed your database, you built one big table with all the pertinent columns. Every time you had a new requirement, you added a new column or started a new table with all the old data plus the new data required to create a specific query. Eventually, your database would collapse from its own weight—not a pretty sight. An alternate design, based on a relational model, would have you put related data into the same table. For example, your customer table would look like this:

```
SELECT *
FROM CUSTOMER

NAME        ADDRESS      STATE  ZIP         PHONE      REMARKS
==========  ==========   ====== ==========  =========  ==========

TRUE WHEEL  550 HUSKER   NE     58702       555-4545   NONE
BIKE SPEC   CPT SHRIVE   LA     45678       555-1234   NONE
LE SHOPPE   HOMETOWN     KS     54678       555-1278   NONE
AAA BIKE    10 OLDTOWN   NE     56784       555-3421   JOHN-MGR
JACKS BIKE  24 EGLIN     FL     34567       555-2314   NONE
```

This table contains all the information you need to describe your customers. The items you sold would go into another table:

114

```
SELECT *
FROM PART
```

```
PARTNUM DESCRIPTION                   PRICE
=========== ==================== ===========

         54 PEDALS                     54.25
         42 SEATS                      24.50
         46 TIRES                      15.25
         23 MOUNTAIN BIKE             350.45
         76 ROAD BIKE                 530.00
         10 TANDEM                   1200.00
```

The orders you take would have their own table:

```
SELECT *
FROM ORDERS
```

```
ORDEREDON NAME         PARTNUM    QUANTITY REMARKS
=========== ========== =========== =========== ==========

15-MAY-1996 TRUE WHEEL        23           6 PAID
19-MAY-1996 TRUE WHEEL        76           3 PAID
 2-SEP-1996 TRUE WHEEL        10           1 PAID
30-JUN-1996 TRUE WHEEL        42           8 PAID
30-JUN-1996 BIKE SPEC         54          10 PAID
30-MAY-1996 BIKE SPEC         10           2 PAID
30-MAY-1996 BIKE SPEC         23           8 PAID
17-JAN-1996 BIKE SPEC         76          11 PAID
17-JAN-1996 LE SHOPPE         76           5 PAID
 1-JUN-1996 LE SHOPPE         10           3 PAID
 1-JUN-1996 AAA BIKE          10           1 PAID
 1-JUL-1996 AAA BIKE          76           4 PAID
 1-JUL-1996 AAA BIKE          46          14 PAID
11-JUL-1996 JACKS BIKE        76          14 PAID
```

One advantage this approach gives you is the ability to have three specialized people or departments responsible for maintaining data they are familiar with. You don't need a database administrator who is conversant with all aspects of your project to shepherd one gigantic, multidepartmental database. Another advantage is that in the age of networks, each table could reside on a different machine. People who understand the data could maintain it, and it could reside on an appropriate machine (rather than that nasty corporate mainframe protected by legions of system administrators). Now join PARTS and ORDERS:

```
SELECT  O.ORDEREDON, O.NAME, O.PARTNUM,
P.PARTNUM, P.DESCRIPTION
FROM ORDERS O, PART P
```

```
ORDEREDON NAME        PARTNUM PARTNUM DESCRIPTION
=========== ========== =========== ======= ====================

15-MAY-1996 TRUE WHEEL        23      54 PEDALS
19-MAY-1996 TRUE WHEEL        76      54 PEDALS
 2-SEP-1996 TRUE WHEEL        10      54 PEDALS
```

6

```
30-JUN-1996 TRUE WHEEL      42        54 PEDALS
30-JUN-1996 BIKE SPEC       54        54 PEDALS
30-MAY-1996 BIKE SPEC       10        54 PEDALS
30-MAY-1996 BIKE SPEC       23        54 PEDALS
17-JAN-1996 BIKE SPEC       76        54 PEDALS
17-JAN-1996 LE SHOPPE       76        54 PEDALS
 1-JUN-1996 LE SHOPPE       10        54 PEDALS
 1-JUN-1996 AAA BIKE        10        54 PEDALS
 1-JUL-1996 AAA BIKE        76        54 PEDALS
 1-JUL-1996 AAA BIKE        46        54 PEDALS
11-JUL-1996 JACKS BIKE      76        54 PEDALS
...
```

 The preceding code is just a portion of the result set. The actual set is 14 (number of rows in ORDERS) × 6 (number of rows in PART), or 84 rows. It is similar to the result from joining TABLE1 and TABLE2 earlier in the chapter, and it is still one statement shy of being useful. Before we tell you what that statement is, we need to regress a little and talk about another use for the alias.

Finding the Right Column

When you joined TABLE1 and TABLE2, you used SELECT *, which returned all the columns in both tables. In joining ORDERS to PART, the SELECT statement is a bit more complicated:

```
SELECT  O.ORDEREDON, O.NAME, O.PARTNUM,
P.PARTNUM, P.DESCRIPTION
```

SQL is smart enough to know that ORDEREDON and NAME exist only in ORDERS, and DESCRIPTION exists only in PART, but what about PARTNUM, which exists in both? If you have a column that has the same name in two tables, you must use an alias in your SELECT clause to specify which one you want to display. A common technique is to assign a single character to each table, as you did in the FROM clause:

```
FROM ORDERS O, PART P
```

You use that character with each column name, as you did in the preceding SELECT clause. The SELECT clause could also be written like this:

```
SELECT  ORDEREDON, NAME, O.PARTNUM, P.PARTNUM, DESCRIPTION
```

But remember, someday you might have to come back and maintain this query. It doesn't hurt to make it more readable. Now back to the missing statement.

Equi-Joins

An extract from the PART/ORDERS join provides you with a clue as to what is missing:

```
30-JUN-1996 TRUE WHEEL      42          54 PEDALS
30-JUN-1996 BIKE SPEC       54          54 PEDALS
30-MAY-1996 BIKE SPEC       10          54 PEDALS
```

Notice the PARTNUM fields that are common to both tables. What if you wrote the following?

```
SELECT  O.ORDEREDON, O.NAME, O.PARTNUM,
P.PARTNUM, P.DESCRIPTION
FROM ORDERS O, PART P
WHERE O.PARTNUM = P.PARTNUM
```

```
ORDEREDON NAME           PARTNUM PARTNUM DESCRIPTION
========== ========== =========== ======= =============

 1-JUN-1996 AAA BIKE         10          10 TANDEM
30-MAY-1996 BIKE SPEC        10          10 TANDEM
 2-SEP-1996 TRUE WHEEL       10          10 TANDEM
 1-JUN-1996 LE SHOPPE        10          10 TANDEM
30-MAY-1996 BIKE SPEC        23          23 MOUNTAIN BIKE
15-MAY-1996 TRUE WHEEL       23          23 MOUNTAIN BIKE
30-JUN-1996 TRUE WHEEL       42          42 SEATS
 1-JUL-1996 AAA BIKE         46          46 TIRES
30-JUN-1996 BIKE SPEC        54          54 PEDALS
 1-JUL-1996 AAA BIKE         76          76 ROAD BIKE
17-JAN-1996 BIKE SPEC        76          76 ROAD BIKE
19-MAY-1996 TRUE WHEEL       76          76 ROAD BIKE
11-JUL-1996 JACKS BIKE       76          76 ROAD BIKE
17-JAN-1996 LE SHOPPE        76          76 ROAD BIKE
```

This is the missing link that makes joins so useful. You have just combined the information you had stored in the ORDERS table with information from the PART table to show a description of the parts the bike shops have ordered from you. Using the WHERE clause to select the combined rows with the desired equality is called an equi-join.

You can further qualify this query with other conditions in the WHERE clause. For example:

```
SELECT  O.ORDEREDON, O.NAME, O.PARTNUM,
P.PARTNUM, P.DESCRIPTION
FROM ORDERS O, PART P
WHERE O.PARTNUM = P.PARTNUM
AND O.PARTNUM = 76
```

```
ORDEREDON NAME           PARTNUM PARTNUM DESCRIPTION
========== ========== =========== ====== ====================

 1-JUL-1996 AAA BIKE         76          76 ROAD BIKE
17-JAN-1996 BIKE SPEC        76          76 ROAD BIKE
19-MAY-1996 TRUE WHEEL       76          76 ROAD BIKE
11-JUL-1996 JACKS BIKE       76          76 ROAD BIKE
17-JAN-1996 LE SHOPPE        76          76 ROAD BIKE
```

The number 76 is not very descriptive, and you wouldn't want your sales people to have to memorize a part number. (This is not that uncommon—we have seen many data information systems in the field that required the end user to know some obscure code for something that had a perfectly good name. Please don't write one of those!) Let's try the query another way:

```
SELECT  O.ORDEREDON, O.NAME, O.PARTNUM,
P.PARTNUM, P.DESCRIPTION
FROM ORDERS O, PART P
WHERE O.PARTNUM = P.PARTNUM
AND P.DESCRIPTION = 'ROAD BIKE'
```

ORDEREDON	NAME	PARTNUM	PARTNUM	DESCRIPTION
1-JUL-1996	AAA BIKE	76	76	ROAD BIKE
17-JAN-1996	BIKE SPEC	76	76	ROAD BIKE
19-MAY-1996	TRUE WHEEL	76	76	ROAD BIKE
11-JUL-1996	JACKS BIKE	76	76	ROAD BIKE
17-JAN-1996	LE SHOPPE	76	76	ROAD BIKE

Let's use your new-found knowledge to find out something really useful, such as how much money you have made from selling road bikes:

```
SELECT SUM(O.QUANTITY * P.PRICE) TOTAL
FROM ORDERS O, PART P
WHERE O.PARTNUM = P.PARTNUM
AND P.DESCRIPTION = 'ROAD BIKE'
```

```
      TOTAL
===========

   19610.00
```

With this setup, the sales people can keep the ORDERS table updated, the production department can keep the PART table current, and you can find your bottom line without redesigning your database.

Can you join more than one table? Suppose you wanted to generate the information you needed to send out an invoice. You could type this:

```
SELECT C.NAME, C.ADDRESS, (O.QUANTITY * P.PRICE) TOTAL
FROM ORDER O, PART P, CUSTOMER C
WHERE O.PARTNUM = P.PARTNUM
AND O.NAME = C.NAME
```

NAME	ADDRESS	TOTAL
TRUE WHEEL	550 HUSKER	1200.00
BIKE SPEC	CPT SHRIVE	2400.00
LE SHOPPE	HOMETOWN	3600.00
AAA BIKE	10 OLDTOWN	1200.00
TRUE WHEEL	550 HUSKER	2102.70
BIKE SPEC	CPT SHRIVE	2803.60
TRUE WHEEL	550 HUSKER	196.00
AAA BIKE	10 OLDTOWN	213.50
BIKE SPEC	CPT SHRIVE	542.50
TRUE WHEEL	550 HUSKER	1590.00
BIKE SPEC	CPT SHRIVE	5830.00
JACKS BIKE	24 EGLIN	7420.00

```
       LE SHOPPE   HOMETOWN      2650.00
       AAA BIKE    10 OLDTOWN    2120.00
```

You could make this more readable by writing it like this:

```
SELECT C.NAME, C.ADDRESS,
O.QUANTITY * P.PRICE TOTAL
FROM ORDERS O, PART P, CUSTOMER C
WHERE O.PARTNUM = P.PARTNUM
AND O.NAME = C.NAME
ORDER BY C.NAME
```

```
NAME        ADDRESS        TOTAL
==========  ==========  ===========

AAA BIKE    10 OLDTOWN      213.50
AAA BIKE    10 OLDTOWN     2120.00
AAA BIKE    10 OLDTOWN     1200.00
BIKE SPEC   CPT SHRIVE      542.50
BIKE SPEC   CPT SHRIVE     2803.60
BIKE SPEC   CPT SHRIVE     5830.00
BIKE SPEC   CPT SHRIVE     2400.00
JACKS BIKE  24 EGLIN       7420.00
LE SHOPPE   HOMETOWN       2650.00
LE SHOPPE   HOMETOWN       3600.00
TRUE WHEEL  550 HUSKER      196.00
TRUE WHEEL  550 HUSKER     2102.70
TRUE WHEEL  550 HUSKER     1590.00
TRUE WHEEL  550 HUSKER     1200.00
```

You can make this nearly perfect by adding what the order was for:

```
SELECT C.NAME, C.ADDRESS,
O.QUANTITY * P.PRICE TOTAL,
P.DESCRIPTION
FROM ORDERS O, PART P, CUSTOMER C
WHERE O.PARTNUM = P.PARTNUM
AND O.NAME = C.NAME
ORDER BY C.NAME
```

```
NAME        ADDRESS        TOTAL DESCRIPTION
==========  ==========  =========== ====================

AAA BIKE    10 OLDTOWN      213.50 TIRES
AAA BIKE    10 OLDTOWN     2120.00 ROAD BIKE
AAA BIKE    10 OLDTOWN     1200.00 TANDEM
BIKE SPEC   CPT SHRIVE      542.50 PEDALS
BIKE SPEC   CPT SHRIVE     2803.60 MOUNTAIN BIKE
BIKE SPEC   CPT SHRIVE     5830.00 ROAD BIKE
BIKE SPEC   CPT SHRIVE     2400.00 TANDEM
JACKS BIKE  24 EGLIN       7420.00 ROAD BIKE
LE SHOPPE   HOMETOWN       2650.00 ROAD BIKE
LE SHOPPE   HOMETOWN       3600.00 TANDEM
TRUE WHEEL  550 HUSKER      196.00 SEATS
TRUE WHEEL  550 HUSKER     2102.70 MOUNTAIN BIKE
TRUE WHEEL  550 HUSKER     1590.00 ROAD BIKE
TRUE WHEEL  550 HUSKER     1200.00 TANDEM
```

6

This information is a result of joining three different tables. Now you could take this information and without too much trouble create an invoice so you could collect all that money you made.

> **Note:** As you start to use joins in your day-to-day life, remember back to the beginning of the chapter where you saw how SQL grouped TABLE1 and TABLE2, creating a new table with X (rows in TABLE1) × Y (rows in TABLE2) number of rows. The SELECT statement has cut down which rows are displayed, but to evaluate the WHERE clause SQL still creates all the possible rows. The sample tables in this chapter had only a handful of rows. Your actual data may have thousands of rows. If you are working on a platform with lots of horsepower, using a multi-table join might not visibly affect performance. However, if you are working in a slower environment, joins could cause a slowdown. We aren't saying don't use joins, because you have seen the advantages to be gained from a relational design. Just be aware of the platform you are designing, and your customer's requirements for speed versus reliability.

Non-Equi-Joins

If there is an equi-join, you might assume there is also a non-equi-join. You would be right! Where the equi-join uses an = sign in the WHERE statement, the non-equi-join uses anything but an = sign. For example

```
SELECT O.NAME, O.PARTNUM, P.PARTNUM,
O.QUANTITY * P.PRICE TOTAL
FROM ORDERS O, PART P
WHERE O.PARTNUM > P.PARTNUM
```

NAME	PARTNUM	PARTNUM	TOTAL
TRUE WHEEL	76	54	162.75
BIKE SPEC	76	54	596.75
LE SHOPPE	76	54	271.25
AAA BIKE	76	54	217.00
JACKS BIKE	76	54	759.50
TRUE WHEEL	76	42	73.50
BIKE SPEC	54	42	245.00
BIKE SPEC	76	42	269.50
LE SHOPPE	76	42	122.50
AAA BIKE	76	42	98.00
AAA BIKE	46	42	343.00
JACKS BIKE	76	42	343.00
TRUE WHEEL	76	46	45.75
BIKE SPEC	54	46	152.50
BIKE SPEC	76	46	167.75
LE SHOPPE	76	46	76.25

```
AAA BIKE          76        46        61.00
JACKS BIKE        76        46       213.50
TRUE WHEEL        76        23      1051.35
TRUE WHEEL        42        23      2803.60
...
```

This listing goes on to describe all the rows in the join WHERE O.PARTNUM > P.PARTNUM. In the context of your bicycle shop, this doesn't have much meaning, and in the real world the equi-join is by far the most common. However, you may encounter an application where a non-equi-join produces the perfect result.

Outer Joins

Just as there is a non-equi-join to balance out the equi-join, there is an OUTER JOIN to complement the INNER JOIN. An INNER JOIN is where the rows of the tables are combined with each other, producing a number of new rows equal to the product of the number of rows in each table. Also ,the INNER JOIN uses these rows to determine the result of the WHERE clause. An OUTER JOIN groups the two tables in a slightly different way. Using the PART and ORDERS tables from the previous examples, perform the INNER JOIN:

```
SELECT P.PARTNUM, P.DESCRIPTION,P.PRICE,
O.NAME, O.PARTNUM
FROM PART P
JOIN ORDERS O ON ORDERS.PARTNUM = 54
```

PARTNUM	DESCRIPTION	PRICE	NAME	PARTNUM
54	PEDALS	54.25	BIKE SPEC	54
42	SEATS	24.50	BIKE SPEC	54
46	TIRES	15.25	BIKE SPEC	54
23	MOUNTAIN BIKE	350.45	BIKE SPEC	54
76	ROAD BIKE	530.00	BIKE SPEC	54
10	TANDEM	1200.00	BIKE SPEC	54

Note: The syntax you used to get this join—JOIN ON—is not ANSI-standard. The implementation you used to perform this example has this additional syntax. You are using it here to specify an INNER and an OUTER JOIN. Most implementations of SQL have similar extensions.

The result is all the rows in PART spliced onto specific rows in ORDERS where the column PARTNUM is 54. Let's try an OUTER JOIN:

```
SELECT P.PARTNUM, P.DESCRIPTION,P.PRICE,
O.NAME, O.PARTNUM
FROM PART P
RIGHT OUTER JOIN ORDERS O ON ORDERS.PARTNUM = 54
```

6

```
PARTNUM      DESCRIPTION          PRICE NAME        PARTNUM
===========  =================  =========== =========== ===========

<null>       <null>             <null> TRUE WHEEL           23
<null>       <null>             <null> TRUE WHEEL           76
<null>       <null>             <null> TRUE WHEEL           10
<null>       <null>             <null> TRUE WHEEL           42
    54       PEDALS              54.25 BIKE SPEC           54
    42       SEATS               24.50 BIKE SPEC           54
    46       TIRES               15.25 BIKE SPEC           54
    23       MOUNTAIN BIKE      350.45 BIKE SPEC           54
    76       ROAD BIKE          530.00 BIKE SPEC           54
    10       TANDEM            1200.00 BIKE SPEC           54
<null>       <null>             <null> BIKE SPEC           10
<null>       <null>             <null> BIKE SPEC           23
<null>       <null>             <null> BIKE SPEC           76
<null>       <null>             <null> LE SHOPPE           76
<null>       <null>             <null> LE SHOPPE           10
<null>       <null>             <null> AAA BIKE            10
<null>       <null>             <null> AAA BIKE            76
<null>       <null>             <null> AAA BIKE            46
<null>       <null>             <null> JACKS BIKE          76
```

This is new. First, you specified a RIGHT OUTER JOIN. This caused SQL to return a full set of the right table, ORDERS, and to place nulls in the fields where ORDERS.PARTNUM <> 54. Following is a LEFT OUTER JOIN:

```
SELECT P.PARTNUM, P.DESCRIPTION,P.PRICE,
O.NAME, O.PARTNUM
FROM PART P
LEFT OUTER JOIN ORDERS O ON ORDERS.PARTNUM = 54
```

```
PARTNUM      DESCRIPTION          PRICE NAME        PARTNUM
===========  =================  =========== =========== ===========

54           PEDALS              54.25 BIKE SPEC           54
42           SEATS               24.50 BIKE SPEC           54
46           TIRES               15.25 BIKE SPEC           54
23           MOUNTAIN BIKE      350.45 BIKE SPEC           54
76           ROAD BIKE          530.00 BIKE SPEC           54
10           TANDEM            1200.00 BIKE SPEC           54
```

You get the same six rows as the INNER JOIN. Because you specified LEFT, the LEFT table, PART, determined the number of rows you would return. Because PART is smaller than ORDERS, SQL saw no need to pad those other fields with blanks.

Don't worry about INNER and OUTER JOINs too much. Most SQL products decide which type of JOIN is the most optimum for your query. In fact, if you are placing your query into a stored procedure (covered in Chapter 15) or using it inside a program (embedded SQL, covered in Chapter 13), we recommend you don't specify a JOIN type even if your SQL provides the proper syntax. If you do specify a JOIN type, the optimizer chooses your way instead of the optimum way.

Joining a Table to Itself

The last topic we cover today is the often-used technique of joining a table to itself. The syntax of this operation is similar to joining two tables. For example, to join the table TABLE1 to itself, type this:

```
SELECT *
FROM TABLE1, TABLE1
```

```
ROW          REMARK       ROW          REMARK
==========   ==========   ==========   ==========

row 1        Table 1      row 1        Table 1
row 1        Table 1      row 2        Table 1
row 1        Table 1      row 3        Table 1
row 1        Table 1      row 4        Table 1
row 1        Table 1      row 5        Table 1
row 1        Table 1      row 6        Table 1
row 2        Table 1      row 1        Table 1
row 2        Table 1      row 2        Table 1
row 2        Table 1      row 3        Table 1
row 2        Table 1      row 4        Table 1
row 2        Table 1      row 5        Table 1
row 2        Table 1      row 6        Table 1
row 3        Table 1      row 1        Table 1
row 3        Table 1      row 2        Table 1
row 3        Table 1      row 3        Table 1
row 3        Table 1      row 4        Table 1
row 3        Table 1      row 5        Table 1
row 3        Table 1      row 6        Table 1
row 4        Table 1      row 1        Table 1
row 4        Table 1      row 2        Table 1
...
```

 In its complete form, this produces the same number of combinations as joining two six-row tables. This type of JOIN could be useful to check the internal consistency of data. What would happen if someone fell asleep in the production department and entered a new part with a PARTNUM that already existed? That would be bad news for everybody: invoices would be wrong; your application would probably blow up; and in general it would be a very bad couple of weeks. And it would all be caused by this table:

```
SELECT * FROM PART
```

```
PARTNUM  DESCRIPTION          PRICE
=======  ===================  ===========

     54  PEDALS                  54.25
     42  SEATS                   24.50
     46  TIRES                   15.25
     23  MOUNTAIN BIKE          350.45
     76  ROAD BIKE              530.00
     10  TANDEM                1200.00
     76  CLIPPLESS SHOE          65.00 <-NOTE SAME #
```

You saved your company from this bad situation by checking PART before anyone used it:

```
SELECT F.PARTNUM, F.DESCRIPTION,
S.PARTNUM,S.DESCRIPTION
FROM PART F, PART S
WHERE F.PARTNUM = S.PARTNUM
AND F.DESCRIPTION <> S.DESCRIPTION
```

```
PARTNUM DESCRIPTION              PARTNUM  DESCRIPTION
====== ====================     ======== ====================

    76  ROAD BIKE                    76 CLIPPLESS SHOE
    76  CLIPPLESS SHOE               76 ROAD BIKE
```

 Now you are a hero until they ask you why there are two entries. You, remembering what you have learned about JOINs, retain your hero status by explaining how the JOIN produced two rows that satisfied the condition WHERE F.PARTNUM = S.PARTNUM AND F.DESCRIPTION <> S.DESCRIPTION.

Summary

Today you learned all about JOINs. You saw how, at its most basic level, a JOIN produces a result combining all the possible combinations of rows present in each table. These new rows are then available for selection based on what you need returned. Congratulations—you have learned almost everything there is to know about the SELECT clause. One more item remains: subqueries, covered in the next chapter.

Q&A

Q Why cover OUTER, INNER, LEFT, and RIGHT JOINs when it is not likely I will use them?

A A little knowledge is a dangerous thing, and no knowledge can be expensive. You now know enough to understand the basics of what your SQL engine might try while optimizing your queries. If you didn't at least have a small understanding of this process, you would never grow past what you have learned here.

Workshop

The workshop provides quiz questions to help solidify your understanding of the material covered, as well as exercises to provide you with experience in using what you have learned. Try to answer the quiz and exercise questions before checking the answers in Appendix F, and make sure you understand the answers before continuing to the next chapter.

Quiz

1. How many rows would a two-table JOIN produce if one table had 50,000 rows and the other had 100,000?

2. Can you join more than one table?

Exercise

1. In the section on joining tables to themselves, the last example returned two combinations. Rewrite the query so only one entry comes up for each redundant part number.

7

Subqueries

Introduction

Today we talk about subqueries. A subquery is just that: a query whose results are passed as the argument for another query. Subqueries are the glue that enables you to bind several queries together. By the end of the day you will understand and be able to do the following:

- ☐ Build a subquery
- ☐ Use the keywords EXISTS, ANY, and ALL with your subqueries
- ☐ Build and use correlated subqueries

Building a Subquery

Simply put, a subquery lets you tie the result set of one query to another. The general syntax is as follows:

```
SELECT *
FROM TABLE1
WHERE TABLE1.SOMECOLUMN =
(SELECT SOMEOTHERCOLUMN
FROM TABLE2
WHERE SOMEOTERCOLUMN = SOMEVALUE)
```

Notice how the second query is nested inside the first. Let's try a real-world example. Look at the PART and ORDERS tables:

```
SELECT *
FROM PART
```

```
      PARTNUM DESCRIPTION                PRICE
  =========== ==================== ===========

           54 PEDALS                      54.25
           42 SEATS                       24.50
           46 TIRES                       15.25
           23 MOUNTAIN BIKE              350.45
           76 ROAD BIKE                  530.00
           10 TANDEM                     1200.00
```

```
SELECT *
FROM ORDERS
```

```
  ORDEREDON NAME        PARTNUM    QUANTITY REMARKS
  ========== ========== =========== =========== ==========

  15-MAY-1996 TRUE WHEEL        23          6 PAID
  19-MAY-1996 TRUE WHEEL        76          3 PAID
   2-SEP-1996 TRUE WHEEL        10          1 PAID
  30-JUN-1996 BIKE SPEC         54         10 PAID
  30-MAY-1996 BIKE SPEC         10          2 PAID
  30-MAY-1996 BIKE SPEC         23          8 PAID
  17-JAN-1996 BIKE SPEC         76         11 PAID
```

```
17-JAN-1996 LE SHOPPE          76          5 PAID
 1-JUN-1996 LE SHOPPE          10          3 PAID
 1-JUN-1996 AAA BIKE           10          1 PAID
 1-JUL-1996 AAA BIKE           76          4 PAID
 1-JUL-1996 AAA BIKE           46         14 PAID
11-JUL-1996 JACKS BIKE         76         14 PAID
```

They share a common field called PARTNUM. Suppose you didn't know or want to know the PARTNUM but instead wanted to work with the description of the part. Using a subquery, you could type this:

```
SELECT *
FROM ORDERS
WHERE PARTNUM =
(SELECT PARTNUM
FROM PART
WHERE DESCRIPTION LIKE "ROAD%")
```

```
ORDEREDON NAME         PARTNUM    QUANTITY REMARKS
========== ========== =========== =========== ==========

19-MAY-1996 TRUE WHEEL        76          3 PAID
17-JAN-1996 BIKE SPEC         76         11 PAID
17-JAN-1996 LE SHOPPE         76          5 PAID
 1-JUL-1996 AAA BIKE          76          4 PAID
11-JUL-1996 JACKS BIKE        76         14 PAID
```

Even better, if you use the concepts you learned on Day 6, "Joins"; you could clarify the PARTNUM column in the final result by including the DESCRIPTION, making it clearer for anyone who hasn't memorized the PARTNUM. Try this:

```
SELECT O.ORDEREDON, O.PARTNUM,
P.DESCRIPTION, O.QUANTITY, O.REMARKS
FROM ORDERS O, PART P
WHERE O.PARTNUM = P.PARTNUM
AND
O.PARTNUM =
(SELECT PARTNUM
FROM PART
WHERE DESCRIPTION LIKE "ROAD%")
```

```
ORDEREDON     PARTNUM DESCRIPTION    QUANTITY REMARKS
========== =========== =========== =========== ==========

19-MAY-1996      76 ROAD BIKE             3 PAID
 1-JUL-1996      76 ROAD BIKE             4 PAID
17-JAN-1996      76 ROAD BIKE             5 PAID
17-JAN-1996      76 ROAD BIKE            11 PAID
11-JUL-1996      76 ROAD BIKE            14 PAID
```

Let's examine this query in some detail to see how you made this magic. The first part is very familiar:

```
SELECT O.ORDEREDON, O.PARTNUM,
P.DESCRIPTION, O.QUANTITY, O.REMARKS
FROM ORDERS O, PART P
```

Here you are using the aliases O and P for tables ORDERS and PART to select the five columns you are interested in. In this case the aliases were not necessary. Why? Because each of the columns you asked to return is unique. However, it is easier to make a readable query now than to have to figure it out later. The first WHERE clause you encounter

```
WHERE O.PARTNUM = P.PARTNUM
```

is standard language for the join of tables PART and ORDERS specified in the FROM clause. If you didn't use this WHERE clause, you would have all the possible row combinations of the two tables. The next section is where the subquery comes in. The statement

```
AND
O.PARTNUM =
(SELECT PARTNUM
FROM PART
WHERE DESCRIPTION LIKE "ROAD%")
```

adds the qualification that O.PARTNUM must be equal to the result of your simple subquery. The subquery is pretty straightforward, finding all the part numbers that are LIKE "ROAD%". The use of LIKE was somewhat lazy, saving you the keystrokes required to type ROAD BIKE. However, it turns out you were lucky this time. What if someone in the Parts department had added a new part called ROADKILL? The revised PART table would look like this:

```
SELECT *
FROM PART
```

```
PARTNUM DESCRIPTION              PRICE
=========== ===================== ===========

        54 PEDALS                  54.25
        42 SEATS                   24.50
        46 TIRES                   15.25
        23 MOUNTAIN BIKE          350.45
        76 ROAD BIKE              530.00
        10 TANDEM                1200.00
        77 ROADKILL                 7.99
```

Let's say you were blissfully unaware of this change and tried your query after this new product was added. If you enter this:

```
SELECT O.ORDEREDON, O.PARTNUM,
P.DESCRIPTION, O.QUANTITY, O.REMARKS
FROM ORDERS O, PART P
WHERE O.PARTNUM = P.PARTNUM
AND
O.PARTNUM =
```

```
(SELECT PARTNUM
FROM PART
WHERE DESCRIPTION LIKE "ROAD%")
```

the SQL engine complains

```
multiple rows in singleton select
```

and you don't get any results. The response from your SQL engine may vary, but it still complains and returns nothing. Why?

To find out why you get this undesirable result, let's play SQL engine. At the SQL engine you will probably evaluate the subquery first. You would return this:

```
SELECT PARTNUM
FROM PART
WHERE DESCRIPTION LIKE "ROAD%"
```

```
      PARTNUM
===========

          76
          77
```

You would take this result and apply it to this:

```
O.PARTNUM =
```

Aha! You have found the problem. How can PARTNUM be equal to both 76 and 77? This must be what the engine meant when it accused you of being a simpleton. When you used the LIKE clause you opened yourself up for this error. When you combine the results of a relational operator with another relational operator such as =, <, or >, you need to make sure the result is singular. In the case of the example we have been using, the solution would be to rewrite the query using an = instead of the LIKE, like this:

```
SELECT O.ORDEREDON, O.PARTNUM,
P.DESCRIPTION, O.QUANTITY, O.REMARKS
FROM ORDERS O, PART P
WHERE O.PARTNUM = P.PARTNUM
AND
O.PARTNUM =
(SELECT PARTNUM
FROM PART
WHERE DESCRIPTION = "ROAD BIKE")
```

7

ORDEREDON	PARTNUM	DESCRIPTION	QUANTITY	REMARKS
19-MAY-1996	76	ROAD BIKE	3	PAID
1-JUL-1996	76	ROAD BIKE	4	PAID
17-JAN-1996	76	ROAD BIKE	5	PAID
17-JAN-1996	76	ROAD BIKE	11	PAID
11-JUL-1996	76	ROAD BIKE	14	PAID

This returns the same result as your pre-ROADKILL query. How can you be sure the query won't run into this problem? Avoiding the use of LIKE would be a start. Another way would be to ensure the uniqueness of the field you were searching during table design. If you are the untrusting type, you could use the method described in Chapter 6 for joining a table to itself to check a given field for uniqueness. If you design the table yourself (described in detail in Chapter 9) or trust the person who designed the table, you could require the column you are searching to have a unique value. You could also use a part of SQL that returns only one answer: the aggregate function.

Using Aggregate Functions with Subqueries

The aggregate functions SUM, COUNT, MIN, MAX, and AVG all return a single value. To find out the average amount of an order, type this:

```
SELECT AVG(O.QUANTITY * P.PRICE)
FROM ORDERS O, PART P
WHERE O.PARTNUM = P.PARTNUM
```

```
        AVG
===========

   2419.16
```

This returns only one value. To find out which orders were above average, make this your subquery. The complete query and result are as follows:

```
SELECT O.NAME, O.ORDEREDON,
O.QUANTITY * P.PRICE TOTAL
FROM ORDERS O, PART P
WHERE O.PARTNUM = P.PARTNUM
AND
O.QUANTITY * P.PRICE  >
(SELECT AVG(O.QUANTITY * P.PRICE)
FROM ORDERS O, PART P
WHERE O.PARTNUM = P.PARTNUM)
```

```
NAME          ORDEREDON        TOTAL
==========  ===========  ===========

LE SHOPPE    1-JUN-1996      3600.00
BIKE SPEC   30-MAY-1996      2803.60
LE SHOPPE   17-JAN-1996      2650.00
BIKE SPEC   17-JAN-1996      5830.00
JACKS BIKE  11-JUL-1996      7420.00
```

Let's digest this in smaller pieces. First, you have an unremarkable SELECT/FROM/ WHERE clause:

```
SELECT O.NAME, O.ORDEREDON,
O.QUANTITY * P.PRICE TOTAL
FROM ORDERS O, PART P
WHERE O.PARTNUM = P.PARTNUM
```

This is the common way of joining these two tables. This JOIN is necessary because the price is in PART and the quantity is in ORDER. The WHERE ensures that you examine only the rows formed by the JOIN that are related. You then add the subquery:

```
AND
O.QUANTITY * P.PRICE  >
(SELECT AVG(O.QUANTITY * P.PRICE)
FROM ORDERS O, PART P
WHERE O.PARTNUM = P.PARTNUM)
```

This compares the total of each order with the average you computed in the subquery. Note that the JOIN in the subquery is required for the same reasons as in the main SELECT statement. This JOIN is also constructed exactly the same. There are no secret handshakes in subqueries; they have exactly the same syntax as a stand-alone query. In fact, most subqueries start out as stand-alone queries and are incorporated as subqueries after their results are tested.

Nesting Subqueries

Nesting is the act of putting several subqueries in serial, such as in the following line:

```
Select * FROM SOMETHING WHERE ( SUBQUERY(SUBQUERY(SUBQUERY)));
```

Subqueries can be nested as deeply as your implementation of SQL allows. For example, to send out special notices to customers who spend more than the average amount of money, you would combine the information in the table CUSTOMER:

```
SELECT *
FROM CUSTOMER
```

```
NAME        ADDRESS     STATE  ZIP         PHONE        REMARKS
==========  ==========  ====== ==========  ===========  ==========

TRUE WHEEL  550 HUSKER  NE     58702       555-4545     NONE
BIKE SPEC   CPT SHRIVE  LA     45678       555-1234     NONE
LE SHOPPE   HOMETOWN    KS     54678       555-1278     NONE
AAA BIKE    10 OLDTOWN  NE     56784       555-3421     JOHN-MGR
JACKS BIKE  24 EGLIN    FL     34567       555-2314     NONE
```

with a slightly modified version of the query you used to find the above average orders:

```
SELECT ALL C.NAME, C.ADDRESS, C.STATE,C.ZIP
FROM CUSTOMER C
WHERE C.NAME IN
(SELECT O.NAME
```

```
FROM ORDERS O, PART P
WHERE O.PARTNUM = P.PARTNUM
AND
O.QUANTITY * P.PRICE  >
(SELECT AVG(O.QUANTITY * P.PRICE)
FROM ORDERS O, PART P
WHERE O.PARTNUM = P.PARTNUM))
```

```
NAME        ADDRESS     STATE  ZIP
==========  ==========  ======  ==========

BIKE SPEC   CPT SHRIVE  LA      45678
LE SHOPPE   HOMETOWN    KS      54678
JACKS BIKE  24 EGLIN    FL      34567
```

Let's look at what you asked for. In the innermost set of parentheses you find a statement we have already discussed:

```
SELECT AVG(O.QUANTITY * P.PRICE)
FROM ORDERS O, PART P
WHERE O.PARTNUM = P.PARTNUM
```

This result feeds into a slightly modified version of what you used before:

```
SELECT O.NAME
FROM ORDERS O, PART P
WHERE O.PARTNUM = P.PARTNUM
AND
O.QUANTITY * P.PRICE  >
(...)
```

Note the SELECT clause has been modified to return a single column, NAME, which, not so coincidentally, is common with the table CUSTOMER. Running this statement by itself you get this:

```
SELECT O.NAME
FROM ORDERS O, PART P
WHERE O.PARTNUM = P.PARTNUM
AND
O.QUANTITY * P.PRICE  >
(SELECT AVG(O.QUANTITY * P.PRICE)
FROM ORDERS O, PART P
WHERE O.PARTNUM = P.PARTNUM)
```

```
NAME
==========

LE SHOPPE
BIKE SPEC
LE SHOPPE
BIKE SPEC
JACKS BIKE
```

We just spent some time discussing why your subqueries should return just one value. The reason this query was able to return more than one value becomes apparent in a moment.

You bring these results to the statement:

```
SELECT C.NAME, C.ADDRESS, C.STATE,C.ZIP
FROM CUSTOMER C
WHERE C.NAME IN
(...)
```

The first two lines are unremarkable. The third reintroduces the keyword IN, last seen on Day 2. IN is the tool that enables you to use the multiple row output of your subquery. IN, as you remember, looks for matches in the following set, which in this case is as follows:

```
LE SHOPPE
BIKE SPEC
LE SHOPPE
BIKE SPEC
JACKS BIKE
```

This gives you the mailing list:

NAME	ADDRESS	STATE	ZIP
========	==========	======	==========
BIKE SPEC	CPT SHRIVE	LA	45678
LE SHOPPE	HOMETOWN	KS	54678
JACKS BIKE	24 EGLIN	FL	34567

This use of IN is very common in subqueries. Because IN uses a set of values for its comparison, it does not cause the SQL engine to feel conflicted and inadequate.

Subqueries can also be used with GROUP BY and HAVING clauses. Examine the following query:

```
SELECT NAME, AVG(QUANTITY)
FROM ORDERS
GROUP BY NAME
HAVING AVG(QUANTITY) >
(SELECT AVG(QUANTITY)
FROM ORDERS)
```

NAME	AVG
==========	===========
BIKE SPEC	8
JACKS BIKE	14

Let's examine this query in the order the SQL engine would. First, look at the subquery:

```
SELECT AVG(QUANTITY)
FROM ORDERS
```

```
         AVG
===========

     6
```

By itself, the query is as follows:

```
SELECT NAME, AVG(QUANTITY)
FROM ORDERS
GROUP BY NAME
```

```
NAME             AVG
==========  ===========

AAA BIKE           6
BIKE SPEC          8
JACKS BIKE        14
LE SHOPPE          4
TRUE WHEEL         5
```

When combined through the HAVING clause:

```
HAVING AVG(QUANTITY) >
(SELECT AVG(QUANTITY)
FROM ORDERS)
```

produces the two rows that have above average QUANTITY:

```
NAME             AVG
==========  ===========

BIKE SPEC          8
JACKS BIKE        14
```

Correlated Subqueries

The subqueries you have written so far are self-contained. None of them have used a reference from outside the subquery. Correlated subqueries enable you to use an outside reference with some strange and wonderful results. Look at the following query:

```
SELECT *
FROM ORDERS O
WHERE 'ROAD BIKE' =
(SELECT DESCRIPTION
FROM PART P
WHERE P.PARTNUM = O.PARTNUM)
```

```
ORDEREDON NAME         PARTNUM    QUANTITY REMARKS
===========  ==========  ===========  ===========  ==========

19-MAY-1996 TRUE WHEEL       76           3 PAID
17-JAN-1996 BIKE SPEC        76          11 PAID
17-JAN-1996 LE SHOPPE        76           5 PAID
 1-JUL-1996 AAA BIKE         76           4 PAID
11-JUL-1996 JACKS BIKE       76          14 PAID
```

Upon closer examination, this query looks a lot like the following JOIN:

```
SELECT O.ORDEREDON, O.NAME,
O.PARTNUM, O.QUANTITY, O.REMARKS
FROM ORDERS O, PART P
WHERE P.PARTNUM = O.PARTNUM
AND P.DESCRIPTION = 'ROAD BIKE'
```

```
   ORDEREDON NAME          PARTNUM    QUANTITY REMARKS
=========== ========== =========== =========== ==========

19-MAY-1996 TRUE WHEEL          76           3 PAID
 1-JUL-1996 AAA BIKE            76           4 PAID
17-JAN-1996 LE SHOPPE           76           5 PAID
17-JAN-1996 BIKE SPEC           76          11 PAID
11-JUL-1996 JACKS BIKE          76          14 PAID
```

In fact, except for the order, the results are identical. The correlated subquery acts very much like a JOIN. The correlation is established by using an element from the query in the subquery. In this example the correlation was established by the statement

```
WHERE P.PARTNUM = O.PARTNUM
```

in which you compare P.PARTNUM, from the table inside your subquery, to O.PARTNUM, from the table outside your query. Because O.PARTNUM can have a different value for every row, the correlated subquery is executed for each row in the query. In this example, each row in the table ORDERS,

```
SELECT *
FROM ORDERS
```

```
   ORDEREDON NAME          PARTNUM    QUANTITY REMARKS
=========== ========== =========== =========== ==========

15-MAY-1996 TRUE WHEEL          23           6 PAID
19-MAY-1996 TRUE WHEEL          76           3 PAID
 2-SEP-1996 TRUE WHEEL          10           1 PAID
30-JUN-1996 TRUE WHEEL          42           8 PAID
30-JUN-1996 BIKE SPEC           54          10 PAID
30-MAY-1996 BIKE SPEC           10           2 PAID
30-MAY-1996 BIKE SPEC           23           8 PAID
17-JAN-1996 BIKE SPEC           76          11 PAID
17-JAN-1996 LE SHOPPE           76           5 PAID
 1-JUN-1996 LE SHOPPE           10           3 PAID
 1-JUN-1996 AAA BIKE            10           1 PAID
 1-JUL-1996 AAA BIKE            76           4 PAID
 1-JUL-1996 AAA BIKE            46          14 PAID
11-JUL-1996 JACKS BIKE          76          14 PAID
```

is processed against the subquery criteria:

```
SELECT DESCRIPTION
FROM PART P
WHERE P.PARTNUM = O.PARTNUM
```

This operation returns the DESCRIPTION of every row in PART where P.PARTNUM = O.PARTNUM. These descriptions are then compared in the WHERE clause:

```
WHERE 'ROAD BIKE' =
```

Because each row is examined, the subquery in a correlated subquery can have more than one value. However, don't try to return multiple columns, or columns that don't make sense in the context of the WHERE clause. The values returned still must match up against the operation specified in the WHERE clause. For example, in the query you just did, returning the PRICE to compare with ROAD BIKE would have the following result:

```
SELECT *
FROM ORDERS O
WHERE 'ROAD BIKE' =
(SELECT PRICE
FROM PART P
WHERE P.PARTNUM = O.PARTNUM)
```

```
conversion error from string "ROAD BIKE"
```

Another example of something not to do would be this:

```
SELECT *
FROM ORDERS O
WHERE 'ROAD BIKE' =
(SELECT *
FROM PART P
WHERE P.PARTNUM = O.PARTNUM)
```

This caused a General Protection Fault on my Windows operating system. The SQL engine simply can't correlate all the columns in PART with the operator =.

Correlated subqueries can also be used with the GROUP BY and HAVING clauses. The query

```
SELECT O.PARTNUM, SUM(O.QUANTITY*P.PRICE), COUNT(PARTNUM)
FROM ORDERS O, PART P
WHERE P.PARTNUM = O.PARTNUM
GROUP BY O.PARTNUM
HAVING SUM(O.QUANTITY*P.PRICE) >
(SELECT AVG(O1.QUANTITY*P1.PRICE)
FROM PART P1, ORDERS O1
WHERE P1.PARTNUM = O1.PARTNUM
AND P1.PARTNUM = O.PARTNUM)
```

PARTNUM	SUM	COUNT
===========	===========	===========
10	8400.00	4
23	4906.30	2
76	19610.00	5

uses a correlated subquery to find the average total order for a particular part and then applies that to filter the total order grouped by PARTNUM. The subquery does not just compute one

```
AVG(O1.QUANTITY*P1.PRICE).
```

Because of the correlation between the query and the subquery,

```
AND P1.PARTNUM = O.PARTNUM,
```

this average is computed for every group of parts and then compared using this:

```
HAVING SUM(O.QUANTITY*P.PRICE) >
```

You need to remember one thing when using correlated subqueries with GROUP BY and HAVING. The columns used in the HAVING clause must exist in either the SELECT clause or the GROUP BY clause. Otherwise you get an error message along the lines of `invalid column reference`. This is because the subquery is evoked for each group, not each row. You cannot make a valid comparison to something that is not used in forming the group.

Using EXISTS, ANY, and ALL

The usage of the keywords EXISTS, ANY, and ALL is not intuitively obvious to the casual observer. EXISTS takes a subquery as an argument and returns TRUE if the subquery returns anything and FALSE if the result set is empty. The following is an example:

```
SELECT NAME, ORDEREDON
FROM ORDERS
WHERE EXISTS
(SELECT *
FROM ORDERS
WHERE NAME ='TRUE WHEEL')
```

```
NAME         ORDEREDON
==========  ===========

TRUE WHEEL  15-MAY-1996
TRUE WHEEL  19-MAY-1996
TRUE WHEEL   2-SEP-1996
TRUE WHEEL  30-JUN-1996
BIKE SPEC   30-JUN-1996
BIKE SPEC   30-MAY-1996
BIKE SPEC   30-MAY-1996
BIKE SPEC   17-JAN-1996
LE SHOPPE   17-JAN-1996
LE SHOPPE    1-JUN-1996
AAA BIKE     1-JUN-1996
AAA BIKE     1-JUL-1996
AAA BIKE     1-JUL-1996
JACKS BIKE  11-JUL-1996
```

7

The subquery inside EXISTS is evaluated only once in this uncorrelated example. Because the return from the subquery has at least one row, EXISTS evaluates to TRUE and all the rows in the query are printed. If you change the subquery to

```
SELECT NAME, ORDEREDON
FROM ORDERS
WHERE EXISTS
(SELECT *
FROM ORDERS
WHERE NAME ='MOSTLY HARMLESS')
```

you don't get back any results. EXISTS evaluates to FALSE because there is no result set from the subquery since MOSTLY HARMLESS is not one of your names.

Note: The use of SELECT * in the subquery is inside the EXISTS. Because of its nature, EXISTS does not care how many columns are returned.

You could use EXISTS in this way to check on the existence of certain rows and control the output of your query based on their existence or nonexistence.

If you use EXISTS in a correlated subquery, it is evaluated for every case inferred by the correlation you set up. The following is an example:

```
SELECT NAME, ORDEREDON
FROM ORDERS O
WHERE EXISTS
(SELECT *
FROM CUSTOMER C
WHERE STATE ='NE'
AND C.NAME = O.NAME)
```

```
NAME         ORDEREDON
==========  ===========

TRUE WHEEL  15-MAY-1996
TRUE WHEEL  19-MAY-1996
TRUE WHEEL   2-SEP-1996
TRUE WHEEL  30-JUN-1996
AAA BIKE     1-JUN-1996
AAA BIKE     1-JUL-1996
AAA BIKE     1-JUL-1996
```

This slight modification of your first, uncorrelated query, returns all the bike shops from Nebraska who made orders. The subquery

```
(SELECT *
FROM CUSTOMER C
WHERE STATE ='NE'
AND C.NAME = O.NAME)
```

is run for every row in the query correlated on the CUSTOMER name and ORDER name. EXISTS is TRUE for those rows that have corresponding names in CUSTOMER located in NE. Otherwise, it returns FALSE.

Closely related to EXISTS are the key words ANY, ALL, and SOME. ANY and SOME are identical in function. An optimist would say this is to provide the user with a choice. A pessimist would see this as one more complication. Look at this query:

```
SELECT NAME, ORDEREDON
FROM ORDERS
WHERE NAME = ANY
(SELECT NAME
FROM ORDERS
WHERE NAME ='TRUE WHEEL')
```

```
NAME            ORDEREDON
==========  ===========

TRUE WHEEL  15-MAY-1996
TRUE WHEEL  19-MAY-1996
TRUE WHEEL   2-SEP-1996
TRUE WHEEL  30-JUN-1996

(SELECT NAME
FROM ORDERS
WHERE NAME ='TRUE WHEEL')
```

ANY took the output of the subquery and compared it to each row in the query, returning TRUE for each row of the query where there is a result from the subquery.

Replacing ANY with SOME produces an identical result:

```
SELECT NAME, ORDEREDON
FROM ORDERS
WHERE NAME = SOME
(SELECT NAME
FROM ORDERS
WHERE NAME ='TRUE WHEEL')
```

```
NAME            ORDEREDON
==========  ===========

TRUE WHEEL  15-MAY-1996
TRUE WHEEL  19-MAY-1996
TRUE WHEEL   2-SEP-1996
TRUE WHEEL  30-JUN-1996
```

You may have already noticed the similarity to IN. The same query using IN is as follows:

```
SELECT NAME, ORDEREDON
FROM ORDERS
WHERE NAME IN
(SELECT NAME
FROM ORDERS
WHERE NAME ='TRUE WHEEL')
```

7

```
NAME          ORDEREDON
==========  ===========

TRUE WHEEL  15-MAY-1996
TRUE WHEEL  19-MAY-1996
TRUE WHEEL   2-SEP-1996
TRUE WHEEL  30-JUN-1996
```

This returns the same result as ANY and SOME. Has the world gone mad? Not yet. Can IN do this?

```
SELECT NAME, ORDEREDON
FROM ORDERS
WHERE NAME > ANY
(SELECT NAME
FROM ORDERS
WHERE NAME ='JACKS BIKE')
```

```
NAME          ORDEREDON
==========  ===========

TRUE WHEEL  15-MAY-1996
TRUE WHEEL  19-MAY-1996
TRUE WHEEL   2-SEP-1996
TRUE WHEEL  30-JUN-1996
LE SHOPPE   17-JAN-1996
LE SHOPPE    1-JUN-1996
```

The answer is no. IN works like multiple equals. ANY and SOME can be used with other relational operators such as greater than or less than. This is another tool in your kit.

ALL takes the results of a subquery and returns TRUE only if all the results meet the condition. Oddly enough, ALL is used most commonly as a double negative, as in this query:

```
SELECT NAME, ORDEREDON
FROM ORDERS
WHERE NAME <> ALL
(SELECT NAME
FROM ORDERS
WHERE NAME ='JACKS BIKE')
```

```
NAME          ORDEREDON
==========  ===========

TRUE WHEEL  15-MAY-1996
TRUE WHEEL  19-MAY-1996
TRUE WHEEL   2-SEP-1996
TRUE WHEEL  30-JUN-1996
BIKE SPEC   30-JUN-1996
BIKE SPEC   30-MAY-1996
BIKE SPEC   30-MAY-1996
BIKE SPEC   17-JAN-1996
LE SHOPPE   17-JAN-1996
LE SHOPPE    1-JUN-1996
AAA BIKE     1-JUN-1996
AAA BIKE     1-JUL-1996
AAA BIKE     1-JUL-1996
```

 This returns everybody except JACKS BIKE. <>ALL evaluates to TRUE only if the result set does not contain what is on the left of the <>.

Summary

Today you performed dozens of examples involving subqueries. You have learned how to use one of the most important parts of SQL. You also tackled one of the most difficult parts of SQL: a correlated subquery. The correlated subquery creates a relationship between the query and the subquery, which is evaluated for every instance of that relationship. Don't be intimidated by how long the queries have become. They can be digested one subquery at a time.

Q&A

Q In this chapter we saw that in some cases there are several ways to get the same result. Isn't this confusing?

A Yes it is! Whenever I am learning something new I look for rules and suffer through the exceptions. I recommend you pick a few simple ways to do what you need and not clutter up your mental landscape with other methods. Just remember there are several ways to achieve the same result.

Workshop

The workshop provides quiz questions to help solidify your understanding of the material covered, as well as exercises to provide you with experience in using what you have learned. Try to answer the quiz and exercise questions before checking the answers in Appendix F, and make sure you understand the answers before continuing to the next chapter.

Quiz

1. In the section on nesting subqueries, the subquery used returned several values:

```
LE SHOPPE
BIKE SPEC
LE SHOPPE
BIKE SPEC
JACKS BIKE
```

Some of these are duplicates. Why aren't these duplicates in the final result set?

Exercise

1. Write a query, using the table ORDERS, to return all the NAMES and ORDEREDON dates for every store that comes after JACKS BIKE in the alphabet.

143

After setting the stage with a quick review of database theory—which taught how good relational databases are (something we tend to forget when our boss or customer tries to drive us to a flat files, or worse yet, our own homegrown database)—we learned SQL's most basic application of the relational and SET theory behind the relational database, the SELECT statement. The following is a summary of the SELECT statement syntax and the days we covered its various bits.

- [ ] SELECT [DISTINCT | ALL] (Day 2); Columns (Day1); Functions(Day 4)

- [ ] FROM(Day 2) Tables or views (Day 1); Aggregate functions (Day 4)

- [ ] WHERE(Day 5); Condition (Day 3); Join (Day 6); Subquery (Day 7)

- [ ] GROUP BY (Day 5) Columns (Day 3)

- [ ] HAVING (Day 5) Aggregate function (Day 4)

- [ ] UNION | INTERSECT (Day 3) (placed between two SELECT statements)

- [ ] ORDER BY (Day 5); columns (Day 1)

If you build a million queries in your programming career, more than 80 percent of them will begin with SELECT.

Preview

The other 20 percent of your queries will fall into the categories covered in Week 2. These new skills will cover database administration. You will learn how to

☐ Create and destroy tables

☐ Assign permissions to your friends and prevent your enemies from even looking at your data

☐ Update and delete data in tables

2

What Is Going to Be Covered During This Week?

During the first week, we essentially covered the basic SQL query using the SELECT statement. Beginning with the simplest SELECT statement, you learned how to retrieve data from the database. Following that accomplishment, we moved on to the SQL functions, which are useful in converting to money or date formats, for instance. You quickly learned that there are many ways to retrieve data from a database. Different clauses such as WHERE, ORDER BY, and GROUP BY enable the programmer to tailor the query to return a specific set of records. A join can be used to return a set of data from a group of tables. Subqueries are especially useful when several queries need to be executed, each of which depends on data returned from an earlier query.

Now that the query has been discussed in great detail, we will cover in some detail the other many useful aspects of SQL. The second week will be used to cover the more advanced uses of SQL.

Chapter 8 shows you how to modify data within a database. Up to this point, we have assumed that the database was populated with data. The astute reader may have been dreading typing all of this data in, but this is not always necessary. SQL provides several useful statements for manipulating data within a database. In addition, modern database systems often supply useful tools for importing and exporting data from different database formats. In Chapter 9, you learn how to create and maintain tables within a database. You also learn how to create a database and manage that database's disk space. Chapter 10 explains how to create, maintain, and use views and indexes within a database. Transaction control is covered in Chapter 11. Transactions are used to commit or roll back changes to a database, and the use of them is essential in on-line transaction processing (OLTP) applications. Database security is the topic of Chapter 12. A knowledge of your database's security capabilities is essential to manage a database effectively. The use of SQL within larger application programs is covered on Chapter 13. Embedded SQL is often used to execute SQL within a host language such as C or COBOL. In addition, the Open Database Connectivity (ODBC) standard enables application programmers to write code that can use database drivers to connect with a variety of database management systems. Cursors are also used to perform operations on a result set returned from a query. Chapter 14 covers a variety of advanced SQL topics, such as writing stored procedures, using triggers effectively within a database, and tuning your SQL statements for optimal performance.

Manipulating Data

Introduction to Data Manipulation Statements

Up to this point, you have learned how to retrieve data from a database using every selection criteria imaginable. Once this data is retrieved, it can be used in an application program or edited by a user. The first week of this book was concerned primarily with retrieving this data. However, you may have wondered how to enter this data into the database in the first place. You may also be wondering what to do with data the user has edited. Today, we discuss three SQL statements that enable you to manipulate the data within a database's table. The three statements are as follows:

- [ ] The INSERT statement
- [ ] The UPDATE statement
- [ ] The DELETE statement

You may have used a PC-based product such as Access, dBASE IV, or FoxPro to enter your data in the past. These products come packaged with excellent tools to enter, edit, and delete records from databases. SQL provides data manipulation statements for several reasons. First, SQL is primarily used within application programs that enable the user to edit the data using the application's own tools. The SQL programmer needs to be able to return the data to the database using SQL. Also, most large-scale database systems are not designed with the database designer or programmer in mind. Because these systems are designed to be used in high-volume, multiuser environments, the primary design emphasis is placed upon the query optimizer and data retrieval engines. All database manipulations that need to be done can be accomplished with these three statements.

In addition, most commercial relational database systems also provide tools for importing and exporting data. This data is traditionally stored in a delimited text file format. Often a format file is stored that contains information about the table being imported. Tools such as Oracle's SQL*Loader, SQL Server's bcp (bulk copy), and Microsoft Access Import/Export are covered at the end of this chapter.

The INSERT Statement

The INSERT statement is provided to enter data into the database. It can be broken down into two statements:

`INSERT...VALUES`

and

`INSERT...SELECT`

The INSERT...VALUES Statement

8

The INSERT...VALUES statement is used to enter data into a table one record at a time. It is useful for small operations dealing with just a few records. The syntax of this statement is as follows:

```
INSERT INTO table_name
(col1, col2...)
VALUES(value1, value2...)
```

This is the basic format of the INSERT...VALUES statement. It basically adds a record to a table using the columns you give it and the corresponding values you instruct it to add. Three rules must be followed when inserting data into a table using this statement:

☐ The values used must be the exact same data type as the fields they are being added to.

☐ The data's size must be within the column's size. For instance, an 80-character string cannot be added to a 40-character column.

☐ The data's location in the VALUES list must correspond to the location in the column list of the column it is being added to. (That is, the first value must be entered into the first column, the second value into the second column, and so on.)

Example 8.1

Assume you have a table called COLLECTION where you list all the important stuff you have collected. You can display what is already in the table by writing

```
SQL> SELECT * FROM COLLECTION;
```

which would yield this:

```
ITEM                    WORTH REMARKS
------------------- -------- ----------------------------
NBA ALL STAR CARDS        300 SOME STILL IN BIKE SPOKES
MALIBU BARBIE             150 TAN NEEDS WORK
STAR WARS GLASS           5.5 HANDLE CHIPPED
LOCK OF SPOUSES HAIR        1 HASN'T NOTICED BALD SPOT YET
```

If you wanted to add a new record to this table you would write

```
SQL> INSERT INTO COLLECTION
    (ITEM, WORTH, REMARKS)
    VALUES('SUPERMANS CAPE', 250.00, 'TUGGED ON IT');
```

```
1 row created.
```

To convince yourself that this statement actually worked, you can execute a simple SELECT statement to verify the insertion:

```
SQL> SELECT * FROM COLLECTION;
```

```
ITEM                      WORTH REMARKS
--------------------      ----- -----------------------------
NBA ALL STAR CARDS          300 SOME STILL IN BIKE SPOKES
MALIBU BARBIE               150 TAN NEEDS WORK
STAR WARS GLASS             5.5 HANDLE CHIPPED
LOCK OF SPOUSES HAIR          1 HASN'T NOTICED BALD SPOT YET
SUPERMANS CAPE              250 TUGGED ON IT
```

When using the INSERT statement, column names are not required. If the column names are not entered, SQL lines up the values with their corresponding column numbers. In other words, SQL inserts the first value into the first column, the second value into the second column, and so on. This statement inserts the values in Example 8.1 into the table using this method:

Example 8.2

```
SQL> INSERT INTO COLLECTION VALUES('STRING',1000.00,'SOME DAY IT WILL BE
VALUABLE');
```

```
1 row created.
```

Once again, the SELECT statement in Example 8.1 verifies that the insertion worked as expected:

```
ITEM                      WORTH REMARKS
--------------------      ----- -----------------------------
NBA ALL STAR CARDS          300 SOME STILL IN BIKE SPOKES
MALIBU BARBIE               150 TAN NEEDS WORK
STAR WARS GLASS             5.5 HANDLE CHIPPED
LOCK OF SPOUSES HAIR          1 HASN'T NOTICED BALD SPOT YET
SUPERMANS CAPE              250 TUGGED ON IT
STRING                     1000 SOME DAY IT WILL BE VALUABLE

6 rows selected.
```

Inserting NULL Values

On Day 9, you learn how to create tables using the SQL CREATE TABLE statement. Suffice it to say that when a column is created it can have several different limitations placed upon it. One of these limitations is that the column should (or should not) be allowed to contain NULL values. A NULL value means that the value is empty. It is not a zero, in the case of an integer, or a space, in the case of a string. Instead, no data at all exists for that record's column. If a column is defined as NOT NULL (that column is not allowed to contain a NULL value), you *must* insert a value for that column when using the INSERT statement.

The INSERT is canceled if this rule is broken, and you should receive a descriptive error message concerning your error.

Assume the column REMARKS in the preceding table has been defined as NOT NULL. Typing

```
SQL> INSERT INTO COLLECTION
     VALUES('SPORES MILDEW FUNGUS',50.00,NULL);
```

produces the following error:

```
INSERT INTO COLLECTION
          *
ERROR at line 1:
ORA-01400: mandatory (NOT NULL) column is missing or NULL during insert
```

Inserting Unique Values

Many database management systems also allow for the creation of a UNIQUE column attribute. This means that within this table, the values within this column must be completely unique and cannot appear more than once. This can cause problems when inserting or updating values into an existing table, as demonstrated by the following exchange:

```
SQL> INSERT INTO COLLECTION VALUES('STRING', 50, 'MORE STRING');
```

```
INSERT INTO COLLECTION VALUES('STRING', 50, 'MORE STRING')
              *
ERROR at line 1:
ORA-00001: unique constraint (PERKINS.UNQ_COLLECTION_ITEM) violated
```

In this example you tried to insert another ITEM called STRING into the collection. Because this table was created with ITEM as a unique value, it returned the appropriate error. ANSI SQL does not offer a solution to this problem, but several commercial implementations include extensions that would allow you to use something like the following:

```
if not exists (select * from COLLECTION WHERE NAME = 'STRING'
```

```
INSERT INTO COLLECTION VALUES('STRING', 50, 'MORE STRING')
```

This particular example is supported in the Sybase system.

As discussed in previous chapters, a properly normalized table should have a unique, or key, field. This is useful for joining data between tables, and it often improves the speed of your queries when using indexes (see Chapter 10).

The INSERT...SELECT Statement

The INSERT...VALUES statement is useful when adding single records to a database table, but it obviously has limitations. Would you like to use it to add 25,000 records to a table? In situations like this, the INSERT...SELECT statement is much more beneficial. It enables the programmer to copy information from a table or group of tables into another table. This is useful in several situations. Often, lookup tables are created for performance gains. Lookup tables can contain data that is spread out across multiple tables in multiple databases. Because multiple-table joins are slower to process than simple queries, it is much quicker to execute a SELECT query against a lookup table than to execute a long, complicated joined query. Lookup tables are often stored on the client machines in client/server environments to reduce network traffic.

Many database systems also support temporary tables (for more information see Chapter 14). Temporary tables exist for the life of your database connection and are deleted when your connection is terminated. The INSERT...SELECT statement can take the output of a SELECT statement and insert these values into a temporary table.

> **Note:** Not all database management systems support temporary tables. Check the documentation for the specific system you are using to determine if this feature is supported. Also, see Chapter 14 for a more detailed treatment of this topic.

The syntax of the INSERT...SELECT statement is as follows:

```
INSERT INTO table_name
(col1, col2...)
SELECT col1, col2...
FROM tablename
WHERE search_condition
```

Essentially, the output of a standard SELECT query is then input into a database table. The same rules that applied to the INSERT...VALUES statement apply to the INSERT...SELECT statement. To copy the contents of the COLLECTION table into a new table called INVENTORY, execute the set of statements in Example 8.3.

Example 8.3

```
SQL> CREATE TABLE INVENTORY
     (ITEM CHAR(20),
     COST NUMBER,
     ROOM CHAR(20),
     REMARKS CHAR(40));
```

Output

```
Table created.
```

This created the new table, INVENTORY. Now let's fill it up with data from COLLECTION.

```
SQL> INSERT INTO INVENTORY (ITEM, COST, REMARKS)
     SELECT ITEM, WORTH, REMARKS
     FROM COLLECTION;
```

```
6 rows created.
```

You can verify this with

```
SQL> SELECT * FROM INVENTORY;
```

```
ITEM                     COST ROOM          REMARKS
--------------------  ------- --------  ------------------------------
NBA ALL STAR CARDS        300           SOME STILL IN BIKE SPOKES
MALIBU BARBIE             150           TAN NEEDS WORK
STAR WARS GLASS           5.5           HANDLE CHIPPED
LOCK OF SPOUSES HAIR        1           HASN'T NOTICED BALD SPOT YET
SUPERMANS CAPE            250           TUGGED ON IT
STRING                   1000           SOME DAY IT WILL BE VALUABLE

6 rows selected.
```

You have successfully, and somewhat painlessly, moved the data from the COLLECTION table to the new INVENTORY table!

There are several new rules to be followed when using the INSERT...SELECT statement:

☐ The SELECT statement cannot select rows from the table that is being inserted into.

☐ The number of columns in the INSERT INTO statement must equal the number of columns returned from the SELECT statement.

☐ The data types of the columns in the INSERT INTO statement must be the same as the data types of the columns returned from the SELECT statement.

Later in this chapter, we discuss how to input data into a table using data from another database format. Nearly all businesses use a variety of database formats to store data for their organizations. Often, the applications programmer is expected to convert back and forth between these formats, and we discuss some common methods for doing just that. For now, we will demonstrate how to edit an existing record's values.

The UPDATE Statement

We have discussed in some detail how to insert new records using the INSERT statement. The UPDATE statement has a similar purpose, but it is used to change the values of existing records. The syntax of the UPDATE statement is as follows:

```
UPDATE table_name
SET columnname1 = value1
[, columname2 = value2]...
WHERE search_condition
```

This statement checks the WHERE clause first. For all records in the given table where the WHERE clause evaluates to TRUE, the corresponding value is updated. Example 8.4 illustrates the use of the UPDATE statement.

Example 8.4

```
SQL> UPDATE COLLECTION
       SET WORTH = 900
       WHERE ITEM = 'STRING';
```

```
1 row updated.
```

To confirm the change, the query

```
SQL> SELECT * FROM COLLECTION
       WHERE ITEM = 'STRING';
```

yields

```
ITEM                        WORTH REMARKS
------------------------    ------- --------------------------------
STRING                        900 SOME DAY IT WILL BE VALUABLE
```

If the WHERE clause is omitted, every record in the inventory table is updated with the value given.

Example 8.5

```
SQL> UPDATE COLLECTION
       SET WORTH = 555;
```

```
6 rows updated.
```

Performing a SELECT query shows that every record in the database was updated with that value:

```
SQL> SELECT * FROM COLLECTION;
```

```
ITEM                    WORTH REMARKS
-------------------     ----- ------------------------------
NBA ALL STAR CARDS        555 SOME STILL IN BIKE SPOKES
MALIBU BARBIE             555 TAN NEEDS WORK
STAR WARS GLASS           555 HANDLE CHIPPED
LOCK OF SPOUSES HAIR      555 HASN'T NOTICED BALD SPOT YET
SUPERMANS CAPE            555 TUGGED ON IT
STRING                    555 SOME DAY IT WILL BE VALUABLE

6 rows selected.
```

As was the case with the INSERT statement, care should be taken to determine whether the column you are updating allows unique values only.

Note: If the WHERE clause is left off the UPDATE statement, all records in the given table are updated.

Some database systems provide an extension to the standard UPDATE syntax. SQL Server's Transact-SQL language, for instance, enables the programmer to update the contents of a table based on the contents of several other tables using a FROM clause. The extended syntax looks like this:

```
UPDATE table_name
SET columnname1 = value1
[, columnname2 = value2]...
FROM table_list
WHERE search_condition
```

Its usage would look like that in Example 8.6.

Example 8.6

```
SQL> UPDATE COLLECTION
  2  SET WORTH = WORTH * 0.005;
```

which changes the table to this:

```
SQL> SELECT * FROM COLLECTION;
```

```
ITEM                    WORTH REMARKS
-------------------     ----- ------------------------------
NBA ALL STAR CARDS      2.775 SOME STILL IN BIKE SPOKES
MALIBU BARBIE           2.775 TAN NEEDS WORK
STAR WARS GLASS         2.775 HANDLE CHIPPED
LOCK OF SPOUSES HAIR    2.775 HASN'T NOTICED BALD SPOT YET
SUPERMANS CAPE          2.775 TUGGED ON IT
STRING                  2.775 SOME DAY IT WILL BE VALUABLE

6 rows selected.
```

Analysis This syntax is useful when the contents of one table need to be updated following the manipulation of the contents of several other tables. Keep in mind that this syntax is nonstandard, and that you need to consult the documentation for your particular database management system before you use it.

The UPDATE statement can also update columns based on the result of an arithmetic expression. When doing this, remember the requirement that the data type of the result of the expression must be the same as the data type of the field that is being modified. Also, the size of the value must fit within the size of the field that is being modified.

Two problems can result from the use of calculated values: truncation and overflow. Truncation results when the database system converts a fractional number to an integer, for instance. Overflow results when the resultant value is larger than the capacity of the modified column. This will result in an overflow error from your database system.

> **Note:** Some database systems handle this problem for you. Oracle7 converts the number to exponential notation and presents the number that way. The possibility for this error should still be kept in mind when using number data types.

The DELETE Statement

As often as data needs to be added to a database, you will also find the need to delete other data based on a specific program's operation. The syntax for the DELETE statement is

```
DELETE FROM tablename
WHERE condition
```

The first thing a new SQL programmer will notice when using this command is that there is no prompting before executing. Users are accustomed to being prompted for assurance when, for instance, a directory or file is deleted at the operating system level. Are you sure? (Y/N) is a common question asked before the operation is performed. Using SQL, when you instruct the DBMS to delete a group of records from a table, it obeys your command without asking. On Day 11, we cover the topic of transaction control. Transactions are database operations that enable the programmer to either COMMIT or ROLLBACK changes to the database. This is very useful in on-line transaction processing applications, where you want to execute a batch of modifications to the database in one logical execution. Data integrity problems will occur if operations are performed while other users are modifying the data at the same time. For now, assume that no transactions are being undertaken. That is, when you tell SQL to delete a group of records, it will really do it!

Depending on the use of the DELETE statement's WHERE clause, SQL can do the following:

☐ Delete single rows
☐ Delete multiple rows
☐ Delete all rows
☐ Delete no rows

Several things should be remembered when using the DELETE clause:

☐ The DELETE statement cannot be used to delete an individual field's values (use UPDATE for this). The DELETE statement deletes entire records from a single table.

☐ Like INSERT and UPDATE, deleting records from one table can cause referential integrity problems within other tables. This should be kept in mind when modifying data within a database.

☐ Using the DELETE statement deletes only records, not the table itself. The DROP TABLE statement (see Chapter 9) is used to remove an entire table.

In Example 8.7, you delete all the records from COLLECTION where WORTH is less than 275.

Example 8.7

```
SQL> DELETE FROM COLLECTION
  2  WHERE WORTH < 275;

4 rows deleted.
```

The result is a table that looks like this:

```
SQL> SELECT * FROM COLLECTION;
```

```
ITEM                    WORTH REMARKS
------------------- -------- -------------------------------
NBA ALL STAR CARDS        300 SOME STILL IN BIKE SPOKES
STRING                   1000 SOME DAY IT WILL BE VALUABLE
```

Note: Like the UPDATE statement, if the WHERE clause is omitted from the DELETE statement, the contents of the entire table are deleted.

Example 8.8 uses all three of the data manipulation statements to perform a set of database operations.

Example 8.8

Starting with COLLECTION as you left it a few paragraphs ago, let's insert some new rows:

```
SQL> INSERT INTO COLLECTION
  2   VALUES('CHIA PET', 5,'WEDDING GIFT');

1 row created.
```

```
SQL> INSERT INTO COLLECTION
  2   VALUES('TRS MODEL III', 50, 'FIRST COMPUTER');

1 row created.
```

Now let's create a new table and copy this data to it:

```
SQL> CREATE TABLE TEMP
  2   (NAME CHAR(20),
  3   VALUE NUMBER,
  4   REMARKS CHAR(40));

Table created.
```

```
SQL> INSERT INTO TEMP(NAME, VALUE, REMARKS)
  2   SELECT ITEM, WORTH, REMARKS
  3   FROM COLLECTION;

4 rows created.
```

```
SQL> SELECT * FROM TEMP;
```

```
NAME                    VALUE REMARKS
-------------------- -------- --------------------------------
NBA ALL STAR CARDS        300 SOME STILL IN BIKE SPOKES
STRING                   1000 SOME DAY IT WILL BE VALUABLE
CHIA PET                    5 WEDDING GIFT
TRS MODEL III              50 FIRST COMPUTER
```

Now, let's change some values:

```
SQL> UPDATE TEMP
  2   SET VALUE = 100
  3   WHERE NAME = 'TRS MODEL III';

1 row updated.
```

```
SQL> UPDATE TEMP
  2   SET VALUE = 8
  3   WHERE NAME = 'CHIA PET';

1 row updated.
```

```
SQL> SELECT * FROM TEMP;
```

```
NAME                     VALUE REMARKS
--------------------     ------- ------------------------------
NBA ALL STAR CARDS         300 SOME STILL IN BIKE SPOKES
STRING                    1000 SOME DAY IT WILL BE VALUABLE
CHIA PET                     8 WEDDING GIFT
TRS MODEL III              100 FIRST COMPUTER
```

Now let's update these values back to the original table:

```
INSERT COLLECTION
SELECT * FROM TEMP;
DROP TABLE TEMP;
```

The DROP TABLE and CREATE TABLE statements are discussed in greater detail on Day 9. For now, these statements basically do what their names imply. CREATE TABLE builds a new table with the format you give it, and DROP TABLE deletes the table. Keep in mind that DROP TABLE permanently removes a table, whereas DELETE FROM <TableName> removes only the records from a table.

To check what you have done, select out the records from the COLLECTION table. You will see that the changes you made now exist in the COLLECTION table.

```
SQL>SELECT * FROM COLLECTION;
```

```
NAME                     VALUE REMARKS
--------------------     ------- ------------------------------
NBA ALL STAR CARDS         300 SOME STILL IN BIKE SPOKES
STRING                    1000 SOME DAY IT WILL BE VALUABLE
CHIA PET                     8 WEDDING GIFT
TRS MODEL III              100 FIRST COMPUTER
```

The previous example used all three data manipulation commands—INSERT, UPDATE, and DELETE—to perform a set of operations on a table. The easiest of the three to use is the DELETE statement. Care should always be taken when using these commands, because the changes they make are permanent. In addition, always keep in mind that modifications you are making could affect the referential integrity of your database. Think through all of your database editing steps to make sure that you have updated all tables correctly.

Importing and Exporting Data from Foreign Sources

The INSERT, UPDATE, and DELETE statements are extremely useful from within a database program. They are used with the SELECT statement to provide the foundation for all other database operations you will perform. However, SQL as a language does not provide for the importing or exporting of data from foreign data sources. For instance, your office may have been using a dBASE application for several years now that has outgrown itself. Now,

your manager would like to convert this application to a client/server application using the Oracle RDBMS. Unfortunately for you, these dBASE files contain thousands of records that must be converted to an Oracle database. Obviously, the INSERT, UPDATE, and DELETE commands will help you once your Oracle database has been populated, but you would rather quit than retype 300,000 records. Fortunately, Oracle and other manufacturers provide tools that will assist you in this task.

Nearly all database systems allow you to import and export data using ASCII text file formats. Although this is not a feature of the SQL language, SQL will not do you (or your boss) much good when you have an empty database. We will examine the import/export products that come packaged with the following products: Microsoft Access, Microsoft and Sybase SQL Server, and Personal Oracle7.

Microsoft Access

Microsoft Access is a PC-only database product that contains many of the features of a relational database management system. Also included with the product are powerful reporting tools, a macro language similar to Visual Basic, and the capability to import and export data from a variety of database and text file formats. We will examine this last feature, particularly the capability to export to delimited text files. By delimited, we mean that each field is separated, or delimited, by some special character. Often, this character is a comma, a quotation mark ("), or a space.

Access allows you to import and export a variety of database formats. Included in their list are dBASE, FoxPro, and SQL Database options. This SQL Database option is actually an ODBC data source connection. The topic of Microsoft's Open Database Connectivity is discussed in Chapter 13. For this discussion, we want to select the Export option and then choose the Text (Fixed Width) option.

After opening an Access database (with the File Open menu command), select the Export menu command. A Destination dialog box (for Exporting) is presented to you. Select the Text (Fixed Width) option. This option allows you to output your Access tables to text files where each data type is a fixed width. For example, a character data field of length 30 will be output to the file as a field 30 characters long. If the field's data takes up less space than 30 characters, it will be padded with spaces. Eventually, you will be asked to set up the export file format. The Import/Export Setup dialog box can be seen in Figure 8.1.

Notice that in this dialog box you can select the Text Delimiter you would like to use. You can also select the Field Separator to be used within your export file. As a final step, save the specification you have used for use later. This specification is stored internally within the database.

Figure 8.1.
*The Import/Export
Setup dialog box.*

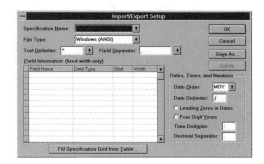

Microsoft and Sybase SQL Server

Microsoft and Sybase have jointly developed a powerful database system that is very popular in client/server application development. The name of this system is SQL Server. Microsoft has agreed to develop versions of the RDBMS for some platforms, and Sybase has developed their version for all the other platforms (usually the larger ones). Although their arrangement has changed somewhat in recent years, we mention this agreement here to help you avoid confusion when you begin examining the different database systems available on the market today.

SQL Server provides file import/export capabilities through the use of the bcp tool. Bcp is short for bulk copy. The basic concept behind bcp is the same as that behind Microsoft Access. Unfortunately, the bcp tool is not graphical in nature. All commands must be done from the operating system command prompt, instead of through dialog boxes or windows.

Bcp imports and exports fixed-width text files. It is possible to export a file using the Microsoft Access method described earlier and then import that same file directly into an SQL Server table using bcp. Bcp uses format files (usually with an .FMT extension) to store the import specification. This specification tells bcp the column names, field widths, and field delimiters. Bcp can be run from within an SQL database build script to completely import data once the database has been built.

Personal Oracle7

Personal Oracle7 allows you to import and export data from ASCII text files containing delimited or fixed-length records. The tool that does this is SQL*Loader. This is a graphical tool that uses a control file (with the extension of .CTL). This file is similar to SQL Server's format (.FMT) file. The information contained in this file tells SQL*Loader what it needs to know to load the data from the file.

The SQL*Loader dialog box can be seen in Figure 8.2.

Figure 8.2.

*The SQL*Loader
dialog box.*

Summary

SQL provides three statements that can be used to manipulate data within a database.

The INSERT statement can be used in two different ways. The INSERT...VALUES statement inserts a set of values into one record. It is used to add a single record at a user's request, for instance. The INSERT...SELECT statement is used in combination with a SELECT statement to insert multiple records into a table based on the contents of one or more tables. The SELECT statement can join together multiple tables, and the results of this join can be added to another table.

The UPDATE statement is used to change one or more columns' values based on some condition. This value can also be the result of an expression or calculation.

The DELETE statement is the simplest of the three statements. It deletes all rows from a table based on the result of a WHERE clause that can be optionally provided. If the WHERE clause is omitted, all records from the table are deleted.

Modern database systems supply a variety of tools for data manipulation. Some of these tools enable the developer to import or export data from foreign sources. This is particularly useful when a database is upsized or downsized to a different system. Specific products discussed were Microsoft Access, Microsoft and Sybase SQL Server, and Personal Oracle7. Within these products, there is a wide range of support and capability.

Q&A

Q Is there an SQL statement for file import/export operations?

A No. This can be thought of as an implementation-specific operation. In other words, the ANSI committee basically leaves this up to the individual manufacturers to create whatever features or enhancements they feel are necessary.

8

Q Can I copy data from a table into itself using the INSERT command? I would like to make duplicate copies of all of the existing records and change the value of one field.

A No, you cannot insert data into the same table that you selected from. However, the operation you would like to do is possible by selecting the original data into a temporary table (true temporary tables are discussed in Chapter 14). The data in this temporary table can be modified and then selected back into the original table. Make sure that you watch out for unique fields you may have already created. A unique field means that only one record can exist having a field with that value.

Workshop

The workshop provides quiz questions to help solidify your understanding of the material covered, as well as exercises to provide you with experience in using what you have learned. Try to answer the quiz and exercise questions before checking the answers in Appendix F, and make sure you understand the answers before continuing to the next chapter.

Quiz

1. What is wrong with the following statements?

    A. `DELETE COLLECTION;`

    B. `INSERT INTO COLLECTION`
       `SELECT * FROM TABLE_2`

    C. `UPDATE COLLECTION ("HONUS WAGNER CARD",`
       `25000, "FOUND IT");`

Exercises

1. Try inserting values with incorrect data types into a table. Note the errors, then insert values with correct data types into the same table.

2. Using your database system, try exporting a table (or an entire database) to some other format. Then import the data back into your database. Familiarize yourself with this capability. Also, export the tables to another database format if your DBMS supports this feature. Then use the other system to open these files and examine them.

Creating and
Maintaining Tables

Introduction

So far, we have covered much of the SQL vocabulary. We have looked at the SQL query in some detail, beginning with its basic syntax. After learning how to select data from the database, on Day 8 you learned how to insert, update, and delete data from the database. Now, nine days into the learning process, you probably have been wondering just where these databases come from. For simplicity's sake, we have ignored the process of creating databases and tables up to this point. We have assumed that these data objects existed currently on your system.

Today, you take the next big step. Topics covered in this chapter are the CREATE DATABASE, CREATE TABLE, ALTER TABLE, DROP TABLE, and DROP DATABASE statements. These statements are often referred to as data definition statements. In contrast, the SELECT, UPDATE, INSERT, and DELETE statements are often described as data manipulation statements.

The CREATE statements' syntax can range from the extremely simple to the complex, depending on what options your DBMS supports and how detailed you would like to get when building your database. By the end of the day, you will actually be able to perform a typical database management task. You begin by creating a database with its associated tables, adding data to the database, modifying the data, copying data to another table, and then deleting the table structures and finally the database itself. Before pursuing this, we will cover the syntax of these statements. Let's begin with CREATE DATABASE.

The CREATE DATABASE Statement

When beginning any database project, the first data management step you take will always be the creation of your database. This task can range from the elementary to the complicated, depending on your needs and the database management system you have chosen. Many modern systems (including Personal Oracle7) come equipped with graphical tools that enable you to completely build the database with the click of a mouse button. Not that this isn't helpful and time-saving, but there are many advantages to learning the SQL statements being executed underneath these mouse clicks.

Through personal experience, I have come to realize the importance of the creation of an SQL install script. This script file contains all of the necessary SQL code to completely rebuild a database or databases, often including all database objects such as indexes, stored procedures, and triggers. You will see the value of this during development as you continually make changes to the underlying database and on occasion want to completely rebuild the database with all the latest changes. Obviously, using the graphical tools each time this task is needed can become extremely time-consuming. After all, you probably are not getting paid to simply create the database. In addition, knowing the SQL syntax for this procedure enables you to apply your knowledge to other database systems in the future.

The syntax for the typical CREATE DATABASE statement looks like this:

```
CREATE DATABASE database_name
```

Because the syntax varies so widely from system to system, we will not expand on the CREATE DATABASE statement's syntax any further. Many systems do not even support an SQL CREATE DATABASE command. However, all of the popular, more powerful relational database management systems do provide it. Instead of focusing on its syntax, we will spend some time discussing the options to consider when creating a database.

CREATE DATABASE Options

As mentioned earlier, the syntax for this statement can vary widely. Many SQL texts skip over the CREATE DATABASE statement and move directly on to the CREATE TABLE statement. Obviously, the smart reader will quickly realize that to build a table, a database must be created first, so this section focuses on some of the concepts a developer must consider when building a database. The first of these considerations is your level of permission. If you are using an RDBMS that supports user permissions, you must make sure that either you have System Administrator-level permission settings or the System Administrator has granted you CREATE DATABASE permission. Contact your RDBMS documentation for more information on this.

Most RDBMSs also allow you to specify a default database size. This size is usually in terms of hard disk space (such as megabytes). You may need to gain some understanding of how your database system stores and locates data on the disk to accurately estimate the size you need. This falls primarily under the area of system administration, and possibly at your location a database administrator will build you a test database to get you started. Don't let this intimidate you. At its simplest, you can create a database named PAYMENTS with the statement shown in Example 9.1.

Example 9.1

```
create database PAYMENTS
```

We assume that this statement will suffice for the remainder of this book. Once again, be sure to consult your database management system's documentation to learn the specifics of building a database.

Database Design

Designing a database properly is extremely important to the success of your application. On Day 1, we touched upon the topics of database normalization and relational database theory. Essentially, normalization is the process of breaking your data into separate components to reduce the repetition of data. There are several levels of normalization, each of which reduces the repetition of data.

Normalizing your data can be an extremely difficult process. Numerous database design tools available on the market allow you to plan this process in a logical fashion. Many factors can influence the design of your database, including the following:

☐ Security

☐ Disk space available

☐ Speed of database searches and retrievals

☐ Speed of database updates

☐ Speed of multiple-table joins to retrieve data

☐ Support of temporary tables by RDBMS

Obviously, disk space is always a factor. Although you may think that, in this age of multi-gigabyte storage, disk space might not be on your list of considerations, remember that the bigger your database is, the longer it takes to retrieve records. If you have done a poor job of designing your table structure, chances are that you have needlessly repeated much of your data.

Often, the opposite problem can occur. You may have sought to completely normalize your tables' design with the database and in doing so may have created a lot of tables. Although in theory you may have approached database design nirvana, the truth is that any query operations done against this database may take a very long time to execute. Databases designed in this manner are sometimes difficult to maintain because it is very difficult to ascertain what the designer had in mind by just looking at the table structure. This underlines the importance of always documenting your code or design, so that others can come in after you (or work with you) and have some idea of what you were thinking at the time you created your database structure. In database designer's terms, this documentation is known as a data dictionary.

Creating a Data Dictionary

A data dictionary is the most important form of documentation to the database designer. It is used to do the following:

☐ Describe the purpose of the database and who will be using it.

☐ Document the specifics behind the database itself. This could mean any of the following: what device it was created on; the database's default size; or the size of the log file (used to store database operations information in some RDBMSs).

☐ Include SQL source code for any database install or un-install scripts. This includes documentation on the use of import/export tools such as those introduced in Day 8.

☐ Provide in-depth description of each table within the database, and their purpose in business process terminology.

9

☐ Document the internal structure of each table. This should include all fields and their data types with comments, all indexes, and all views. (See Day 10.)

☐ Include SQL source code for all stored procedures and triggers.

☐ Provide some description of database constraints such as the use of unique values or NOT NULL values. Also, it should mention whether these constraints are enforced at the RDBMS level, or whether the database programmer is expected to check for these constraints within his or her source code.

Many CASE (Computer Aided Software Engineering) tools aid the database designer in the creation of this data dictionary. For instance, Microsoft Access comes prepackaged with a Database Documentor tool that prints out a detailed description of every object in the database.

Creating Key Fields

Along with documenting your database design, the most important design goal you should have is to separate your table structure so that each table has a primary key and a foreign key. The primary key should be designed to meet the following goals:

☐ Each record is unique within a table (no other record within the table has all of its columns equal to any other).

☐ For a record to be unique, all of the columns are necessary. This means that only one column ideally would have data that is not repeated anywhere else in the table.

Regarding the second goal, the column that has completely unique data throughout the table is known as the primary key field. A foreign key field is a field that is used to link a table to another table's primary or foreign key. Example 9.2 should clarify this situation.

Example 9.2

Assume you have three tables: BILLS, BANK_ACCOUNTS, and COMPANY. The format of these three tables is shown in Table 9.1.

Table 9.1. Table structure for the PAYMENTS database.

BILLS	BANK_ACCOUNTS	COMPANY
NAME, CHAR(30) CHAR(30)	ACCOUNT_ID, NUMBER	NAME,
AMOUNT, NUMBER	TYPE, CHAR(30)	ADDRESS, CHAR(50)
ACCOUNT_ID, NUMBER	BALANCE, NUMBER	CITY, CHAR(20)
	BANK, CHAR(30)	STATE, CHAR(2)

Take a moment to examine these tables. Which fields do you think are the primary keys? Which are the foreign keys?

The primary key in the BILLS table is the NAME field. This field should not be duplicated because you have only one bill with this amount. (In reality, you would probably have a check number or a date to make this record truly unique, but assume for now that the NAME field works.) The ACCOUNT_ID field in the BANK_ACCOUNTS table is the primary key for that table. The NAME field is the primary key for the COMPANY table.

The foreign keys in this example are probably easy to spot also. The ACCOUNT_ID field in the BILLS table is used to join the BILLS table with the BANK_ACCOUNTS table. The NAME field in the BILLS table is used to join the BILLS table with the COMPANY table. If this were a full-fledged database design you would have many more tables and data breakdowns. For instance, the BANK field in the BANK_ACCOUNTS table could point to a BANK table containing bank information such as addresses and phone numbers. The COMPANY table could be linked with another table (or database for that matter) containing information about the company and its products.

Exercise 9.1

Let's take a moment to examine an incorrect database design using the same information contained in the BILLS, BANK_ACCOUNTS, and COMPANY tables. A mistake many beginning users make is not breaking down their data into as many logical groups as possible. For instance, one poorly designed BILLS table might look like this:

Column Names	Comments
NAME, CHAR(30)	Name of company that bill is owed to
AMOUNT, NUMBER	Amount of bill in dollars
ACCOUNT_ID, NUMBER	Bank account number of bill (linked to BANK_ACCOUNTS table)
ADDRESS	Address of company that bill is owed to
CITY	City of company that bill is owed to
STATE	State of company that bill is owed to

This might look correct, but take a moment to really look at the data here. If over several months you wrote several bills to the company in the NAME field, each time a new record was added for a bill, the company's ADDRESS, CITY, and STATE information would be duplicated. Now multiply that duplication over several hundred or thousand records, then multiply that by 10, 20, or 30 tables, and you can begin to see the importance of a properly normalized database.

Before you actually fill these tables with data, we will discuss how to create a table.

The CREATE TABLE Statement

I am happy to say that the process of creating a table is far more standardized than the CREATE DATABASE statement. The basic syntax for the CREATE TABLE statement looks like the following:

```
CREATE TABLE table_name
(     field1 datatype [ NOT NULL ],
      field2 datatype [ NOT NULL ],
      field3 datatype [ NOT NULL ]...)
```

A simple example of a CREATE TABLE statement is shown in Example 9.3.

Example 9.3

```
CREATE TABLE BILLS (
    NAME CHAR(30),
    AMOUNT NUMBER,
    ACCOUNT_ID NUMBER);
```

This creates a table named BILLS. Within the BILLS table are three fields: NAME, AMOUNT, and ACCOUNT_ID. The NAME field has a data type of character and can store strings up to 30 characters long. The AMOUNT and ACCOUNT_ID fields can contain number values only.

Let's examine this command by breaking it down into its different components.

The Table Name

When creating a table using Personal Oracle7, several constraints apply when naming the table. First, the table name can be no more than 30 characters long. Because Oracle is case-insensitive, it makes no difference whether you use upper- or lowercase for the individual characters. However, the first character of the name must be a letter between A and Z. The remaining characters can be letters or the symbols _, #, $, and @. Of course, the table name must be unique within the database you create it in. The name also cannot be one of the Oracle or SQL reserved words (such as SELECT).

The Field Name

The same constraints that apply to the table name also apply to the field name. However, a field name can be duplicated within the database. The restriction is that the field name must be unique within the table it is in. For instance, assume that you have two tables in your database: Table1 and Table2. Both of these tables could have fields called ID. You cannot, however, have two fields within Table1 called ID, even if they are different data types.

The Field's Data Type

If you have ever programmed in any language, you are familiar with the concept of data types. This means the type of data that is to be stored in this specific field. For instance, a character data type constitutes a field that stores only character string data. The data types supported by Oracle are shown in Table 9.2.

Table 9.2. Data types supported by Personal Oracle7.

Data Type	Comments
CHAR	Alphanumeric data with a length between 1 and 255 characters
DATE	Included as part of the date are century, year, month, day, hour, minute, and second
LONG	Variable-length alphanumeric strings up to 2 gigabytes in size (see the following note)
LONG RAW	Binary data up to 2 gigabytes in size (see the following note)
NUMBER	Numeric zero, positive, or negative fixed or floating point data
RAW	Binary data up to 255 bytes in size
ROWID	Hexadecimal string representing the unique address of a row in a table (see the following note)
VARCHAR2	Alphanumeric data that is variable length; this field must be between 1 and 2,000 characters in length

The LONG data type is often called a MEMO data type in other database management systems. It is primarily used to store large amounts of text for retrieval at some later time.

The LONG RAW data type is often called a BLOB (Binary Large Object) in other database management systems. It is typically used to store graphics, sound, or video data. Although relational database management systems were not originally designed to serve this type of data, many multimedia systems today store their data in LONG RAW, or BLOB, fields.

The ROWID field type is used to give each record within your table a unique, nonduplicating value. Many other database systems support this concept through the use of a COUNTER (MS Access) field or an IDENTITY field (SQL Server).

The NULL Value

SQL enables you to identify what can be stored within a column, in addition to specifying the data type you would like to use. A NULL value is almost an oxymoron, because having a field with a value of NULL means that the field actually has no value stored in it.

When building a table, most database systems enable you to denote a column with the NOT NULL keywords. This means that there can be no NULL values stored in this column for any records in the table. Conversely, this means that every record must have an actual value in this column. Example 9.4 illustrates the use of the NOT NULL keywords.

Example 9.4

```
CREATE TABLE BILLS (
    NAME CHAR(30) NOT NULL,
    AMOUNT NUMBER,
    ACCOUNT_ID NOT NULL);
```

In this table, we would like to save the name of the company we owe the money to, along with the bill's amount. If the NAME field were not stored, the record would be meaningless. You would end up with a record with a bill that you owed to someone, but you would have no idea who that someone was.

Example 9.5

```
INSERT INTO BILLS VALUES("Joe's Computer Service", 25, 1);
INSERT INTO BILLS VALUES("", 25000, 1);
```

Example 9.5 inserted a valid record containing data for a bill to be sent to Joe's Computer Service for $25. However, the next record contains no NAME value. You might think this is a good thing because the bill amount is $25,000, but we won't take that into consideration. If the table had been created with a NOT NULL value for the NAME field (as in Example 9.4), the second insert would have raised an error.

A good rule of thumb is that the primary key field and all foreign key fields should never be allowed to contain NULL values.

Unique Fields

Earlier in this chapter, we stated that one of your design goals should be to have one unique column within each table. We called this column or field a primary key field. Some database systems allow you to set a field as unique. Other DBMSs, such as Oracle and SQL Server, allow you to create a unique index on a field. (See Day 10.) This keeps you from inserting duplicate key field values into the database.

Several things should be noticed when choosing a key field. As we mentioned, Oracle provides a ROWID field that is incremented for each row that is added. This makes this field by default always a unique key. These fields make excellent key fields for several reasons. First, it is much faster to join on an integer value than an 80-character string. It results in smaller database sizes over time if you store an integer value in every primary and foreign key as opposed to a long CHAR value. Also, using CHAR values leaves you open to a number of data entry problems. For instance, what would happen if one person entered 111 First Street, another entered 111 1st Street, and yet another entered 111 First St.? With today's graphical user environments, the correct string could be entered into a list box. Then, when a user selected one of these, the code would convert this string to a unique ID and save this ID to the database.

Now let's create the tables used in Example 9.2. Because these tables will be used for the remainder of this chapter, let's also fill them with some data. Use the INSERT command covered in Chapter 8.

Example 9.6

```
SQL> create database BILLS;
SQL> create table BILLS (
     NAME CHAR(30) NOT NULL,
     AMOUNT NUMBER,
     ACCOUNT_ID NUMBER NOT NULL);
SQL> create table BANK_ACCOUNTS (
     ACCOUNT_ID NUMBER NOT NULL,
     TYPE CHAR(30),
     BALANCE NUMBER,
     BANK CHAR(30));
SQL> create table COMPANY (
     NAME CHAR(30) NOT NULL,
     ADDRESS CHAR(50),
     CITY CHAR(30),
     STATE CHAR(2));
```

Table 9.3. Sample data for the BILLS table.

NAME	AMOUNT	ACCOUNT_ID
Phone Company	125	1
Power Company	75	1
Record Club	25	2
Software Company	250	1
Cable TV Company	35	3

Table 9.4. Sample data for the BANK_ACCOUNTS table.

ACCOUNT_ID	TYPE	BALANCE	BANK
1	Checking	500	First Federal
2	Money Market	1200	First Investor's
3	Checking	90	Credit Union

Table 9.5. Sample data for the COMPANY table.

NAME	ADDRESS	CITY	STATE
Phone Company	111 1st Street	Atlanta	GA
Power Company	222 2nd Street	Jacksonville	FL
Record Club	333 3rd Avenue	Los Angeles	CA
Software Company	444 4th Drive	San Francisco	CA
Cable TV Company	555 5th Drive	Austin	TX

Creating a Table from an Existing Table

Creating a table is usually done using the CREATE TABLE command. However, some DBMSs provide for other methods of creating tables using the format and data of an existing table. This is useful when you would like to select the data out of a table for temporary modification. It can also be useful when you have to create a similar table to the existing one that also has similar data. To keep from re-entering all of this information, this method can be used. The syntax for Oracle looks like the following:

```
CREATE TABLE NEW_TABLE(FIELD1, FIELD2, FIELD3)
AS (SELECT FIELD1, FIELD2, FIELD3
    FROM OLD_TABLE <WHERE...>
```

This syntax allows you to create a new table with the same data types as those of the fields that are selected from the old table. It also allows you to rename the fields in the new table by giving them new names.

Example 9.7

```
SQL> CREATE TABLE NEW_BILLS(NAME, AMOUNT, ACCOUNT_ID)
     AS (SELECT * FROM BILLS WHERE AMOUNT < 50);
```

Example 9.7 creates a new table (NEW_BILLS) with all the records from the BILLS table that have an AMOUNT less than 50.

Some database systems also allow you to use the following syntax:

```
INSERT NEW_TABLE
SELECT <field1, field2... ¦ *> from OLD_TABLE
<WHERE...>
```

This syntax would create a new table with the exact field structure and data found in the old table. Using SQL Server's Transact-SQL language, Example 9.8 illustrates this.

Example 9.8

```
INSERT NEW_BILLS
1> select * from BILLS where AMOUNT < 50
2> go
```

(The GO statement in SQL Server is used to process the SQL statements in the command buffer. It is equivalent to the semicolon (;) used in Oracle7.)

The ALTER TABLE Statement

Many times your design may have not accounted for everything it should have. Also, requirements for applications and databases in particular are always subject to change. The ALTER TABLE statement enables the database administrator or designer to change the structure of a table after it has been created.

The ALTER TABLE command allows the programmer to do two things:

☐ Add a column to an existing table

☐ Modify a column that already exists

The syntax for the ALTER TABLE statement is as follows:

```
ALTER TABLE table_name
  <ADD column_name data_type; ¦
  MODIFY column_name data_type;>
```

For instance, to change the NAME field of the BILLS table to hold 40 characters, the following command would be issued:

```
SQL> ALTER TABLE BILLS
     MODIFY NAME CHAR(40);
```

To add a new column to the NEW_BILLS table that was created in Example 9.7, the statement would look like the following:

```
SQL> ALTER TABLE NEW_BILLS
     ADD COMMENTS CHAR(80);
```

This statement would add a new column, named COMMENTS, capable of holding 80 characters. The field would be added to the right of all the existing fields.

Several restrictions apply to using the ALTER TABLE statement. You cannot use it to add or delete fields from a database. It can be used to change a column from NOT NULL to NULL, but not necessarily the other way around. A column specification can be changed from NULL to NOT NULL only if there are currently no NULL values in that column. To change a column from NOT NULL to NULL, use the following syntax:

```
ALTER TABLE table_name
MODIFY (column_name data_type NULL);
```

To change a column from NULL to NOT NULL, you might have to take several steps:

1. Make sure there are no NULL values in that column.
2. If there are NULL values, make a decision about what to do (delete those records, update the column's value, and so on).
3. Issue the ALTER TABLE command.

> **Note:** Some database management systems allow the use of the MODIFY clause; others do not. Still others have added other clauses to the ALTER TABLE statement. Check the documentation of the system you are using to determine the implementation of the ALTER TABLE statement.

The DROP TABLE Statement

SQL provides a command to completely get rid of a table from a database. By issuing the DROP TABLE command, you can delete a table along with all of its associated views and indexes (see Chapter 10). Once this command has been issued, there is no turning back. The most common use of the DROP TABLE statement is when you have created a table for temporary use. When you have completed all operations on the table that you planned to do, issue the DROP TABLE statement with the following syntax:

```
DROP TABLE table_name;
```

For instance, to drop the NEW_BILLS table created in Example 9.7, issue the following command:

```
SQL> DROP TABLE NEW_BILLS;
```

Notice that there was no prompting from the system. It did not ask you Are you sure? (Y/N). Once this command has been issued, the table is permanently deleted.

The DROP DATABASE Statement

Some database management systems also provide the DROP DATABASE statement, which is identical in usage to the DROP TABLE statement. The syntax for this statement is as follows:

```
DROP TABLE database_name
```

We won't drop the BILLS database now because it will be used for the rest of this chapter, as well as on Day 10.

Exercise 9.2

Create a database with one table in it. Issue the DROP TABLE command, followed by the DROP DATABASE command. Does your database system allow you to do this? Single-file–based systems such as MS Access do not support this command. The database is actually contained in a single file. To create a database, you must use the menu options provided in the product itself. To delete a database, simply delete the file from the hard drive.

Summary

This chapter covered much of what is known as SQL's Data Manipulation Language (DML). In particular, we covered five statements: CREATE DATABASE, CREATE TABLE, ALTER TABLE, DROP TABLE, and DROP DATABASE. We also discussed the importance of creating a good database design.

A data dictionary is one of the most important pieces of documentation you can create when designing a database. This dictionary should include a complete description of all objects in the database, including tables, fields, views, indexes, stored procedures, and triggers. It is often a good idea to include a brief comment explaining the purpose behind each item within the database. Once the data dictionary has been created, it should be continually updated as new changes are made to the database.

Before using any of the data manipulation statements, it is also important to create a good database design. This can be done by breaking down required information into logical groups. Within each logical group, try to identify a primary key field that other groups (or tables) can reference this group by. Use foreign key fields to point to the primary or foreign key fields in other tables.

You learned that the CREATE DATABASE statement is fairly nonstandard among the different database systems. This is primarily because of the many different ways each vendor stores their database on the disk. Each one enables a different set of features and options, which in the end results in a completely different CREATE DATABASE statement. Simply issuing `CREATE DATABASE database_name` creates a default database with a default size on most systems. The DROP DATABASE statement permanently removes that database.

The CREATE TABLE statement is used to create a new table. With this command, you can create the fields you need and identify their data types. Some DBMSs also allow the programmer to specify other attributes for the field, such as whether it can allow NULL values or whether that field should be unique throughout the table. The ALTER TABLE statement can alter the structure of an existing table. The DROP TABLE statement can delete a table from a database.

Q&A

Q Why does the CREATE DATABASE statement vary so much from one system to another?

A This statement varies so much because the actual process of creating a database varies so much among the different database systems. Small PC-based databases usually rely on files that are created within some type of application program. To distribute the database, these files are simply distributed. When your code accesses these databases, there is no database process running on the computer, just your application accessing the files directly. More powerful database systems must take into account disk space management as well as support features such as security, transaction control, and stored procedures embedded within the database itself. When your application program accesses a database, a database server manages your requests (along with many others' requests) and returns data to you through a sometimes complex layer of middleware. These topics are discussed toward the end of this book. For now, learn all you can about how your particular database management system creates and manages databases.

Q Is there any type of table that can be created temporarily and automatically be dropped when I am done with it?

A Yes. Many database management systems support the concept of a temporary table. This type of table is created for temporary usage and is automatically deleted when your user's process ends or when you issue the DROP TABLE command. The use of temporary tables is discussed on Day 14.

Q Can I remove columns with the ALTER TABLE statement?

A No. The ALTER TABLE command can be used only to add or modify columns within a table. To remove columns, a new table should be created with the desired format, and then the records from the old table should be selected into that new table.

Workshop

The workshop provides quiz questions to help solidify your understanding of the material covered, as well as exercises to provide you with experience in using what you have learned. Try to answer the quiz and exercise questions before checking the answers in Appendix F, and make sure you understand the answers before continuing to the next chapter.

Quiz

1. Answer the following questions (true or false):

   A. The ALTER DATABASE statement is often used to modify an existing table's structure.

   B. The DROP TABLE command is functionally equivalent to the DELETE FROM <table_name> command.

   C. To add a new table to a database, use the CREATE TABLE command.

2. What is wrong with the following statements?

   A.
   ```
   CREATE TABLE new_table (
   ID NUMBER,
   FIELD1 char(40),
   FIELD2 char(80),
   ID char(40);
   ```

   B.
   ```
   ALTER DATABASE BILLS (
   COMPANY char(80));
   ```

Exercises

1. Add two tables to the BILLS database named BANK and ACCOUNT_TYPE using any format you like. The BANK table should contain information about the BANK field used in the BANK_ACCOUNTS table in the examples. The ACCOUNT_TYPE table should contain information about the ACCOUNT_TYPE field in the BANK_ACCOUNTS table also. Try to reduce the data as much as possible.

2. With the five tables that you have created—BILLS, BANK_ACCOUNTS, COMPANY, BANK, and ACCOUNT_TYPE—change the table structure so that instead of using CHAR fields as keys, you use integer ID fields as keys.

3. Using your knowledge of SQL joins (as discussed on Day 6), write several queries to join the tables in the BILLS database together.

Creating Views and Indexes

Introduction

On Day 10, we begin to cover topics that may be new even to the programmer or database user who had already had some exposure to SQL before reading this book. To this date, we have covered nearly all the introductory material to get you started using SQL and relational databases. On Day 9, we spent an entire chapter discussing database design, table creation, and other data manipulation commands. All of this discussion dealt with databases, tables, records, and fields. What these objects have in common is that they are all physical objects located on a hard disk. Today we focus on two features of SQL that enable you to view or present data in a different format than it appears on the disk. These two features are the view and the index.

A view is often referred to as a virtual table. Views enable the SQL programmer to create a "view" of data that may be different than what physically exists on the disk. After the view has been created, you can use the following SQL commands to refer to that view:

- ☐ SELECT
- ☐ INSERT
- ☐ INPUT
- ☐ UPDATE
- ☐ DELETE

Views are created by using the CREATE VIEW statement. We spend the first part of this chapter discussing the view and all of its functionality.

An index is another way of presenting data differently than it appears on the disk. There are also special types of indexes that actually reorder the record's physical location within a table. Indexes can be created on a column within a table, or on a combination of columns within a table. When an index is used, the data is presented to the user in a sorted order. This order can be controlled by the programmer through the CREATE INDEX statement. Substantial performance improvements can usually be gained by indexing on the correct fields, particularly fields that are being joined between tables. We discuss the index in much greater detail later in the chapter. We begin with the view.

Using Views

Views, as mentioned earlier, are essentially virtual tables. They can be used to encapsulate complex queries. Once a view on a set of data has been created, you can treat that view as another table. You will learn, however, that there are special restrictions placed on modifying the data within views.

The syntax for the CREATE VIEW statement is

```
CREATE VIEW <view_name> [(column1, column2...)] AS
SELECT <table_name column_names>
FROM <table_name>
```

As usual, this syntax may look a little cryptic at first glance. Rest assured that we include many examples that show you the many uses of views and their many advantages. This command tells SQL to create a view (with the name of your choice) composed of columns (with the names of your choice, if you like). The fields in these columns, and their data types, are determined by an SQL SELECT statement. Yes, this is the same SELECT statement we have used repeatedly for the first nine days.

Before you can actually do anything useful with views (or indexes), you need to populate the BILLS database with a little more data. Don't worry if you got excited and took advantage of your newfound knowledge of the DROP DATABASE command. You can simply re-create it. (See Table 10.1 for sample data.)

```
SQL> create database BILLS;
SQL> create table BILLS (
     NAME CHAR(30) NOT NULL,
     AMOUNT NUMBER,
     ACCOUNT_ID NUMBER NOT NULL);
SQL> create table BANK_ACCOUNTS (
     ACCOUNT_ID NUMBER NOT NULL,
     TYPE CHAR(30),
     BALANCE NUMBER,
     BANK CHAR(30));
SQL> create table COMPANY (
     NAME CHAR(30) NOT NULL,
     ADDRESS CHAR(50),
     CITY CHAR(30),
     STATE CHAR(2));
```

Table 10.1. Sample data for the BILLS table.

NAME	AMOUNT	ACCOUNT_ID
Phone Company	125	1
Power Company	75	1
Record Club	25	2
Software Company	250	1
Cable TV Company	35	3
Joe's Car Palace	350	5
S.C. Student Loan	200	6
Florida Water Company	20	1
U-O-Us Insurance Company	125	5
Debtor's Credit Card	35	4

Table 10.2. Sample data for the BANK_ACCOUNTS table.

ACCOUNT_ID	TYPE	BALANCE	BANK
1	Checking	500	First Federal
2	Money Market	1200	First Investor's
3	Checking	90	Credit Union
4	Savings	400	First Federal
5	Checking	2500	Second Mutual
6	Business	4500	Fidelity

Table 10.3. Sample data for the COMPANY table.

NAME	ADDRESS	CITY	STATE
Phone Company	111 1st Street	Atlanta	GA
Power Company	222 2nd Street	Jacksonville	FL
Record Club	333 3rd Avenue	Los Angeles	CA
Software Company	444 4th Drive	San Francisco	CA
Cable TV Company	555 5th Drive	Austin	TX
Joe's Car Palace	1000 Govt. Blvd	Miami	FL
S.C. Student Loan	25 College Blvd	Columbia	SC
Florida Water Company	1883 Hwy 87	Navarre	FL
U-O-Us Insurance Company	295 Beltline Hwy	Macon	GA
Debtor's Credit Card	115 2nd Avenue	Newark	NJ

Now that you have successfully used the CREATE DATABASE, CREATE TABLE, and INSERT commands to input all this information, you are ready for an in-depth discussion of the view.

A Simple View

Let's begin with the simplest of all views. Suppose, for some unknown reason, you would like to make a view on the BILLS table that looked identical to the table but had a different name (we call it DEBTS). This statement would look like this:

```
SQL> CREATE VIEW DEBTS AS
     SELECT * FROM BILLS;
```

To confirm that this operation did what it should, you can treat the view just like a table:

```
SQL> SELECT * FROM DEBTS;
```

```
NAME                      AMOUNT  ACCOUNT_ID
Phone Company                125  1
Power Company                 75  1
Record Club                   25  2
Software Company             250  1
Cable TV Company              35  3
Joe's Car Palace             350  5
S.C. Student Loan            200  6
Florida Water Company         20  1
U-O-Us Insurance Company     125  5
Debtor's Credit Card          35  4
```

You can even create new views from existing views. Remember, once the view has been created, think of it as a virtual table.

```
SQL> CREATE VIEW CREDITCARD_DEBTS AS
     SELECT * FROM DEBTS
     WHERE ACCOUNT_ID = 4;
SQL> SELECT * FROM CREDITCARD_DEBTS;
```

```
NAME                      AMOUNT  ACCOUNT_ID
Debtor's Credit Card          35  4
```

CREATE VIEW also enables the programmer to select individual columns from a table and place them in a view. The following example selects the NAME and STATE fields from the COMPANY table.

```
SQL> CREATE VIEW COMPANY_INFO (NAME, STATE) AS
     SELECT * FROM COMPANY;
SQL> SELECT * FROM COMPANY_INFO;
```

```
NAME                      STATE
Phone Company                GA
Power Company                FL
Record Club                  CA
Software Company             CA
Cable TV Company             TX
Joe's Car Palace             FL
S.C. Student Loan            SC
Florida Water Company        FL
U-O-Us Insurance Company     GA
Debtor's Credit Card         NJ
```

Renaming Columns

Views are used to simplify the representation of data. The SQL syntax for the CREATE VIEW statement enables you to rename selected columns in addition to naming the view. Examine the previous example a little more closely. What if you wanted to combine the ADDRESS, CITY, and STATE fields from the COMPANY table to print them on an envelop? The following example illustrates this. This example uses the SQL + operator to combine the address fields into one long address using spaces and commas combined with the character data.

```
SQL> CREATE VIEW ENVELOPE (COMPANY, MAILING_ADDRESS) AS
     SELECT NAME, ADDRESS + " " + CITY + ", " + STATE
     FROM COMPANY;
SQL> SELECT * FROM ENVELOPE;
```

```
COMPANY                     MAILING_ADDRESS
Phone Company               111 1st Street Atlanta, GA
Power Company               222 2nd Street Jacksonville, FL
Record Club                 333 3rd Avenue Los Angeles, CA
Software Company            444 4th Drive San Francisco, CA
Cable TV Company            555 5th Drive Austin, TX
Joe's Car Palace            1000 Govt. Blvd Miami, FL
S.C. Student Loan           25 College Blvd. Columbia, SC
Florida Water Company       1883 Hwy. 87 Navarre, FL
U-O-Us Insurance Company    295 Beltline Hwy. Macon, GA
Debtor's Credit Card        115 2nd Avenue Newark, NJ
```

The SQL syntax requires you to supply a virtual field name whenever the view's virtual field is created using a calculation or SQL function. This makes sense because you wouldn't want a view's column name to be COUNT(*) or AVG(PAYMENT).

SQL View Processing

Views can represent data within tables in a more convenient fashion than what actually exists in the database's table structure. They can also be extremely convenient when performing several complex queries in a series (such as within a stored procedure or application program). To solidify your understanding of the view and the SELECT statement, we break down how SQL actually processes a query against a view. Suppose you have the following query that occurs often. Perhaps you must routinely join the BILLS table with the BANK_ACCOUNTS table to retrieve information on your payments.

```
SQL> SELECT BILLS.NAME, BILLS.AMOUNT, BANK_ACCOUNTS.BALANCE,
     BANK_ACCOUNTS.BANK FROM BILLS, BANK_ACCOUNTS
     WHERE BILLS.ACCOUNT_ID = BANK_ACCOUNTS.ACCOUNT_ID;
```

```
BILLS.NAME                BILLS.AMOUNT   BANK_ACCOUNTS.BALANCE
BANK_ACCOUNTS.BANK
Phone Company             125            500                    First
Federal
Power Company             75             500                    First
Federal
Record Club               25             1200                   First
Investor's
Software Company          250            500                    First
Federal
Cable TV Company          35             90                     Credit
Union
Joe's Car Palace          350            2500                   Second
Mutual
S.C. Student Loan         200            4500                   Fidelity
Florida Water Company     20             500                    First
Federal
U-O-Us Insurance Company  125            2500                   Second
Mutual
```

This process could be turned into a view using the following statement:

```
SQL> CREATE VIEW BILLS_DUE (NAME, AMOUNT, ACCT_BALANCE, BANK) AS
     SELECT BILLS.NAME, BILLS.AMOUNT, BANK_ACCOUNTS.BALANCE,
     BANK_ACCOUNTS.BANK FROM BILLS, BANK_ACCOUNTS
     WHERE BILLS.ACCOUNT_ID = BANK_ACCOUNTS.ACCOUNT_ID;
```

If you then took the BILLS_DUE view and queried it using some condition, it would look something like this:

```
SQL> SELECT * FROM BILLS_DUE
     WHERE ACCT_BALANCE > 500;
```

```
NAME                          AMOUNT    ACCT_BALANCE    BANK
Record Club                   25        1200            First Investor's
Joe's Car Palace              350       2500            Second Mutual
S.C. Student Loan             200       4500            Fidelity
U-O-Us Insurance Company      125       2500            Second Mutual
```

SQL processes the preceding statement using several steps. Because BILLS_DUE is a view, not an actual table, SQL first looks for a table named BILLS_DUE and finds nothing. Depending on what database system you are using, the SQL processor will probably find out from a system table that BILLS_DUE is actually a view. It will then use the view's plan to construct the following query:

```
SQL> SELECT BILLS.NAME, BILLS.AMOUNT, BANK_ACCOUNTS.BALANCE,
     BANK_ACCOUNTS.BANK FROM BILLS, BANK_ACCOUNTS
     WHERE BILLS.ACCOUNT_ID = BANK_ACCOUNTS.ACCOUNT_ID
     AND BANK_ACCOUNTS.BALANCE > 500;
```

Exercise 10.1

Construct a view that will show all states that the bills are being sent to. Along with this, display the total amount of money and the total number of bills being sent to each state.

First of all, you know that the CREATE VIEW part of the statement will look like this:

```
CREATE VIEW EXAMPLE (STATE, TOTAL_BILLS, TOTAL_AMOUNT) AS...
```

Now you must determine what the SELECT query will look like. You know that you want to select the STATE field first using the SELECT DISTINCT syntax based on the requirement to show the states that bills are being sent to. This would look something like this:

```
SQL> SELECT DISTINCT STATE FROM COMPANY;
```

```
STATE
GA
FL
CA
TX
SC
NJ
```

In addition to selecting the STATE field, you need to total the number of payments sent to that STATE. This would require you to join the BILLS table and the COMPANY table together.

```
SQL> SELECT DISTINCT COMPANY.STATE, COUNT(BILLS.*) FROM BILLS, COMPANY
        GROUP BY COMPANY.STATE
        HAVING BILLS.NAME = COMPANY.NAME;
```

This returns the following:

```
STATE      COUNT(BILLS.*)
GA         2
FL         3
CA         2
TX         1
SC         1
NJ         1
```

Now that you have successfully returned two-thirds of the desired result, you can add the final required return value. The amount of money sent to each state can be totaled using the SUM function.

```
SQL> SELECT DISTINCT COMPANY.STATE, COUNT(BILLS.NAME), SUM(BILLS.AMOUNT)
        FROM BILLS, COMPANY
        GROUP BY COMPANY.STATE
        HAVING BILLS.NAME = COMPANY.NAME;
```

This returns the following:

```
STATE      COUNT(BILLS.*)      SUM(BILLS.AMOUNT)
GA         2                   250
FL         3                   445
CA         2                   275
TX         1                   35
SC         1                   200
NJ         1                   35
```

As the final step, you can combine this SELECT statement with the CREATE VIEW statement you created in the beginning to complete this exercise.

```
SQL> CREATE VIEW EXAMPLE (STATE, TOTAL_BILLS, TOTAL_AMOUNT) AS
     SELECT DISTINCT COMPANY.STATE, COUNT(BILLS.NAME), SUM(BILLS.AMOUNT)
     FROM BILLS, COMPANY
     GROUP BY COMPANY.STATE
     HAVING BILLS.NAME = COMPANY.NAME;
```

```
SQL> SELECT * FROM EXAMPLE;
```

STATE	TOTAL_BILLS	TOTAL_AMOUNT
GA	2	250
FL	3	445
CA	2	275
TX	1	35
SC	1	200
NJ	1	35

Exercise 10.2

Assume that all of your creditors charge a 10-percent service charge for all late payments, and unfortunately you are late on everything this month. Because of your tardiness, you would like to see this charge along with the type of accounts all these payments are coming out of.

This is a straightforward join (you don't need to use anything like COUNT or SUM). However, you will discover one of the primary benefits of using views. You can add the 10 percent service charge and present it as a field within the view. From that point on, you can select records from the view and already have the total amount calculated for you. The syntax would look like this:

```
SQL> CREATE VIEW LATE_PAYMENT (NAME, NEW_TOTAL, ACCOUNT_TYPE) AS
     SELECT BILLS.NAME, BILLS.AMOUNT * 1.10, BANK_ACCOUNTS.TYPE
     FROM BILLS, BANK_ACCOUNTS
     WHERE BILLS.ACCOUNT_ID = BANK_ACCOUNTS.ACCOUNT_ID;

SQL> SELECT * FROM LATE_PAYMENT;
```

NAME	NEW_TOTAL	ACCOUNT_TYPE
Phone Company	137.50	Checking
Power Company	82.50	Checking
Record Club	27.50	Money Market
Software Company	275	Checking
Cable TV Company	38.50	Checking
Joe's Car Palace	385	Checking
S.C. Student Loan	220	Business
Florida Water Company	22	Checking
U-O-Us Insurance Company	137.50	Business
Debtor's Credit Card	38.50	Savings

Restrictions on Using SELECT

SQL places certain restrictions on using the SELECT statement to formulate a view. The following two rules apply when using the SELECT statement:

☐ You cannot use the UNION operator

☐ You cannot use the ORDER BY clause

Modifying Data Using Views

As you have learned, by creating a view on one or more physical tables within a database, you can create a virtual table for use throughout an SQL script or a database application. After the view has been created using the CREATE VIEW...SELECT statement, you can update, insert, or delete view data using the UPDATE, INSERT, and DELETE commands you learned about on Day 8.

There are many limitations to modifying a view's data, and we discuss those limitations in greater detail later. For now, we will go through several examples to illustrate data manipulation using views.

To continue on the work you did in Exercise 10.2, update the BILLS table to reflect that unfortunate 10-percent late charge.

```
SQL> CREATE VIEW LATE_PAYMENT AS
        SELECT * FROM BILLS;
SQL> UPDATE LATE_PAYMENT
        SET AMOUNT = AMOUNT * 1.10;
SQL> SELECT * FROM LATE_PAYMENT;
```

NAME	NEW_TOTAL	ACCOUNT_ID
Phone Company	137.50	1
Power Company	82.50	1
Record Club	27.50	2
Software Company	275	1
Cable TV Company	38.50	3
Joe's Car Palace	385	5
S.C. Student Loan	220	6
Florida Water Company	22	1
U-O-Us Insurance Company	137.50	5
Debtor's Credit Card	38.50	4

To verify that the UPDATE command actually updated the underlying table BILLS, query the BILLS table.

```
SQL> SELECT * FROM BILLS;
```

NAME	NEW_TOTAL	ACCOUNT_ID
Phone Company	137.50	1
Power Company	82.50	1
Record Club	27.50	2
Software Company	275	1
Cable TV Company	38.50	3
Joe's Car Palace	385	5
S.C. Student Loan	220	6
Florida Water Company	22	1
U-O-Us Insurance Company	137.50	5
Debtor's Credit Card	38.50	4

Now delete a row from the view:

```
SQL> DELETE FROM LATE_PAYMENT
     WHERE ACCOUNT_ID = 4;
SQL> SELECT * FROM LATE_PAYMENT;
```

```
NAME                        NEW_TOTAL      ACCOUNT_ID
Phone Company               137.50         1
Power Company               82.50          1
Record Club                 27.50          2
Software Company            275            1
Cable TV Company            38.50          3
Joe's Car Palace            385            5
S.C. Student Loan           220            6
Florida Water Company       22             1
U-O-Us Insurance Company    137.50         5
```

Finally, test the UPDATE function. For all bills that have a NEW_TOTAL greater than 100, add an additional 10.

```
SQL> UPDATE LATE_PAYMENT
     SET NEW_TOTAL = NEW_TOTAL + 10
     WHERE NEW_TOTAL > 100;
SQL> SELECT * FROM LATE_PAYMENT;
```

```
NAME                        NEW_TOTAL      ACCOUNT_ID
Phone Company               147.50         1
Power Company               82.50          1
Record Club                 27.50          2
Software Company            285            1
Cable TV Company            38.50          3
Joe's Car Palace            395            5
S.C. Student Loan           230            6
Florida Water Company       22             1
U-O-Us Insurance Company    147.50         5
```

Problems with Modifying Data Using Views

Because what you see through a view can actually be some set of a group of tables, modifying the data in the underlying tables is not always as straightforward as the previous examples. A number of rules should be followed. Following is a list of the most common things you will encounter while working with views:

- ☐ DELETE statements are not allowed on multiple table views.
- ☐ The INSERT statement is not allowed unless all NOT NULL columns used in the underlying table are included in the view. This is because the SQL processor does not know what values to insert into the NOT NULL columns.
- ☐ If you do insert or update records through a join view, all records that are updated must belong to the same physical table.

☐ If the DISTINCT clause is used to create a view, you cannot update or insert records within that view.

☐ A virtual column (a column that is the result of an expression or function) cannot be updated.

Common Applications of Views

Views are commonly used to perform a number of tasks, including the following:

☐ Performing user security functions

☐ Converting between units

☐ Creating a new virtual table format

☐ Simplifying building of complex queries

Views and Security

Although we have put off a complete discussion of database security until Day 12, we briefly touch on the topic now to explain how views can be used in performing security functions.

Today, all relational database systems provide a full suite of security features that are built into the system itself. Generally, users of the database system are broken into groups based on their use of the database. Common group types are Database Administrators, Database Developers, Data Entry Personnel, and Public Users. Like any other type of secure system, these groups have varying degrees of privileges when using the database. The Database Administrator will probably have complete control of the system, including UPDATE, INSERT, DELETE, and ALTER database privileges. The Public group may be granted only SELECT privileges—and perhaps may be allowed to SELECT only from certain tables within certain databases.

Views are commonly used in this situation to control what the database user has access to. For instance, if you wanted users to have access only to the NAME field of the BILLS table, you could simply create a view called BILLS_NAME:

```
SQL> CREATE VIEW BILLS_NAME AS
     SELECT NAME FROM BILLS;
```

Someone with System Administrator-level privileges could grant the Public group SELECT privileges on the BILLS_NAME view. This group would not have any privileges on the underlying BILLS table. As you might guess, SQL has provided data security statements for your use also. Keep in mind that views are a very useful tool when implementing database security.

Using Views to Convert Units

Views are also useful in situations where you need to present the user with data that is different than what actually exists within the database. For instance, let's assume that the AMOUNT field is actually stored in U.S. dollars. However, we don't want our Canadian users to have to continually do calculations in their heads to see the AMOUNT total in Canadian dollars. A simple view called CANADIAN_BILLS could be created as follows:

```
SQL> CREATE VIEW CANADIAN_BILLS (NAME, CAN_AMOUNT) AS
     SELECT NAME, AMOUNT / 1.10
     FROM BILLS;
SQL> SELECT * FROM CANADIAN_BILLS;
```

```
NAME                       CAN_AMOUNT
Phone Company              125
Power Company              75
Record Club                25
Software Company           250
Cable TV Company           35
Joe's Car Palace           350
S.C. Student Loan          200
Florida Water Company      20
U-O-Us Insurance Company   125
```

When converting between different units, keep in mind the possible problems we discussed concerning modifying the underlying data when a calculation was used to create one of the virtual columns. As always, make sure you consult your database system's documentation to determine exactly how they implemented the CREATE VIEW command.

Simplifying Complex Queries Using Views

Views can also be used in situations where many queries have to be performed in a row to arrive at a result. The following example illustrates the use of a view in this situation.

To give the name of all banks that had bills sent to the state of Texas with an amount less than $50, you would break the problem into two separate problems:

- ☐ Retrieve all bills that were sent to Texas
- ☐ Retrieve all bills less than $50

Let's solve this using two separate views: BILLS_1 and BILLS_2.

```
SQL> CREATE TABLE BILLS1 AS
     SELECT * FROM BILLS
     WHERE AMOUNT < 50;
SQL> CREATE TABLE BILLS2 (NAME, AMOUNT, ACCOUNT_ID) AS
     SELECT BILLS.* FROM BILLS, COMPANY
     WHERE BILLS.NAME = COMPANY.NAME AND COMPANY.STATE = "TX";
```

Because you want to find all bills sent to Texas *and* all bills that were less than $50, you can now use the SQL IN clause to find which bills in BILLS1 were sent to Texas. Use this to create a view called BILLS3:

```
SQL> CREATE VIEW BILLS3 AS
     SELECT * FROM BILLS2 WHERE NAME IN
     (SELECT * FROM BILLS1);
```

Now combine the preceding query with the BANK_ACCOUNTS table to satisfy the original requirements of this example:

```
SQL> CREATE VIEW BANKS_IN_TEXAS (BANK) AS
     SELECT BANK_ACCOUNTS.BANK
     FROM BANK_ACCOUNTS, BILLS3
     WHERE BILLS3.ACCOUNT_ID = BANK_ACCOUNTS.ACCOUNT_ID;
SQL> SELECT * FROM BANK_IN_TEXAS;
```

```
BANK
Credit Union
```

As you can see, once the queries were broken down into separate views, the final query was rather simple. Also, the individual views can be reused over and over again.

The DROP VIEW Statement

As with every other SQL CREATE... command, there is also a DROP... command. CREATE VIEW and DROP VIEW are no exceptions. The syntax is as follows:

```
DROP VIEW view_name;
```

The only thing to remember when using the DROP VIEW command is that all other views that reference that view are now invalid. Some database systems even drop all views that used the view you dropped. Using Personal Oracle7 and the following example, if view BILLS1 were dropped, the final query would result in the following error:

```
SQL> DROP VIEW BILLS1;
SQL> SELECT * FROM BANKS_IN_TEXAS;
         *
```

```
ERROR at line 1:
ORA-04063: view "PERKINS.BANKS_IN_TEXAS" has errors
```

Using Indexes

If you have ever used indexes to sort a table, it may have seemed out of place to put the topic of indexes in the same chapter as the topic of views. However, take a moment to think about these two tools. Views provide a view of the data that actually exists in the underlying tables. The view can be dropped without any of the actual tables being modified. This is why we often refer to views as virtual tables. (The same logic can be applied to the technology of virtual reality.) Indexes can also be used to present data in a different format than it physically exists on the disk. In addition, indexes can also actually reorder the data stored on the disk (something views cannot do).

Indexes are used in an SQL database for three primary reasons:

☐ To enforce referential integrity constraints by using the UNIQUE keyword (we discuss this in more detail later in the chapter)

☐ To facilitate the ordering of data based on the contents of the index's field or fields

☐ To optimize the execution speed of queries

What Are Indexes?

Data can be retrieved from a database using two methods. The first method, often called the Sequential Access Method, requires SQL to go through each record looking for a match. This is an inefficient search method, but it is the only way for SQL to locate the correct record. Think back to the days when libraries had massive card catalog filing systems. Suppose the librarian removed the alphabetical index cards, tossed the cards into the air, then placed them back into the filing cabinets. When you wanted to look up this book's shelf location, you would probably start at the very beginning, then go through one card at a time until you found the information you were looking for. (Chances are, a human would probably give up shortly into the search and just find another book on the same topic!)

Now suppose the librarian went through and sorted the book titles alphabetically. You could quickly access this book's information by using your knowledge of the alphabet to search through the catalog.

Imagine the flexibility if the librarian was diligent enough not only to sort the books by title, but also to create another catalog sorted by author's name, and another one sorted by topic. This would provide you, the library user, with a great deal of flexibility in retrieving information. Also, you would be able to retrieve your information in a fraction of the time it originally would have taken.

Adding these indexes to your database enables SQL to use the Direct Access Method. If you have never taken a data structures class (or if you have and have long since forgotten what you learned), SQL uses a tree-like structure to store and retrieve the index's data. At the top of

10

the tree, pointers to a group of data are stored. These groups are called *nodes*. Within each of these nodes, pointers to other nodes are stored. The nodes pointing to the left contain values that are less than the parent node. The pointers to the right point to values greater than the parent node.

The database system first looks at the top node to find what it is looking for. If it doesn't find it, it simply follows the pointers until it is successful.

Fortunately for the SQL programmer, you are not required to actually implement the tree structure yourself, just as you are not required to write the implementation for saving and reading in tables or databases. The basic SQL syntax to create an index is as follows:

```
CREATE INDEX index_name
ON table_name(column_name1, [column_name2], ...);
```

As you have seen many times before, the syntax for CREATE INDEX can vary widely among database systems. For instance, the CREATE INDEX statement under Oracle7 looks like this:

```
CREATE INDEX [schema.]index
ON { [schema.]table (column [!!under!!ASC¦DESC]
    [, column [!!under!!ASC¦DESC]] ...)
  ¦ CLUSTER [schema.]cluster }
[INITRANS integer] [MAXTRANS integer]
[TABLESPACE tablespace]
[STORAGE storage_clause]
[PCTFREE integer]
[NOSORT]
```

The syntax for CREATE INDEX using Sybase SQL Server is as follows:

```
create [unique] [clustered ¦ nonclustered]
      index index_name
on [[database.]owner.]table_name (column_name
    [, column_name]...)
[with {fillfactor = x, ignore_dup_key, sorted_data,
      [ignore_dup_row ¦ allow_dup_row]}]
[on segment_name]
```

Informix SQL implements the command like this:

```
CREATE [UNIQUE ¦ DISTINCT] [CLUSTER] INDEX index_name
ON table_name (column_name [ASC ¦ DESC],
              column_name [ASC ¦ DESC]...)
```

Notice that all of these implementations have several things in common, starting with the basic statement

```
CREATE INDEX index_name ON table_name (column_name, ...)
```

SQL Server and Oracle allow you to create a clustered index, which is discussed later. Oracle and Informix allow you to designate whether the column name should be sorted in ascending or descending order. We hate to sound like a broken record, but, once again, you should definitely consult your database management system's documentation when using the CREATE INDEX command.

For instance, to create an index on the ACCOUNT_ID field of the BILLS table, the CREATE INDEX statement would look like this:

```
SQL> SELECT * FROM BILLS;
```

```
NAME                       AMOUNT      ACCOUNT_ID
Phone Company              125         1
Power Company              75          1
Record Club                25          2
Software Company           250         1
Cable TV Company           35          3
Joe's Car Palace           350         5
S.C. Student Loan          200         6
Florida Water Company      20          1
U-O-Us Insurance Company   125         5
Debtor's Credit Card       35          4
```

```
SQL> CREATE INDEX ID_INDEX ON BILLS( ACCOUNT_ID );
SQL> SELECT * FROM BILLS;
```

```
NAME                       AMOUNT      ACCOUNT_ID
Phone Company              125         1
Power Company              75          1
Software Company           250         1
Florida Water Company      20          1
Record Club                25          2
Cable TV Company           35          3
Debtor's Credit Card       35          4
Joe's Car Palace           350         5
U-O-Us Insurance Company   125         5
S.C. Student Loan          200         6
```

The results of the ID_INDEX being created can be plainly seen. Now the BILLS table is sorted by the ACCOUNT_ID field until the index is dropped using the DROP INDEX statement. As usual, the DROP statement is very straightforward:

```
DROP INDEX index_name;
```

Let's look at what happens when the index is dropped:

```
SQL> DROP INDEX ID_INDEX;
SQL> SELECT * FROM BILLS;
```

```
NAME                        AMOUNT      ACCOUNT_ID
Phone Company               125         1
Power Company               75          1
Record Club                 25          2
Software Company            250         1
Cable TV Company            35          3
Joe's Car Palace            350         5
S.C. Student Loan           200         6
Florida Water Company       20          1
U-O-Us Insurance Company    125         5
Debtor's Credit Card        35          4
```

Now the BILLS table is back in its original form. The CREATE INDEX statement did not physically change the way the table was stored using the CREATE INDEX statement in its simplest form.

At this point, you may wonder why database systems even provide indexes if they also enable you to use the ORDER BY clause.

```
SQL> SELECT * FROM BILLS ORDER BY ACCOUNT_ID;
```

```
NAME                        AMOUNT      ACCOUNT_ID
Phone Company               125         1
Power Company               75          1
Software Company            250         1
Florida Water Company       20          1
Record Club                 25          2
Cable TV Company            35          3
Debtor's Credit Card        35          4
Joe's Car Palace            350         5
U-O-Us Insurance Company    125         5
S.C. Student Loan           200         6
```

This SELECT statement resulted in the exact same data returned as when you created the ID_INDEX on the BILLS table. The difference is that when you use an ORDER BY clause, the data is resorted and ordered for you each time the SQL statement using the ORDER BY clause is executed. When using an index, the database system creates a physical index object (using the tree structure we already talked about) and can reuse this index each time the table is queried.

Indexing Tips

Listed here are several tips to keep in mind when using indexes:

☐ For small tables, using indexes does not result in any performance improvement.

☐ Indexes bring the greatest improvement when the columns you have indexed on contain a wide variety of data or many NULL values.

☐ Indexes can optimize your queries when those queries are returning a small amount of data (a good rule of thumb is less than 25 percent of the data). If you are returning more than that most of the time, indexes simply add overhead.

☐ Indexes can improve the speed of data retrieval. However, they slow data updates. Keep this in mind when doing many updates in a row with an index.

☐ Indexes take up space within your database. If you are using a database management system that enables you to manage the disk space taken up your database, factor in the size of indexes when planning your database's size.

☐ Always index on fields that are used in joins between tables. This can greatly increase the speed of a join.

☐ Most database systems do not allow you to create an index on a view. If your database system allows it, use the ORDER BY clause with the SELECT statement that builds the view to order the data within the view. (Unfortunately, many systems don't enable the ORDER BY clause with the CREATE VIEW statement either.)

☐ Do not index on fields that are updated or modified regularly. The overhead required to constantly update the index will offset any performance gain you hope to acquire.

Indexing on More Than One Field

SQL also enables you to index on more than one field. We call this type of index a composite index. The following code illustrates a simple composite index. Note that even though two fields are being combined, only one physical index is created (called ID_CMPD_INDEX).

```
SQL> CREATE INDEX ID_CMPD_INDEX ON BILLS( ACCOUNT_ID, AMOUNT );
SQL> SELECT * FROM BILLS;
```

```
NAME                        AMOUNT      ACCOUNT_ID
Florida Water Company       20          1
Power Company               75          1
Phone Company               125         1
Software Company            250         1
Record Club                 25          2
Cable TV Company            35          3
Debtor's Credit Card        35          4
U-O-Us Insurance Company    125         5
Joe's Car Palace            350         5
S.C. Student Loan           200         6
SQL> DROP INDEX ID_CMPD_INDEX;
```

Analysis Performance gains are achieved when you select the column with the most unique values. For instance, every value in the NAME field of the BILLS table is unique. When using a compound index, place the most selective field first in the column list. What this means is that the field that you expect to select most often should be placed first. (The order in which the column names appear in the CREATE INDEX statement does not have to be the order they are in within the table.) Assume you are routinely using a statement such as the following:

```
SQL> SELECT * FROM BILLS WHERE NAME = "Cable TV Company";
```

To achieve performance gains, you must create an index using the NAME field as the leading column. Here are two examples of this:

```
SQL>CREATE INDEX NAME_INDEX ON BILLS(NAME, AMOUNT);
```

or

```
SQL>CREATE INDEX NAME_INDEX ON BILLS(NAME);
```

The NAME field is the left-most column for both of these indexes, so the preceding query would be optimized to search on the NAME field.

Composite indexes are also used to combine two or more columns that by themselves may have low selectivity. For an example of what we mean by selectivity, examine the BANK_ACCOUNTS table:

ACCOUNT_ID	TYPE	BALANCE	BANK
1	Checking	500	First Federal
2	Money Market	1200	First Investor's
3	Checking	90	Credit Union
4	Savings	400	First Federal
5	Checking	2500	Second Mutual
6	Business	4500	Fidelity

Notice that out of six records, the value Checking appears in three of them. This column has a lower selectivity than the ACCOUNT_ID field. Notice that every value of the ACCOUNT_ID field is unique. To improve the selectivity of your index, you could combine the TYPE and ACCOUNT_ID fields in a new index. This would create a unique index value (which, of course, is the highest selectivity you can get).

Using the UNIQUE Keyword with CREATE INDEX

Composite indexes are often used in combination with the UNIQUE keyword to prevent multiple records from appearing with the exact same data. Suppose you wanted to force the

BILLS table to have the following built-in "rule": Only one bill should ever be sent to a company from an account. (Once one bill has been paid to a company from a bank account, the next bill to that company must come from a different account.) You would create a UNIQUE index on the NAME and ACCOUNT_ID fields. Unfortunately, Oracle7 does not support the UNIQUE syntax. Instead, they have chosen to implement the UNIQUE feature using the UNIQUE integrity constraint. We illustrate the use of the UNIQUE keyword with CREATE INDEX using Sybase's Transact-SQL language.

```
1> create unique index unique_id_name
2>on BILLS(ACCOUNT_ID, NAME)
3>go
1>select * from BILLS
2>go
```

```
NAME                        AMOUNT      ACCOUNT_ID
Florida Water Company       20          1
Power Company               75          1
Phone Company               125         1
Software Company            250         1
Record Club                 25          2
Cable TV Company            35          3
Debtor's Credit Card        35          4
U-O-Us Insurance Company    125         5
Joe's Car Palace            350         5
S.C. Student Loan           200         6
```

Now let's try to insert a record into the BILLS table that duplicates data that already exists.

```
1>insert BILLS (NAME, AMOUNT, ACCOUNT_ID)
2>values("Power Company", 125, 1)
3>go
```

You should have received an error message telling you that the INSERT command was not allowed. Within an application program, this type of error message can be trapped, and a message could be displayed to the user telling them that the data they inserted was not allowed.

Exercise 10.3

Create an index on the BILLS table that will sort the AMOUNT field in descending order.

```
SQL> CREATE INDEX DESC_AMOUNT
     ON  BILLS(AMOUNT DESC);
```

This is the first time you have used the DESC operator. This tells SQL to sort the index in descending order. (By default, a number field is sorted in ascending order.) Now you can examine your handiwork.

```
SQL> SELECT * FROM BILLS;
```

```
NAME                          AMOUNT     ACCOUNT_ID
Joe's Car Palace              350        5
Software Company             250         1
S.C. Student Loan            200         6
Phone Company                125         1
U-O-Us Insurance Company     125         5
Power Company                75          1
Cable TV Company             35          3
Debtor's Credit Card         35          4
Record Club                  25          2
Florida Water Company        20          1
```

Indexes and Joins

When using complicated joins in queries, your SELECT statement can take a long time. With large tables, this amount of time can approach several seconds (as compared to the milliseconds you are used to waiting). This type of performance in a client/server environment with many users becomes extremely frustrating to the user of your application. Creating an index on fields that are frequently used in joins can optimize the performance of your query considerably. However, it should be noted here that if too many indexes are created, they can actually slow down the performance of your system, rather than speeding it up. We recommend that you experiment with using indexes on several large tables (on the order of thousands of records). Use a stopwatch to time several complex queries with and without indexes and record your results. This type of experimentation leads to a better understanding of optimizing SQL statements.

Let's create an index on the ACCOUNT_ID fields in the BILLS and BANK_ACCOUNTS tables:

```
SQL> CREATE INDEX BILLS_INDEX ON BILLS(ACCOUNT_ID);
SQL> CREATE INDEX BILLS_INDEX2 ON BANK_ACCOUNTS(ACCOUNT_ID);
SQL> SELECT BILLS.NAME NAME, BILLS.AMOUNT AMOUNT, BANK_ACCOUNTS.BALANCE
     ACCOUNT_BALANCE
     FROM BILLS, BANK_ACCOUNTS
     WHERE BILLS.ACCOUNT_ID = BANK_ACCOUNTS.ACCOUNT_ID;
```

```
NAME                          AMOUNT     ACCOUNT_BALANCE
Phone Company                125         500
Power Company                75          500
Software Company             250         500
Florida Water Company        20          500
Record Club                  25          1200
Cable TV Company             35          90
Debtor's Credit Card         35          400
Joe's Car Palace             350         2500
U-O-Us Insurance Company     125         2500
S.C. Student Loan            200         4500
```

Using Clusters

Although we originally said that indexes can be used to present a different view of a table to a user than what physically exists, this is not entirely accurate. A special type of index supported by many database systems allows the database manager or developer to cluster data. When a clustered index is used, the physical arrangement of the data within a table is modified. Using a clustered index almost always results in faster data retrieval than using a traditional, nonclustered index. However, many database systems (such as Sybase SQL Server) allow only one clustered index per table. The field used to create the clustered index is almost always the primary key field. Using Sybase Transact-SQL, you could create a clustered, unique index on the ACCOUNT_ID field of the BANK_ACCOUNTS table using the following syntax:

```
1> create unique clustered index id_index
2> on BANK_ACCOUNTS(ACCOUNT_ID)
3> go
```

Oracle treats the concept of clusters differently. When using the Oracle relational database, a cluster is a database object like a database or table. A cluster is used to store tables with common fields so that their access speed is improved.

Here is the syntax to create a cluster using Oracle7:

```
CREATE CLUSTER [schema.]cluster
(column datatype [,column datatype] ... )
[PCTUSED integer] [PCTFREE integer]
[SIZE integer [K¦M] ]
[INITRANS integer] [MAXTRANS integer]
[TABLESPACE tablespace]
[STORAGE storage_clause]
[!!under!!INDEX
¦ [HASH IS column] HASHKEYS integer]
```

Once this cluster has been created, an index should be created within it based on which tables will be added to it. After the index has been created, tables can be added to it. You should add tables only to clusters that are frequently joined together. Do not add tables to clusters that are accessed individually through a simple SELECT statement.

Obviously, clusters are a vendor-specific feature of SQL. We will not go into more detail here on their use or on the syntax that creates them. However, consult your database vendor's documentation to determine if these useful objects are supported under your database management system.

Summary

Today we went beyond the beginning aspects of using relational databases. Through Day 9, we covered the many, many ways to use the SELECT query as well as the data manipulation statements INSERT, UPDATE, and DELETE. After that, you learned to create a database and the tables within it. On Day 10, the concepts of the view and the index were introduced. As you have seen, much of the material we covered in detail at the beginning can now be used to create views and indexes.

Views can be thought of as virtual tables. They are simply another way of presenting data in a different format than what actually exists in the database. The syntax of the CREATE VIEW statement uses a standard SELECT statement to create the view (with some exceptions). Once the view has been created, it can be treated as a regular table. Inserts, updates, deletes, and selects can be performed on the view. We briefly discussed the use of database security and how views are commonly used to implement this security. Database security is covered in greater detail on Day 12.

The basic syntax used to create a view is

```
CREATE VIEW view_name AS
SELECT field_name(s) FROM table_name(s);
```

The following list illustrates the most common ways that views are used:

- ☐ Performing user security functions
- ☐ Converting between units
- ☐ Creating a new virtual table format
- ☐ Simplifying building of complex queries

Indexes are another tool made available to the database designer or SQL programmer. Indexes are physical database objects stored by your database management system that can be used to retrieve data already sorted from the database. In addition, thanks to the way indexes are mapped out, if indexes are used in conjunction with properly formed queries, significant performance improvements can be achieved.

The basic syntax used to create an index looks like this:

```
CREATE INDEX index_name
ON table_name(field_name(s));
```

Depending on the database system you are using, other options are often provided, such as the UNIQUE and CLUSTERED keywords.

Q&A

Q If the data within my table is already in sorted order, should I use an index on that table?

A If your query conditions meet those discussed in this chapter, an index still gives you a performance benefit. This is because the index looks quickly through key values in a tree. It can still locate records faster than a Direct Access search through each record within your database. Remember—just because your data is in sorted order doesn't mean the SQL query processor knows this!

Q Can I create an index that contains fields from multiple tables?

A No, you cannot. However, Oracle7, for instance, allows you to create a cluster. Once a cluster has been created, tables can be placed within it and cluster indexes can be created on fields common between tables. This is the exception, not the rule, so be sure to study your documentation on this topic in more detail.

Workshop

The workshop provides quiz questions to help solidify your understanding of the material covered, as well as exercises to provide you with experience in using what you have learned. Try to answer the quiz and exercise questions before checking the answers in Appendix F, and make sure you understand the answers before continuing to the next chapter.

Quiz

1. What will happen is a unique index is created on a non-unique field?

Exercises

1. Examine the database system you are using. Does it support views? What options are you allowed to use when creating a view? Write a simple SQL statement that will create a view using the appropriate syntax. Perform some traditional operations such as SELECT or DELETE, then DROP the view.

2. Examine the database system you are using to determine how it supports indexes. You will undoubtedly have a wide range of options such as those discussed in this chapter. Try out some of these options on a table that exists within your database. In particular, determine whether you are allowed to create UNIQUE or CLUSTERED indexes on a table within your database.

3. If possible, locate a table that has several thousand records. Use a stopwatch or clock to time a variety of operations against the database. Add some indexes and see if you notice a performance improvement. Try to follow the tips given to you within this chapter.

11

Transaction
Control

Introduction

We have spent the first 10 days covering virtually everything you can do with data within a relational database. As of today, you have become an intermediate-level SQL and database user. If required, you could build a database with its associated tables. Each of these tables would contain several fields of different data types. Using proper design techniques, the information contained within this database could be leveraged into a powerful application. We have thoroughly covered the SQL SELECT statement, which retrieves data from one or more tables based on a number of conditions supplied by the user. Data modification statements such as INSERT, UPDATE, and DELETE have also been presented with several practical examples.

Finally, on Day 10 we introduced two new tools: views and indexes. Both of these can be used to present data in a format of your choice (as opposed to the way the data exists in the database). If you have never worked much with databases, you may be wondering where we will go from here. The next four days include more advanced topics such as transaction control, security, embedded SQL programming, and database procedures. If you are only a casual user of SQL who occasionally needs to retrieve data from a database, the topics of the first ten days provide the vast majority of information you will use. However, if you ever intend to (or are currently required to) develop a professional application using any type of relational database, the topics covered over the next four days will help you a great deal. We begin with transaction control.

Transaction Control

Transaction control, or transaction management, refers to the capability of a relational database management system to perform database transactions. Transactions are units of work that must be done successfully as a group or not at all. By a unit of work, we mean that a transaction has a beginning and an end. If anything were to go wrong during the transaction, the entire unit of work can be canceled if desired. If everything looks good, the entire unit of work can be saved off to the database.

If you have not yet worked in a multi-user environment, the chances are very good that in the coming months or years you will be implementing applications for multiple users to use across a network. As we mentioned on Day 1, client/server environments are designed specifically for this purpose. Traditionally, there is a server (in this case, let's say a database server) that can support multiple network connections to it. As is often the case with technology, with this new-found flexibility comes a new degree of complexity. Consider Example 11.1.

Example 11.1

You are employed with First Federal Financial Bank to set up an application that handles checking account transactions. As you are undoubtedly aware, these transactions consist of debits and credits to customer's checking accounts. You have set up a nice database, which has been tested and verified to work correctly. After calling up your application, you verify that when you take $20 out of the account, $20 actually disappears from the database. When you add $50.25 to the checking account, this deposit shows up as expected. Proud of your new accomplishment, you announce to your bosses that the system is ready to go, and several computers are set up in a local branch to begin work.

Within minutes, you notice big problems. It seems that as one teller was depositing a check, another was withdrawing money. This was something you had never really taken into consideration. Within minutes, many depositor's balances are incorrect due to multiple users updating tables simultaneously. Unfortunately, these multiple updates resulted in the overwriting of other worker's changes. Shortly thereafter, your application is pulled off-line due to obvious difficulties. Let's work through an actual exercise to help you visualize the problem at hand.

Exercise 11.1

Create a database called CHECKING. Within this database are two tables, shown in Tables 11.1 and 11.2.

Table 11.1. The CUSTOMERS table.

Name	Address	City	State	Zip	Customer_ID
Bill Turner	725 N. Deal Parkway	Washington	DC	20085	1
John Keith	1220 Via De Luna Dr.	Jacksonville	FL	33581	2
Mary Rosenberg	482 Wannamaker Avenue	Williamsburg	VA	23478	3
David Blanken	405 N. Davis Highway	Greenville	SC	29652	4
Rebecca Little	7753 Woods Lane	Houston	TX	38764	5

Table 11.2. The BALANCES table.

Average_Bal	Curr_Bal	Account_ID
1298.53	854.22	1
5427.22	6015.96	2
211.25	190.01	3
73.79	25.87	4
1285.90	1473.75	5
1234.56	1543.67	6
345.25	348.03	7

Assume now that your application program does a SELECT operation and retrieves the data for Bill Turner.

```
NAME:  Bill Turner
ADDRESS:  725 N. Deal Parkway
CITY:  Washington
STATE:  DC
ZIP:  20085
CUSTOMER_ID:  1
```

While this information is being retrieved, another user with a connection to this database updates Bill Turner's address information:

```
SQL> UPDATE CUSTOMERS SET Address = "11741 Kingstowne Road"
     WHERE Name = "Bill Turner";
```

As you can see, the information you retrieved earlier could be invalid if the update occurred during the middle of your SELECT. If your application fired off a letter to be sent to Mr. Bill Turner, the address it used would be wrong. Obviously, if the letter has already been sent, there is nothing you can do about a change of address. However, if you had used a transaction, this data change could have been detected, and all your other operations could have been rolled back.

Beginning a Transaction

Transactions are actually quite simple to implement. We will examine the syntax used to perform transactions using the Oracle RDBMS SQL syntax as well as the Sybase SQL Server SQL syntax.

Under all database systems that support transactions, there must be a way to explicitly tell the system that you are beginning a transaction. (Remember that a transaction is a logical grouping of work that has a beginning and an end.) Using Personal Oracle7, the syntax looks like this:

```
SET TRANSACTION {READ ONLY ¦ USE ROLLBACK SEGMENT segment}
```

The SQL standard specifies that each database's SQL implementation must support statement-level read consistency. This means that data must stay consistent while one statement is executing. However, we realize that there are many instances where data must remain valid across a single unit of work, not just a single statement. Oracle enables the user to specify when the transaction will begin by using the SET TRANSACTION statement. If, as in Example 11.1, you wanted to examine Bill Turner's information and make sure that the data was not changed, you could do the following:

```
SQL> SET TRANSACTION READ ONLY;
SQL> SELECT * FROM CUSTOMERS
     WHERE NAME = "Bill Turner";
—Do Other Operations—
SQL> COMMIT;
```

We discuss the COMMIT statement later in this chapter. The SET TRANSACTION READ ONLY option enables the programmer to effectively lock a set of records until the transaction ends. The READ ONLY option can be used with the following commands:

SELECT

LOCK TABLE

SET ROLE

ALTER SESSION

ALTER SYSTEM

The option USE ROLLBACK SEGMENT segment is used to tell Oracle what database segment to use for rollback storage space. Because this is an Oracle extension to standard SQL syntax, we do not cover this aspect of the command. Consult your Oracle documentation for more information on using segments to maintain your database.

SQL Server's Transact-SQL language implements the BEGIN TRANSACTION command with the following syntax:

```
begin {transaction ¦ tran} [transaction_name]
```

This is a little different from the Oracle implementation. (Sybase does not allow you to specify the READ ONLY option.) However, Sybase does allow you to give a transaction a name, as long as that transaction is the outermost of a set of nested transactions. Example 11.2 should illustrate the use of nested transactions.

11

Example 11.2

The following group of statements illustrates the use of nested transactions using Sybase's Transact-SQL language:

```
1> begin transaction new_account
2> insert CUSTOMERS values ("Izetta Parsons", "1285 Pineapple Highway",
"Greenville", "AL"  32854, 6)
3> if exists(select * from CUSTOMERS where Name = "Izetta Parsons")
4> begin
5> begin transaction
6> insert BALANCES values(1250.76, 1431.26, 8)
7> end
8> else
9> rollback transaction
10> if exists(select * from BALANCES where Account_ID = 8)
11> begin
12> begin transaction
13> insert ACCOUNTS values(8, 6)
14> end
15> else
16> rollback transaction
17> if exists (select * from ACCOUNTS where Account_ID = 8 and Customer_ID = 6)
18> commit transaction
19> else
20> rollback transaction
21> go
```

For now, don't worry about the ROLLBACK TRANSACTION and COMMIT TRANS-ACTION statements. What should be remembered from Example 11.2 is the capability to perform nested transactions. This is essentially a transaction within a transaction.

Notice that the original transaction (new_account) begins on Line 1. After the first insert, we then check to make sure the INSERT was executed properly. Another transaction is begun on Line 5. This "transaction-within-a-transaction" is termed a nested transaction.

Other databases support the AUTOCOMMIT option. This option can be used with the SET command, as in

```
SET AUTOCOMMIT [ON ¦ OFF]
```

By default, the SET AUTOCOMMIT ON command is executed at startup. This tells SQL to automatically commit all statements you execute. If you do not want these commands to be automatically executed, set the AUTOCOMMIT option to off:

```
SET AUTOCOMMIT OFF
```

Check your database system's documentation to determine how you would begin a transaction.

Finishing a Transaction

As you may have guessed by now, you use the following command to end a transaction with Oracle SQL syntax:

```
COMMIT [WORK]
[ COMMENT 'text'
¦ FORCE 'text' [, integer] ] ;
```

Using Sybase syntax, this command looks like this:

```
commit [transaction ¦ tran ¦ work] [transaction_name]
```

The COMMIT command saves all changes made during the course of a transaction. It is often wise to execute a COMMIT statement before beginning a transaction. This ensures that no errors were made and no previous transactions are left hanging.

Example 11.3 verifies that the COMMIT command can be used by itself without receiving an error back from the database system.

Example 11.3

```
SQL> COMMIT;
SQL> SET TRANSACTION READ ONLY;
SQL> SELECT * FROM CUSTOMERS
     WHERE NAME = "Bill Turner";
—Do Other Operations—
SQL> COMMIT;
```

Example 11.4

An Oracle SQL use of the COMMIT statement would look like this:

```
SQL> SET TRANSACTION;
SQL> INSERT INTO CUSTOMERS VALUES("John MacDowell", "2000 Lake Lunge Road",
"Chicago", "IL", 42854, 7);
SQL> COMMIT;
SQL> SELECT * FROM CUSTOMERS;
```

Table 11.3. The CUSTOMERS table.

Name	Address	City	State	Zip	Customer_ID
Bill Turner	725 N. Deal Parkway	Washington	DC	20085	1
John Keith	1220 Via De Luna Dr.	Jacksonville	FL	33581	2
Mary Rosenberg	482 Wannamaker Avenue	Williamsburg	VA	23478	3
David Blanken	405 N. Davis Highway	Greenville	SC	29652	4
Rebecca Little	7753 Woods Lane	Houston	TX	38764	5
Izetta Parsons	1285 Pineapple Highway	Greenville	AL	32854	6
John MacDowell	2000 Lake Lunge Road	Chicago	IL	42854	7

A Sybase SQL use of the COMMIT statement would look like this:

```
1> begin transaction
2> insert into CUSTOMERS values("John MacDowell", "2000 Lake Lunge Road",
   "Chicago", "IL", 42854, 7)
3> commit transaction
4> go
1> select * from CUSTOMERS
2> go
```

Table 11.4. The CUSTOMERS table.

Name	Address	City	State	Zip	Customer_ID
Bill Turner	725 N. Deal Parkway	Washington	DC	20085	1
John Keith	1220 Via De Luna Dr.	Jacksonville	FL	33581	2
Mary Rosenberg	482 Wannamaker Avenue	Williamsburg	VA	23478	3
David Blanken	405 N. Davis Highway	Greenville	SC	29652	4
Rebecca Little	7753 Woods Lane	Houston	TX	38764	5

Name	Address	City	State	Zip	Customer_ID
Izetta Parsons	1285 Pineapple Highway	Greenville	AL	32854	6
John MacDowell	2000 Lake Lunge Road	Chicago	IL	42854	7

The preceding statements accomplished the exact same thing as they did earlier using the Oracle7 syntax. However, by putting the COMMIT command soon after the transaction was begun, you made sure that the transaction you were beginning would be executed correctly.

> **Note:** The COMMIT WORK command performs the same operation as the COMMIT command (or Sybase's COMMIT TRANSACTION command). It is provided simply to comply with ANSI SQL syntax.

Remember that every COMMIT command must correspond with an earlier executed SET TRANSACTION or BEGIN TRANSACTION command. Note the errors you receive with the following statements:

Oracle SQL:

```
SQL> INSERT INTO BALANCES values (18765.42, 19073.06, 8);
SQL> COMMIT WORK;
```

Sybase SQL:

```
1> insert into BALANCES values (18765.42, 19073.06, 8)
2> commit work
```

Canceling the Transaction

After a transaction has begun, some type of error checking is usually performed to determine whether the transaction has been executing successfully thus far. SQL provides the ROLLBACK statement for just this purpose. The ROLLBACK statement must be executed from within a transaction. The ROLLBACK statement rolls the transaction back to its

beginning. This means that the state of the database is returned to what it was at the transaction's beginning. The syntax for this command using Oracle7 is the following:

```
ROLLBACK [WORK]
[ TO [SAVEPOINT] savepoint
¦ FORCE 'text' ]
```

As you can see, this command makes use of a transaction savepoint. We discuss this technique later today.

Sybase Transact-SQL's ROLLBACK command looks very similar to the COMMIT command:

```
rollback {transaction ¦ tran ¦ work}
  [transaction_name ¦ savepoint_name]
```

Example 11.5

An Oracle SQL sequence of commands might look like this:

```
SQL> SET TRANSACTION;
SQL> INSERT INTO CUSTOMERS VALUES("Bubba MacDowell", "2222 Blue Lake Way",
"Austin", "TX", 39874, 8);
SQL> ROLLBACK;
SQL> SELECT * FROM CUSTOMERS;
```

Table 11.5. The CUSTOMERS table.

Name	Address	City	State	Zip	Customer_ID
Bill Turner	725 N. Deal Parkway	Washington	DC	20085	1
John Keith	1220 Via De Luna Dr.	Jacksonville	FL	33581	2
Mary Rosenberg	482 Wannamaker Avenue	Williamsburg	VA	23478	3
David Blanken	405 N. Davis Highway	Greenville	SC	29652	4
Rebecca Little	7753 Woods Lane	Houston	TX	38764	5
Izetta Parsons	1285 Pineapple Highway	Greenville	AL	32854	6
John MacDowell	2000 Lake Lunge Road	Chicago	IL	42854	7

A Sybase SQL sequence of commands might look like this:

```
1> begin transaction
2> insert into CUSTOMERS values("Bubba MacDowell", "2222 Blue Lake Way",
   "Austin", "TX", 39874, 8)
3> rollback transaction
4> go
1> SELECT * FROM CUSTOMERS
2> go
```

Table 11.6. The CUSTOMERS table.

Name	Address	City	State	Zip	Customer_ID
Bill Turner	725 N. Deal Parkway	Washington	DC	20085	1
John Keith	1220 Via De Luna Dr.	Jacksonville	FL	33581	2
Mary Rosenberg	482 Wannamaker Avenue	Williamsburg	VA	23478	3
David Blanken	405 N. Davis Highway	Greenville	SC	29652	4
Rebecca Little	7753 Woods Lane	Houston	TX	38764	5
Izetta Parsons	1285 Pineapple Highway	Greenville	AL	32854	6
John MacDowell	2000 Lake Lunge Road	Chicago	IL	42854	7

As you can see, the new record was not added. This is because the ROLLBACK statement rolled the insert back.

Let's do an example making use of your new-found transaction control knowledge. Example 11.6a uses Oracle SQL syntax. Example 11.6b uses Sybase SQL syntax.

Suppose you are writing an application for a graphical user interface, such as Microsoft Windows. You have a dialog box that queries a database and allows the user to change these values. If the user chooses OK, the database saves the changes. If the user chooses CANCEL, the changes are canceled. Obviously, this is an excellent chance for you to use a transaction.

Example 11.6a

When the dialog box is loaded, these SQL statements are executed:

```
SQL> SET TRANSACTION;
SQL> SELECT CUSTOMERS.NAME, BALANCES.CURR_BAL, BALANCES.ACCOUNT_ID
     FROM CUSTOMERS, BALANCES
     WHERE CUSTOMERS.NAME = "Rebecca Little"
     AND CUSTOMERS.CUSTOMER_ID = BALANCES.ACCOUNT_ID;
```

The dialog box allows the user to change the current account balance, so let's store this value back to the database.

On OK:

```
SQL> UPDATE BALANCES SET CURR_BAL = 'new-value' WHERE ACCOUNT_ID = 6;
SQL> COMMIT;
```

On CANCEL:

```
SQL> ROLLBACK;
```

Example 11.6b

When the dialog box is loaded, these SQL statements are executed:

```
1> begin transaction
2> select CUSTOMERS.Name, BALANCES.Curr_Bal, BALANCES.Account_ID
3> from CUSTOMERS, BALANCES
4> where CUSTOMERS.Name = "Rebecca Little"
5> and CUSTOMERS.Customer_ID = BALANCES.Account_ID
6> go
```

The dialog box allows the user to change the current account balance, so let's store this value back to the database.

On OK:

```
1> update BALANCES set Curr_BAL = 'new-value' WHERE Account_ID = 6
2> commit transaction
3> go
```

On CANCEL:

```
1> rollback transaction
2> go
```

The ROLLBACK statement cancels the entire transaction. When you are nesting transactions one within another, the ROLLBACK statement completely cancels all the transactions, rolling them back to the beginning of the outermost transaction.

If no transaction is currently active, issuing the ROLLBACK command or the COMMIT command has no effect on the database system (think of them as dead commands with no purpose).

Once the COMMIT statement has been executed, all actions with the transaction are executed. At this point, it is too late to roll back the transaction.

Using Transaction Savepoints

We just mentioned that rolling back a transaction cancels the entire transaction. However, in some instances, you might want to "semi-commit" your transaction midway through its statements. To do this, you would use a savepoint. Both Sybase and Oracle SQL allow you to save the transaction with a savepoint. From that point on, if a rollback is issued, the transaction is rolled back to the savepoint. All statements that were executed up to the point of the savepoint are saved. The syntax for creating a savepoint using Oracle SQL is as follows:

```
SAVEPOINT savepoint_name;
```

Sybase SQL Server's syntax to create a savepoint is the following:

```
save transaction savepoint_name
```

If this sounds somewhat confusing, study Examples 11.7a and 11.7b.

Example 11.7a

This example uses Oracle SQL syntax.

```
SQL> SET TRANSACTION;
SQL> UPDATE BALANCES SET CURR_BAL = 25000 WHERE ACCOUNT_ID = 5;
SQL> SAVEPOINT save_it;
SQL> DELETE FROM BALANCES WHERE ACCOUNT_ID = 5;
SQL> ROLLBACK TO SAVEPOINT save_it;
SQL> COMMIT;
SQL> SELECT * FROM BALANCES;
```

Table 11.7. The BALANCES table.

Average_Bal	Curr_Bal	Account_ID
1298.53	854.22	1
5427.22	6015.96	2

continues

221

Table 11.7. continued

Average_Bal	Curr_Bal	Account_ID
211.25	190.01	3
73.79	25.87	4
1285.90	25000.00	5
1234.56	1543.67	6
345.25	348.03	7
1250.76	1431.26	8

Example 11.7b

This example uses Sybase SQL syntax.

```
1> begin transaction
2> update BALANCES set Curr_Bal = 25000 where Account_ID = 5
3> save transaction save_it
4> delete from BALANCES where Account_ID = 5
5> rollback transaction save_it
6> commit transaction
7> go
1> select * from BALANCES
2> go
```

Table 11.8. The BALANCES table.

Average_Bal	Curr_Bal	Account_ID
1298.53	854.22	1
5427.22	6015.96	2
211.25	190.01	3
73.79	25.87	4
1285.90	25000.00	5
1234.56	1543.67	6
345.25	348.03	7
1250.76	1431.26	8

The previous examples created a savepoint called SAVE_IT. An update was made to the database that changed the value of the CURR_BAL column of the BALANCES table. We then saved this change as a savepoint. Following this save, we executed a DELETE statement, but just after this we rolled the transaction back to the savepoint. Following this we executed COMMIT TRANSACTION, which committed all commands up to the savepoint. Had we

executed a ROLLBACK TRANSACTION after the ROLLBACK TRANSACTION savepoint_name command, the entire transaction would have been rolled back, and no changes would have been made.

Example 11.8a

This example uses Oracle SQL syntax.

```
SQL> SET TRANSACTION;
SQL> UPDATE BALANCES SET CURR_BAL = 25000 WHERE ACCOUNT_ID = 5;
SQL> SAVEPOINT save_it;
SQL> DELETE FROM BALANCES WHERE ACCOUNT_ID = 5;
SQL> ROLLBACK TO SAVEPOINT save_it;
SQL> ROLLBACK;
SQL> SELECT * FROM BALANCES;
```

Table 11.9. The BALANCES table.

Average_Bal	Curr_Bal	Account_ID
1298.53	854.22	1
5427.22	6015.96	2
211.25	190.01	3
73.79	25.87	4
1285.90	1473.75	5
1234.56	1543.67	6
345.25	348.03	7
1250.76	1431.26	8

Example 11.8b

This example uses Sybase SQL syntax:

```
1> begin transaction
2> update BALANCES set Curr_Bal = 25000 where Account_ID = 5
3> save transaction save_it
4> delete from BALANCES where Account_ID = 5
5> rollback transaction save_it
6> rollback transaction
7> go
1> select * from BALANCES
2> go
```

Table 11.10. The BALANCES table.

Average_Bal	Curr_Bal	Account_ID
1298.53	854.22	1
5427.22	6015.96	2
211.25	190.01	3
73.79	25.87	4
1285.90	1473.75	5
1234.56	1543.67	6
345.25	348.03	7
1250.76	1431.26	8

Summary

A transaction can be thought of as an organized unit of work. Typically, the work done during a transaction is a series of operations that are dependent on previous operations that have already been executed. If one of these operations is not executed properly, or if data is changed for some reason, the rest of the work in a transaction should be canceled. Otherwise, if all statements are executed correctly, the transaction's work should be saved.

The process of canceling a transaction is called a rollback. The process of saving the work of a correctly executed transaction is called a commit. SQL syntax supports these two processes through syntax similar to the following two statements:

```
BEGIN TRANSACTION
      statement 1
      statement 2
      statement 3
ROLLBACK TRANSACTION
```

or

```
BEGIN TRANSACTION
      statement 1
      statement 2
      statement 3
COMMIT TRANSACTION
```

Workshop

The workshop provides quiz questions to help solidify your understanding of the material covered, as well as exercises to provide you with experience in using what you have learned. Try to answer the quiz and exercise questions before checking the answers in Appendix F, and make sure you understand the answers before continuing to the next chapter.

Quiz

1. When nesting transactions, does issuing a ROLLBACK TRANSACTION command cancel the current transaction and roll the batch of statements back into the upper-level transaction? And why?

2. Can savepoints be used to *save off* portions of a transaction? And why?

Database Security

Today, we discuss database security. We specifically look at various SQL statements and constructs that enable you to administer and effectively manage a relational database. Like many other topics you have studied thus far, how a database management system implements security varies widely among products. Focusing on the popular database product Oracle7 gives you an excellent introduction to this topic.

Wanted: Database Administrator

Security is an often-overlooked aspect of database design. Because most computer professionals enter the computer world with some knowledge of computer programming or hardware, these are the areas they tend to concentrate on. For instance, if your boss brought a brand new project to you that obviously required some type of relational database design, what would be your first step? After choosing some type of hardware and software baseline to begin with, you would probably begin by designing the basic database that would be used throughout the project. Gradually, this design phase would be split up among several people, one of them a Graphical User Interface designer, another a low-level component builder. Perhaps you, after reading this book, would be asked to code the SQL queries required to provide the guts of the application. Along with this task comes the responsibility of actually administering and maintaining the database. We have all been caught up in this whirlwind atmosphere and have often found that, before we know it, our deadline is upon us.

Many times, little thought or planning has been put into the actual production phase of the application. What happens when many users are allowed to use the application across a Wide-Area Network (WAN)? With today's powerful personal computer software and with technologies such as Microsoft's Open Database Connectivity (ODBC), any user with access to your network can find a way to get at your database. (We won't even bring up the complexities involved when your company decides to hook your LAN up to the Internet or some other wide-ranging computer network!) Are you prepared to face this situation?

Fortunately for you, software manufacturers provide you with most of the tools needed to handle this security problem. Network operating systems are designed to face more stringent security requirements with every release. On top of this, most major database vendors build some degree of security into their products. This security exists independently of your operating system or network security. How the different manufacturers implement these security features varies widely from product to product.

Popular Database Products and Security

As you know by now, there are myriad choices on the market for you to consider when the time comes to choose a relational database system. All of these vendors want your business for short- and long-term reasons. During the development phase of a project, you might purchase a small number of product licenses for testing, development, and so forth. However, the total number of licenses required for your production database can number in the hundreds or even thousands. In addition, once you have chosen to use a particular database product, the chances are good that you will stay with that product for years to come. You should remember when examining these products that they are all designed with certain usages in mind. Let's examine some of these:

- [ ] The Microsoft FoxPro database management system is a powerful database system that is used primarily in single-user environments. FoxPro uses a limited subset of SQL. No security measures are provided with the system. It also uses an Xbase file format, with each file containing one table. Indexes are also stored in separate files.

- [ ] The Microsoft Access relational database management system implements more of SQL. It is still intended for use on the PC platform, although it does contain a rudimentary security system. The product enables you to build queries and store them within the database. In addition, the entire database with all its objects exists within one file.

- [ ] The Oracle7 relational database management system supports nearly the full SQL standard. In addition, Oracle has added its own extensions to SQL, called PL*SQL. It contains full security features, including the capability to create roles and assign permissions and privileges on objects in the database.

- [ ] Sybase SQL Server is similar in power and features to the Oracle relational database. It also provides a wide range of security features and has its own extensions to the SQL language, called Transact-SQL.

The purpose behind explaining these is to illustrate that not all products are created equal. If you are undertaking your first database project, some decisions have probably already been made for you to point you in the direction your company would like you to go. Factors such as cost and performance are extremely important when making this decision. However, without adequate security measures, any savings your database creates can be easily offset by security problems.

12

How Does a Database Become Secure?

You may be wondering what it means exactly for a database to become secure. Up to this point, you have been creating databases at will and entering the appropriate information into various tables you have created. Has it occurred to you that you might not want other users to come in and tamper with the database information you have so carefully entered? What would your reaction be if you logged on one morning and discovered that the database you had slaved over had been dropped (remember how silent the DROP DATABASE command is)? We examine in some detail how one popular database management system enables you to set up a secure database. The database chosen for these examples is Personal Oracle7. As in the previous eleven chapters, most of what we cover can be applied to other database management systems as well, so make sure you read this information even if Oracle is not your system of choice.

Personal Oracle7 and Security

Oracle7 implements security by using three constructs:

- ☐ Users
- ☐ Roles
- ☐ Privileges

Creating Users

A user is basically exactly what it sounds like. Users are account names that are allowed to log in to the Oracle database. The SQL syntax used to create a new user is this:

```
CREATE USER user
IDENTIFIED {BY password ¦ EXTERNALLY}
[DEFAULT TABLESPACE tablespace]
[TEMPORARY TABLESPACE tablespace]
[QUOTA {integer [K¦M] ¦ UNLIMITED} ON tablespace] ...
[PROFILE profile]
```

If the BY password option is chosen, the system prompts the user to enter a password each time he or she logs in. As an example, create a user named for yourself. My example is as follows:

```
SQL> CREATE USER Bryan IDENTIFIED BY CUTIGER;
User created.
```

Each time I log in (using my clever alias "Bryan"), I am prompted to enter my password: CUTIGER.

If the EXTERNALLY option was chosen, Oracle relies on your computer system logon name and password. When you log on to your system, you have essentially logged in to Oracle.

As you can see from looking at the rest of the CREATE USER syntax, Oracle also allows you to set up default tablespaces and quotas. These topics are beyond the scope of this book and can be studied in more detail by examining the Oracle documentation.

As with every other CREATE command you have learned about in this book, there is also an ALTER USER command. It looks like this:

```
ALTER USER user
[IDENTIFIED {BY password ¦ EXTERNALLY}]
[DEFAULT TABLESPACE tablespace]
[TEMPORARY TABLESPACE tablespace]
[QUOTA {integer [K¦M] ¦ UNLIMITED} ON tablespace] ...
[PROFILE profile]
[DEFAULT ROLE { role [, role] ...
  ¦ ALL [EXCEPT role [, role] ...] ¦ NONE}]
```

This command can be used to change all of the user's options, including the password and profile. For example, to change the user Bryan's password, you type this:

```
SQL> ALTER USER Bryan
  2  IDENTIFIED BY ROSEBUD;
User altered.
```

To remove a user, simply issue the DROP USER command. This removes the user's entry in the system database. Let's look at the syntax for this command:

```
DROP USER user_name [CASCADE];
```

If the CASCADE option is used, all objects owned by user_name are dropped along with the user's account. If CASCADE is not used, and the user denoted by user_name still owns objects, that user is not dropped. This is somewhat confusing, but make a note of this feature in case you are ever required to drop users.

Creating Roles

To grant a role to a user, use the following syntax:

```
GRANT role TO user [WITH ADMIN OPTION];
```

If WITH ADMIN OPTION is used, that user can then grant roles to other users. Isn't power exhilarating?

To remove a role, use the REVOKE command:

```
REVOKE role FROM user;
```

Once you have logged in to the system using the account you created earlier, you have exhausted the limits of your permissions. You can log in, but that is about all you can do. Oracle lets you register as one of three roles:

☐ Connect

☐ Resource

☐ DBA (or Database Administrator)

These three roles have varying degrees of privileges. We examine each of these more closely.

The Connect Role

The Connect role can be thought of as the entry-level role. Once a user has been granted Connect role access, they can be granted different privileges that actually allow them to do something with a database.

```
SQL> GRANT CONNECT TO BRYAN;
Grant succeeded.
```

The Connect role enables the user to select, insert, update, and delete records from tables belonging to other users (once the appropriate permissions have been granted). The user can also create tables, views, sequences, clusters, and synonyms.

The Resource Role

The Resource role gives the user more access to Oracle databases. In addition to the permissions that can be granted to the Connect role, Resource roles can also be granted permission to create procedures, triggers, and indexes.

```
SQL> GRANT RESOURCE TO BRYAN;
Grant succeeded.
```

The DBA Role

As expected, the DBA role includes all privileges. Users with this role are able to do essentially anything they want to the database system. The number of users with this role should be kept to a minimum to ensure system integrity.

```
SQL> GRANT DBA TO BRYAN;
Grant succeeded.
```

After the three preceding steps, user Bryan was granted the Connect, Resource, and DBA roles. This is somewhat redundant because the DBA role encompasses the other two roles. Let's drop them now:

```
SQL> REVOKE CONNECT FROM BRYAN;
Revoke succeeded.
```

```
SQL> REVOKE RESOURCE FROM BRYAN;
Revoke succeeded.
```

Now, the user Bryan is left with only the DBA role, which is good enough for anything he needs to do.

User Privileges

Once you have decided what roles your users should be granted, your next step is deciding what permissions these users will have on database objects. These permissions are called privileges under Oracle7. The types of privileges vary depending on what role you have been granted. If you actually create an object, you can grant privileges on that object to other users, as long as their role enables access to that privilege. Oracle defines two types of privileges that can be granted to users: system privileges and object privileges. Tables 12.1 and 12.2 illustrate common types of each of these.

System privileges are system-wide privileges. The syntax used to grant a system privilege is as follows:

```
GRANT system_privilege TO {user_name ¦ role ¦ PUBLIC}
[WITH ADMIN OPTION];
```

WITH ADMIN OPTION enables the grantee to grant this privilege to someone else.

Exercise 12.1

Suppose you would like to enable every user of the system to have CREATE VIEW access within their own schema. The syntax for this command would look like this:

```
SQL> GRANT CREATE VIEW
  2   TO PUBLIC;
Grant succeeded.
```

The PUBLIC keyword means that everyone has CREATE VIEW privileges. Obviously, these system privileges enable the grantee to have a lot of access to nearly all the system settings. System privileges should be granted only to special users or users who have a need to use these privileges. Table 12.1 shows the system privileges you will find in the help files included with Personal Oracle7.

Table 12.1. Common system privileges in Oracle7.

System Privilege	Operations Permitted
ALTER ANY INDEX	Allows the grantee to alter any index in any schema.
ALTER ANY PROCEDURE	Allows the grantee to alter any stored procedure, function, or package in any schema.

continues

233

Table 12.1. continued

System Privilege	Operations Permitted
ALTER ANY ROLE	Allows the grantee to alter any role in the database.
ALTER ANY TABLE	Allows the grantee to alter any table or view in the schema.
ALTER ANY TRIGGER	Allows the grantee to enable, disable, or compile any database trigger in any schema.
ALTER DATABASE	Allows the grantee to alter the database.
ALTER USER	Allows the grantee to alter any user. This privilege authorizes the grantee to change another user's password or authentication method, assign quotas on any tablespace, set default and temporary tablespaces, and assign a profile and default roles.
CREATE ANY INDEX	Allows the grantee to create an index on any table in any schema.
CREATE ANY PROCEDURE	Allows the grantee to create stored procedures, functions, and packages in any schema.
CREATE ANY TABLE	Allows the grantee to create tables in any schema.
	The owner of the schema containing the table must have space quota on the tablespace to contain the table.
CREATE ANY TRIGGER	Allows the grantee to create a database trigger in any schema associated with a table in any schema.
CREATE ANY VIEW	Allows the grantee to create views in any schema.
CREATE PROCEDURE	Allows the grantee to create stored procedures, functions, and packages in their own schema.
CREATE PROFILE	Allows the grantee to create profiles.

System Privilege	Operations Permitted
CREATE ROLE	Allows the grantee to create roles.
CREATE SYNONYM	Allows the grantee to create synonyms in their own schema.
CREATE TABLE	Allows the grantee to create tables in their own schema. To create a table, the grantee must also have space quota on the tablespace to contain the table.
CREATE TRIGGER	Allows the grantee to create a database trigger in their own schema.
CREATE USER	Allows the grantee to create users. This privilege also allows the creator to assign quotas on any tablespace, set default and temporary tablespaces, and assign a profile as part of a CREATE USER statement.
CREATE VIEW	Allows the grantee to create views in their own schema.
DELETE ANY TABLE	Allows the grantee to delete rows from tables or views in any schema or truncate tables in any schema.
DROP ANY INDEX	Allows the grantee to drop indexes in any schema.
DROP ANY PROCEDURE	Allows the grantee to drop stored procedures, functions, or packages in any schema.
DROP ANY ROLE	Allows the grantee to drop roles.
DROP ANY SYNONYM	Allows the grantee to drop private synonyms in any schema.
DROP ANY TABLE	Allows the grantee to drop tables in any schema.
DROP ANY TRIGGER	Allows the grantee to drop database triggers in any schema.
DROP ANY VIEW	Allows the grantee to drop views in any schema.
DROP USER	Allows the grantee to drop users.

12

continues

Table 12.1. continued

System Privilege	Operations Permitted
EXECUTE ANY PROCEDURE	Allows the grantee to execute procedures or functions (stand-alone or packaged) or reference public package variables in any schema.
TRANSACTION	Allows back of own in-doubt distributed transactions in the local database.
GRANT ANY PRIVILEGE	Allows the grantee to grant any system privilege.
GRANT ANY ROLE	Allows the grantee to grant any role in the database.
INSERT ANY TABLE	Allows the grantee to insert rows into tables and views in any schema.
LOCK ANY TABLE	Allows the grantee to lock tables and views in any schema.
SELECT ANY SEQUENCE	Allows the grantee to reference sequences in any schema.
SELECT ANY TABLE	Allows the grantee to query tables, views, or snapshots in any schema.
UPDATE ANY	Allows the grantee to update rows in tables.

Object privileges are privileges that can be used against specific database objects. Table 12.2 lists the object privileges in Oracle7.

Table 12.2. Object privileges enabled under Oracle7.

ALL

ALTER

DELETE

EXECUTE

INDEX

INSERT

REFERENCES

SELECT

UPDATE

To give other users access to your tables, there is a slightly different form of the GRANT statement:

```
GRANT {object_priv ¦ ALL [PRIVILEGES]} [ (column
[, column]...) ]
[, {object_priv ¦ ALL [PRIVILEGES]} [ (column
[, column] ...) ] ] ...
ON [schema.]object
TO {user ¦ role ¦ PUBLIC} [, {user ¦ role ¦ PUBLIC}] ...
[WITH GRANT OPTION]
```

To remove the object privileges you have granted to someone, use the REVOKE command with the following syntax:

```
REVOKE {object_priv ¦ ALL [PRIVILEGES]}
[, {object_priv ¦ ALL [PRIVILEGES]} ] ...
ON [schema.]object
FROM {user ¦ role ¦ PUBLIC} [, {user ¦ role ¦ PUBLIC}] ...
[CASCADE CONSTRAINTS]
```

For an example, see Exercise 12.2.

Exercise 12.2

Create a table named SALARIES with the following structure:

```
NAME, CHAR(30)
SALARY, NUMBER
AGE, NUMBER

SQL> CREATE TABLE SALARIES (
  2       NAME CHAR(30),
  3       SALARY NUMBER,
  4       AGE NUMBER);
Table created.
```

Now, create two users: Jack and Jill.

```
SQL> create user Jack identified by Jack;
User created.
SQL> create user Jill identified by Jill;
User created.
SQL> grant connect to Jack;
Grant succeeded.
SQL> grant resource to Jill;
Grant succeeded.
```

So far, you have created two users. Each of these users has been granted a different role, meaning that they will have different capabilities when working with the database. First create the SALARIES table with the following information:

```
SQL> SELECT * FROM SALARIES;
```

```
NAME                              SALARY      AGE
--------------------------------  --------  --------
JACK                               35000       29
JILL                               48000       42
JOHN                               61000       55
```

You could then grant different privileges to this table based on some arbitrary reasons for this example. We are assuming that you currently have DBA privileges and can grant any system privilege. Even if you do not have DBA privileges, you can still grant object privileges on the SALARIES table because you own it (assuming you just created it).

Let's assume that because Jack belongs only to the Connect role, you want him to have only SELECT privileges.

```
SQL> GRANT SELECT ON SALARIES TO JACK;
Grant succeeded.
```

Because Jill belongs to the Resource role, you allow her to select and insert some data into the table. To liven things up a bit, allow Jill to update values only in the SALARY field of the SALARIES table.

```
SQL> GRANT SELECT, UPDATE(SALARY) ON SALARIES TO Jill;
Grant succeeded.
```

Now that this table and these users have been created, you need to look at how a user accesses a table that was created by another user. Both Jack and Jill have been granted SELECT access on the SALARIES table. However, if Jack tries to access the SALARIES table, he will be told that it does not exist. This is because Oracle requires the table name to be preceded by the username of the table's owner.

Exercise 12.3

First, make a note of the username you used to create the SALARIES table (mine was Bryan). For Jack to select data out of the SALARIES table, he must address the SALARIES table with that username.

```
SQL> SELECT * FROM SALARIES;
```

```
SELECT * FROM SALARIES
               *
ERROR at line 1:
ORA-00942: table or view does not exist
```

Here, Jack was warned that the table did not exist. Now use the owner's username to identify the table:

```
SQL> SELECT *
  2  FROM BRYAN.SALARIES;
```

```
NAME                                   SALARY      AGE
------------------------------------   --------   --------
JACK                                    35000       29
JILL                                    48000       42
JOHN                                    61000       55
```

You can see that now the query worked. Now test out Jill's access privileges. First, log out of Jack's login and log in again as Jill (using the password created in Exercise 12.2).

```
SQL> SELECT *
  2  FROM BRYAN.SALARIES;
```

```
NAME                                   SALARY      AGE
------------------------------------   --------   --------
JACK                                    35000       29
JILL                                    48000       42
JOHN                                    61000       55
```

That worked just fine. Now let's try to insert a new record into the table.

```
SQL> INSERT INTO BRYAN.SALARIES
  2  VALUES('JOE',85000,38);
```

```
INSERT INTO BRYAN.SALARIES
                  *
ERROR at line 1:
ORA-01031: insufficient privileges
```

This did not work because Jill does not have INSERT privileges on the SALARIES table.

```
SQL> UPDATE BRYAN.SALARIES
  2  SET AGE = 42
  3  WHERE NAME = 'JOHN';
```

```
UPDATE BRYAN.SALARIES
       *
ERROR at line 1:
ORA-01031: insufficient privileges
```

Once again, Jill tried to go around the privileges that she had been given. Naturally, Oracle caught this error and corrected her quickly.

```
SQL> UPDATE BRYAN.SALARIES
  2  SET SALARY = 35000
  3  WHERE NAME = 'JOHN';

1 row updated.
SQL> SELECT *
  2  FROM BRYAN.SALARIES;
```

```
NAME                              SALARY      AGE
- - - - - - - - - - - - - - - - - - - - - -   - - - - - - - -   - - - - - - - -
JACK                               35000       29
JILL                               48000       42
JOHN                               35000       55
```

You can see now that the update works as long as Jill abides by the privileges she has been given.

Using Views for Security Purposes

As we mentioned on Day 10, views are useful virtual tables that can be used to present a different view of data than what actually physically exists in the database. We mentioned on Day 10 that views are often used to implement security measures. Now we try to explain that in more detail. First, let's look at how views can simplify SQL statements.

In Exercise 12.3, you learned that when a user must access a table or database object that another user owns, that object must be referenced with a username. As you can imagine, this can get wordy when writing several SQL queries in a row. More importantly, beginning-level users would be required to determine the owner of a table before they could select the contents of a table. This is a step you probably don't want all your users to have to make. One simple way around this is shown in Exercise 12.4.

Exercise 12.4

Assume that you are logged in as Jack, your friend from earlier examples. You learned that for Jack to look at the contents of the SALARIES table, he must use the following statement:

```
SQL> SELECT *
  2  FROM BRYAN.SALARIES;
```

```
NAME                              SALARY      AGE
- - - - - - - - - - - - - - - - - - - - - -   - - - - - - - -   - - - - - - - -
JACK                               35000       29
JILL                               48000       42
JOHN                               35000       55
```

This can be changed by using views. If you were to create a view named SALARY_VIEW, a user could simply select from that view.

```
SQL> CREATE VIEW SALARY_VIEW
  2  AS SELECT *
  3  FROM BRYAN.SALARIES;

View created.

SQL> SELECT * FROM SALARY_VIEW;
```

NAME	SALARY	AGE
JACK	35000	29
JILL	48000	42
JOHN	35000	55

Note that this returned the same values as the records returned from BRYAN.SALARIES.

Using Synonyms in Place of Views

SQL also provides for an object known as a synonym. A synonym works exactly like a view. The syntax looks like this:

```
CREATE [PUBLIC] SYNONYM [schema.]synonym
FOR [schema.]object[@dblink]
```

In Exercise 12.4, you could have issued the following command to achieve the same results:

```
SQL> CREATE PUBLIC SYNONYM SALARY FOR SALARIES; Synonym created.
```

Then log back in to Jack and type this:

```
SQL> SELECT * FROM SALARY;
```

NAME	SALARY	AGE
JACK	35000	29
JILL	48000	42
JOHN	35000	55

We have discussed how to use views to ease query statements, but you have not yet seen how views can be implemented to solve security problems. Study Exercise 12.5 to see an example of this technique.

Exercise 12.5

Suppose you changed your mind about Jack and Jill and decided that neither of them should be able to look at the SALARIES table completely. You can change this and allow them to examine only their own information. This can be done using views.

```
SQL> CREATE VIEW JACK_SALARY AS
  2  SELECT * FROM BRYAN.SALARIES
  3  WHERE NAME = 'JACK';

View created.

SQL> CREATE VIEW JILL_SALARY AS
  2  SELECT * FROM BRYAN.SALARIES
  3  WHERE NAME = 'JILL';

View created.
```

12

```
SQL> GRANT SELECT ON JACK_SALARY
  2  TO JACK;
Grant succeeded.

SQL> GRANT SELECT ON JILL_SALARY
  2  TO JILL;
Grant succeeded.

SQL> REVOKE SELECT ON SALARIES FROM JACK;
Revoke succeeded.

SQL> REVOKE SELECT ON SALARIES FROM JILL;
Revoke succeeded.
```

Now log in as Jack and test out the view you created for him.

```
SQL> SELECT * FROM BRYAN.JACK_SALARY;
```

```
NAME        SALARY      AGE
----------  ----------  ----
Jack        35000       29
```

```
SQL> SELECT * FROM PERKINS.SALARIES;
```

```
SELECT * FROM PERKINS.SALARIES
                      *
ERROR at line 1:
ORA-00942: table or view does not exist
```

Log out of Jack's account and test Jill's now:

```
SQL> SELECT * FROM BRYAN.JILL_SALARY;
```

```
NAME             SALARY          AGE
---------------  --------------  ----
Jill             48000           42
```

You can see that access to the SALARIES table was completely controlled using views. SQL enables you to create these views as you like, then assign permissions to other users. This allows a great deal of flexibility.

By now, you should have seen the importance of keeping to a minimum the number of people with DBA roles. A user with this access level can have complete access to all commands and operations within the database. Note, however, that with Oracle and Sybase you must have DBA-level access (or SA-level in Sybase) to import or export data on the database.

Taking Advantage of WITH GRANT OPTION

What do you think would happen if Jill attempted to pass her UPDATE privilege on to Jack? At first glance, you might think that because Jill was entrusted with the UPDATE privilege, she should be able to pass it on to other users, as long as their role allowed them that specific privilege. However, using the GRANT statement as you did in Exercise 12.2, Jill cannot pass her privileges onto others:

```
SQL> GRANT SELECT, UPDATE(SALARY) ON BRYAN.SALARIES TO Jill;
```

Think back to several pages ago, when you were introduced to the GRANT statement. The syntax for it looks like this:

```
GRANT {object_priv ¦ ALL [PRIVILEGES]} [ (column
[, column]...) ]
[, {object_priv ¦ ALL [PRIVILEGES]} [ (column
[, column] ...) ] ] ...
ON [schema.]object
TO {user ¦ role ¦ PUBLIC} [, {user ¦ role ¦ PUBLIC}] ...
[WITH GRANT OPTION]
```

What you are looking for is the WITH GRANT OPTION clause at the end of the GRANT statement. When object privileges are granted and WITH GRANT OPTION is used, these privileges can then be passed on to others. So, if you wanted to allow Jill to pass this privilege on to Jack, you would do the following:

```
SQL> GRANT SELECT, UPDATE(SALARY)
  2  ON BRYAN.SALARIES TO JILL
  3  WITH GRANT OPTION;
```

```
Grant succeeded.
```

Jill could then log in and issue the following command:

```
SQL> GRANT SELECT, UPDATE(SALARY)
  2  ON BRYAN.SALARIES TO JACK;
Grant succeeded.
```

Summary

Today we covered a topic that was probably entirely new to even intermediate-level SQL users. Security is an often-overlooked topic that can cause many problems if not properly thought out and administered. Fortunately, SQL provides several useful commands for implementing security on a database.

Users are originally created using the CREATE USER command. This sets up a username and password for a user. Once the user account has been set up, this user must be assigned to a role in order to accomplish any work. The three roles available within Oracle7 are Connect, Resource, and DBA. Each of these has different levels of access to the database, with Connect being the simplest and DBA having access to everything.

The GRANT command is used to give permission or a privilege to a user. The REVOKE command can take that permission or privilege away from the user. There are two types of privileges: object privileges and system privileges. The system privileges should be monitored closely and should not be granted to inexperienced users. Doing this gives inexperienced users access to commands that could destroy data or databases you have painstakingly set up. Object privileges can be granted to give users access to individual objects existing in the owner's database schema.

All of these techniques and SQL statements provide the SQL user with a broad range of tools to use when setting up system security. Although the security features of Oracle7 were focused on in this chapter, we hope much of the information will carry over to the database system of your choice. Just remember that no matter what product you are using, it is important to enforce some level of database security.

Workshop

The workshop provides quiz questions to help solidify your understanding of the material covered, as well as exercises to provide you with experience in using what you have learned. Try to answer the quiz and exercise questions before checking the answers in Appendix F, and make sure you understand the answers before continuing to the next chapter.

Quiz

1. What is wrong with the following statement:

   ```
   SQL> GRANT CONNECTION TO DAVID;
   ```

2. True or false (and why): Dropping a user will cause all objects owned by that user to be dropped as well.

Exercise

1. Experiment with your database system's security by creating a table, and then by creating a user. Experiment with this user by giving it different privileges and then taking them away.

13

Embedded SQL

Introduction

The first 12 days introduced you to the many features of SQL. You have by now learned the many intricacies of the SELECT statement, including new and exciting ways to retrieve data already sorted, filtered, and modified. Depending on what database system you have chosen to work with, you probably have already explored your system's many functions and features and have learned something about creating new databases, and tables within those databases.

All this newly found information is required to begin to learn to program with SQL. Chances are, however, that by now you no longer consider yourself to be a beginner. It might have already occurred to you that you would like to do more with SQL than write simple SELECT or UPDATE queries to a database. For the casual database user, these statements are important tools used to retrieve data from the database. However, for the professional programmer, additional code must be added around these queries to give your application program smarts. These smarts are often referred to as the logic within the application. In other words, retrieving data from a database is only part of the problem. Analyzing that data and displaying it to the user are also complex tasks—and are topics of additional books.

On Day 13 and Day 14, we discuss programming with SQL. Day 13 focuses on procedures or functions that can encapsulate entire business processes or function points. We also focus on extensions to SQL that enable the programmer to add logic and functional flow to his code. Day 14 presents the reader with the concept of Dynamic SQL. This is the process of embedding SQL statements within application program code. It is dynamic because the queries can be built at runtime based on user input. Dynamic SQL has become extremely popular using products such as Microsoft's Open Database Connectivity, and programming tools such as Microsoft Visual Basic and Visual C++, Powersoft Powerbuilder, and Borland Delphi and C++.

Because the term *Embedded SQL* means different things to different people, we discuss what it means and how this chapter treats the topic.

What Exactly is Embedded SQL?

When this book uses the term Embedded SQL, we refer to the larger topic of writing actual program code using SQL. This can mean writing stored procedures embedded in the database that can be called by an application program to perform some task. Some database systems come with complete tool kits that enable you to build simple screens and menu objects using a combination of a proprietary programming language and SQL. The SQL code is embedded within this code.

The most common usage of the term Embedded SQL actually refers to what is technically known as Static SQL.

Static and Dynamic SQL

Static SQL refers to the usage of SQL statements embedded directly within programming code. This code cannot be modified at runtime. In fact, most implementations of Static SQL require the use of a precompiler that fixes your SQL statement at runtime. Both Oracle and Informix have developed Static SQL packages for their database systems. These products contain precompilers for use with several languages, including the following:

- [ ] C
- [ ] Pascal
- [ ] Ada
- [ ] COBOL
- [ ] FORTRAN

There are advantages and disadvantages to using Static SQL. Some advantages are as follows:

- [ ] Improved runtime speed
- [ ] Compile-time error checking

The disadvantages to using this technique are as follows:

- [ ] It is inflexible.
- [ ] It leads to a greater amount of code (because queries cannot be formulated at runtime).
- [ ] Code is not portable to other database systems (something that should always be considered).

If you were to print out a copy of this code, the SQL statements would appear side by side with C language (or whatever language you chose to use) code. Program variables are bound to database fields using a precompiler command. See Example 13.1 for a simple example of Static SQL code.

Dynamic SQL, on the other hand, enables the programmer to build an SQL statement at runtime and pass this statement off to the database engine. The engine then returns data back into program variables, which are also bound at runtime. This topic is discussed thoroughly on Day 14.

A Static SQL Example

Let's look at an example of using Static SQL in an application program.

13

Example 13.1

This example illustrates the use of Static SQL in a C function. Please note that the syntax used here is basically pseudo-code. This Static SQL syntax does not actually comply with any commercial product, although the syntax used is similar to that of most commercial products.

```
BOOL Print_Employee_Info (void)
{
int Age = 0;
char Name[41] = "\0";
char Address[81] = "\0";
/* Now Bind Each Field We Will Select To a Program Variable */
#SQL BIND(AGE, Age)
#SQL BIND(NAME, Name);
#SQL BIND(ADDRESS, Address);
/* The above statements "bind" fields from the database to variables from
the program.
 After we query the database, we will scroll the records returned and then
print them to the screen */
#SQL SELECT AGE, NAME, ADDRESS FROM EMPLOYEES;
#SQL FIRST_RECORD
if (Age == NULL)
{
    return FALSE;
}
while (Age != NULL)
{
    printf("AGE = %d\n, Age);
    printf("NAME = %s\n, Name);
    printf("ADDRESS = %s\n", Address);
    #SQL NEXT_RECORD
}
return TRUE;
}
```

After you have typed in your code and the file has been saved, the code is usually run through some type of precompiler. This precompiler converts the lines that begin with the #SQL precompiler directive to actual C code. This code can then be compiled with the rest of your program to accomplish the task at hand.

If you have never seen or written a C program, don't worry about the syntax used in Example 13.1. (As was stated earlier, the Static SQL syntax is only pseudo-code. Consult your Static SQL documentation for your product's actual syntax.)

Programming with SQL

So far, we have discussed two uses for programming with SQL. The first, which was the focus of the first 12 days of this book, used SQL to write queries and modify data. The second is the capability to embed SQL statements within third- or fourth-generation language code. Obviously, the first use for SQL is important to becoming truly knowledgeable about the language and database programming in general. We have already discussed the drawbacks to

using Embedded or Static SQL as opposed to Dynamic SQL. However, there is still another way to write sophisticated code using SQL.

As we have mentioned during the discussion of virtually every topic in this book, database vendors almost without exception have added many extensions to the language. The Sybase and Microsoft SQL Server database product is called Transact-SQL. Oracle has named theirs PL/SQL. Each of these languages contains the complete functionality of everything discussed in this book to this point. In addition, each of these contains many extensions to the ANSI SQL standard. The remainder of this chapter explores these extensions in detail.

Extensions to ANSI SQL

To illustrate the use of these SQL extensions to create actual programming logic, we have chosen to use Sybase and Microsoft SQL Server's Transact-SQL language. It contains most of the constructs found in third-generation (3GL) languages, as well as some SQL Server-specific features that turn out to be very handy tools for the database programmer. (Other manufacturers' extensions contain many of these features and more. Transact-SQL was chosen simply because we have more experience with this language than any other.) To actually run these examples, the following database tables need to be built in a database named BASEBALL.

The BASEBALL Database

The BASEBALL database consists of three tables used to track typical baseball information: the BATTERS table, the PITCHERS table, and the TEAMS table. This database will be used in examples throughout the rest of this chapter.

The Batters Table

```
NAME char(30)
TEAM int
AVERAGE float
HOMERUNS int
RBIS int
```

This table can be created using the following Transact-SQL syntax:

```
1> create database BASEBALL on default
2> go
1> use BASEBALL
2> go
1> create table BATTERS (
2> NAME char(30),
3> TEAM int,
4> AVERAGE float,
```

```
5> HOMERUNS int,
6> RBIS int)
7> go
```

Enter the data in Table 13.1 into the Batters table.

Table 13.1. The Batters table.

Name	Team	Average	Homeruns	RBIs
Billy Brewster	1	.275	14	46
John Jackson	1	.293	2	29
Phil Hartman	1	.221	13	21
Jim Gehardy	2	.316	29	84
Tom Trawick	2	.258	3	51
Eric Redstone	2	.305	0	28

The Pitchers Table

```
NAME char(30)
TEAM int
WON int
LOST int
ERA float
```

The Pitchers table can be created using the following Transact-SQL syntax:

```
1> use BASEBALL
2> go
1> create table PITCHERS (
2> NAME char(30),
3> TEAM int,
4> WON int,
5> LOST int,
6> ERA float)
7> go
```

Enter the data in Table 13.2 into the Pitchers table.

Table 13.2. The Pitchers table.

Name	Team	Won	Lost	Era
Tom Madden	1	7	5	3.46
Bill Witter	1	8	2	2.75
Jeff Knox	2	2	8	4.82
Hank Arnold	2	13	1	1.93
Tim Smythe	3	4	2	2.76

The Teams Table

```
TEAM_ID int
CITY char(30)
NAME char(30)
WON int
LOST int
TOTAL_HOME_ATTENDANCE int
AVG_HOME_ATTENDANCE int
```

The Teams table can be created using the following Transact-SQL syntax:

```
1> use BASEBALL
2> go
1> create table TEAMS (
2> TEAM_ID int,
3> CITY char(30),
4> NAME char(30),
5> WON int,
6> LOST int,
7> TOTAL_HOME_ATTENDANCE int,
8> AVG_HOME_ATTENDANCE int)
9> go
```

Enter the data in Table 13.3 into the Teams table.

Table 13.3 The Teams table.

Team_ID	City	Name	Won	Lost	Total_Home_Attendance	Avg_Home_Attendance
1	Portland	Beavers	72	63	1,226,843	19473
2	Washington	Representatives	50	85	941,228	14048
3	Tampa	Sharks	99	36	2,028,652	30278

Declaring Local Variables

Every programming language enables some method for declaring local (or global) variables that can be used to store data. Transact-SQL is no exception. Declaring a variable using Transact-SQL is an extremely simple procedure. The keyword that must be used is the DECLARE keyword. The syntax looks like this:

```
declare @variable_name data_type.
```

To declare a character string variable to store players' names, use the following statement:

```
1> declare @name char(30)
2> go
```

Note the @ symbol before the variable's name. This symbol is required and is used by the query processor to identify variables.

Declaring Global Variables

If you delve further into the Transact-SQL documentation, you will notice certain system-level variables with the @@ symbol preceding the variable's name. This syntax is used to denote SQL Server global variables that are used to store information.

The programmer can declare his or her own global variables (they are particularly useful when using stored procedures, which are covered on the Bonus Day at the end of this book). SQL Server also maintains several system global variables that contain information that might be useful to the database system user. Table 13.4 contains the complete list of these variables. The source for this list is the Sybase SQL Server System 10 documentation.

Table 13.4. SQL Server global variables.

Variable Name	Purpose
@@char_convert	0 if character set conversion is in effect
@@client_csid	Client's character set ID
@@client_csname	Client's character set name
@@connections	Number of logins since SQL Server was started
@@cpu_busy	Amount of time, in ticks, the CPU has been busy since SQL Server was started
@@error	Contains error status
@@identity	Last value inserted into an identity column
@@idle	Amount of time, in ticks, that SQL Server has been idle since started
@@io_busy	Amount of time, in ticks, that SQL Server has spent doing I/O
@@isolation	Current isolation level of the Transact-SQL program
@@langid	Defines local language ID
@@language	Defines the name of the local language
@@maxcharlen	Maximum length of a character
@@max_connections	Maximum number of connections that can be made with SQL Server
@@ncharsize	Average length of a national character
@@nestlevel	Nesting level of current execution
@@pack_received	Number of input packets read by SQL Server since it was started

Variable Name	Purpose
@@pack_sent	Number of output packets sent by SQL Server since it was started
@@packet_errors	Numbers of errors that have occurred since SQL Server was started
@@procid	ID of the currently executing stored procedure
@@rowcount	Number of rows affected by the last command
@@servername	Name of the local SQL Server
@@spid	Process ID number of the current process
@@sqlstatus	Contains status information
@@textsize	Maximum length of text or image data returned with SELECT statement
@@thresh_hysteresis	Change in free space required to activate a threshold
@@timeticks	Number of microseconds per tick
@@total_errors	Number of errors that have occurred while reading or writing
@@total_read	Number of disk reads since SQL Server was started
@@total_write	Number of disk writes since SQL Server was started
@@tranchained	Current transaction mode of the Transact-SQL program
@@trancount	Nesting level of transactions
@@transtate	Current state of a transaction after a statement executes
@@version	Date of the current version of SQL Server

Using Variables

Using the DECLARE keyword, the programmer can declare several variables with a single statement (although this can sometimes look confusing when you look at your code later). An example of this type of statement appears here:

```
1> declare @batter_name char(30), @team int, @average float
2> go
```

Once the variable has been declared, you probably want to do something with it. Now that you know how to declare the variable, you will learn how to use it to perform useful programming operations.

13

Using Variables to Store Data

The first thing you should remember when using variables is that they are available only within the current statement block. To execute a block of statements using the Transact-SQL language, the go statement is executed. (As you remember, Oracle uses the semicolon for the same purpose.) The scope of a variable refers to the statements between when it is declared and when the go command is executed.

Variables cannot be initialized simply by using the = sign. Try this and note the error that is returned.

```
1> declare @name char(30)
2> @name = "Billy Brewster"
3> go
```

You should have received an error informing you of the improper syntax used in line 2. The proper way to initialize a variable is by using the SELECT command (yes, the same command you have already mastered). Repeat the preceding example using the correct syntax:

```
1> declare @name char(30)
2> select @name = "Billy Brewster"
3> go
```

This statement was executed correctly, and if you had inserted additional statements before executing the go statement, the @name variable could have been used.

Retrieving Data into Local Variables

Variables are often used to store data that has been retrieved from the database. They can be used with the common SQL commands we have already examined in some detail, such as SELECT, INSERT, UPDATE, and DELETE. Example 13.2 illustrates the use of variables in this manner.

Example 13.2

This example retrieves the name of the player in the BASEBALL database who has the highest batting average and plays for the Portland Beavers.

```
1> declare @team_id int, @player_name char(30), @max_avg float
2> select @team_id = TEAM_ID from TEAMS where CITY = "Portland"
3> select @max_avg = max(AVERAGE) from BATTERS where TEAM = @team_id
4> select @player_name = NAME from BATTERS where AVERAGE = @max_avg
5> go
```

This example was broken down into three queries to illustrate the use of variables. One other useful feature of Transact-SQL should be mentioned at this point: the PRINT command.

The PRINT Command

Transact-SQL enables the programmer to print output to the display device using the PRINT command. This command has the following syntax:

```
PRINT character_string
```

Although PRINT displays only character strings, Transact-SQL provides a number of useful functions that can be used to convert different data types to strings (and vice versa).

Example 13.3 repeats Example 13.2 but prints the player's name when finished.

Example 13.3

```
1> declare @team_id int, @player_name char(30), @max_avg float
2> select @team_id = TEAM_ID from TEAMS where CITY = "Portland"
3> select @max_avg = max(AVERAGE) from BATTERS where TEAM = @team_id
4> select @player_name = NAME from BATTERS where AVERAGE = @max_avg
5> print @player_name
6> go
```

Note that a variable can be used within a WHERE clause (or any other clause) just as if it were a constant value.

BEGIN and END Statements

Transact-SQL uses the BEGIN and END statements to signify the beginning and ending points of blocks of code. Other languages use brackets ({}) or some other operator to signify the beginning and ending points of functional groups of code. These statements are often used in conjunction with IF...ELSE statements and WHILE loops.

IF...ELSE Statements

One of the most basic programming constructs is the IF statement. Nearly every programming language supports it, and it is extremely useful for checking the value of data retrieved from the database. The Transact-SQL syntax for this statement looks like this:

```
if (condition)
begin
    (statement block)
end
else if (condition)
begin
    statement block)
end
.
.
.
else
```

```
begin
   (statement block)
end
```

Note that for each condition that might be true, a new begin/end block of statements was entered. Also, it is considered good programming practice to indent statement blocks a set amount of spaces and to keep this number of spaces the same throughout your application. This greatly improves the readability of the program and cuts down on silly errors that are often caused by simply misreading the code.

Example 13.4 takes Example 13.3 a step further by adding a check of the player's batting average. If the player's average is over .300, the owner would like to give him a raise. Otherwise, the owner could really care less about the player!

Example 13.4

```
1> declare @team_id int, @player_name char(30), @max_avg float
2> select @team_id = TEAM_ID from TEAMS where CITY = "Portland"
3> select @max_avg = max(AVERAGE) from BATTERS where TEAM = @team_id
4> select @player_name = NAME from BATTERS where AVERAGE = @max_avg
5> if (@max_avg > .300)
6> begin
7>    print @player_name
8>    print "Give this guy a raise!"
9> end
10> else
11> begin
12>    print @player_name
13>    print "Come back when you're hitting better!"
14> end
15> go
```

With this new IF statement, you are able to add some programming logic to the simple BASEBALL database queries. Example 13.5 extends Example 13.4 just slightly by adding an IF...ELSE IF...ELSE branch to your code.

Example 13.5

```
1> declare @team_id int, @player_name char(30), @max_avg float
2> select @team_id = TEAM_ID from TEAMS where CITY = "Portland"
3> select @max_avg = max(AVERAGE) from BATTERS where TEAM = @team_id
4> select @player_name = NAME from BATTERS where AVERAGE = @max_avg
5> if (@max_avg > .300)
6> begin
7>    print @player_name
8>    print "Give this guy a raise!"
9> end
10> else if (@max_avg > .275)
11> begin
12>    print @player_name
13>    print "Not bad. Here's a bonus!"
14> end
```

```
15> else
16> begin
17>    print @player_name
18>    print "Come back when you're hitting better!"
19> end
20> go
```

Transact-SQL also enables the programmer to check for a condition in conjunction with an IF statement. These functions can test for certain conditions or values. If the function returns TRUE, the IF branch is executed. Otherwise, if provided, the ELSE branch is executed, as you saw in the previous example.

The EXISTS Condition

Using the EXISTS keyword ensures that a value is returned from a SELECT statement. If it is, the IF statement is executed. Example 13.6 illustrates this.

Example 13.6

```
1> if exists (select * from TEAMS where TEAM_ID > 5)
2> begin
3>    print "IT EXISTS!!"
4> end
5> else
6> begin
7>    print "NO ESTA AQUI!"
8> end
```

Testing a Query's Result

The IF statement can also be used to test the result returned from a SELECT query. Example 13.7 implements this feature to check for the maximum batting average among players.

Example 13.7

```
1> if (select max(AVG) from BATTERS) > .400
2> begin
3>    print "UNBELIEVABLE!!"
4> end
5> else
6>    print "TED WILLIAMS IS GETTING LONELY!"
7> end
```

We recommend experimenting with your SQL implementation's use of the IF statement. Think of several conditions you would be interested in checking in the BASEBALL database (or a database of your own creation). Run some queries making use of the IF statement to familiarize yourself with its use.

13

The WHILE Loop

Another popular programming construct supported by Transact-SQL is the WHILE loop. This command has the following syntax:

```
WHILE logical_expression
    statement(s)
```

The WHILE loop continues to loop through its statements until the logical expression it is checking returns a FALSE. Example 13.8 uses a simple WHILE loop to increment a local variable (named COUNT).

Example 13.8

```
1> declare @COUNT int
2> select @COUNT = 1
3> while (@COUNT < 10)
4> begin
5>    select @COUNT = @COUNT + 1
6>    print "LOOP AGAIN!"
7> end
8> print "LOOP FINISHED!"
```

> **Note:** Programmers who are familiar with the FOR loop (supported in C and other languages) should notice that Example 13.8 implements a simple FOR loop. Other implementations of SQL, such as Oracle's PL/SQL, actually provide a FOR loop statement. Check your documentation to determine whether the system you are using supports this useful command.

The BREAK Command

The BREAK command can be issued within a WHILE loop to force an immediate exit from the loop. The BREAK command is often used along with an IF test to check some condition. If the condition check succeeds, the BREAK command can be used to exit out of the WHILE loop. Commands immediately following the END command are then executed. Example 13.9 illustrates a simple use of the BREAK command. We will check for some arbitrary number (say @COUNT = 8). When this condition is met, we will break out of the WHILE loop.

Example 13.9

```
1> declare @COUNT int
2> select @COUNT = 1
3> while (@COUNT < 10)
4> begin
5>    select @COUNT = @COUNT + 1
6>    if (@COUNT = 8)
7>    begin
8>       break
9>    end
10>   else
11>   begin
12>      print "LOOP AGAIN!"
13>   end
14> end
15> print "LOOP FINISHED!"
```

In this example, the BREAK command caused the loop to be exited when the @COUNT variable equaled eight. The following example will illustrate the use of the CONTINUE command.

The CONTINUE Command

The CONTINUE command is also a special command that can be executed from within a WHILE loop. The CONTINUE command forces the loop to immediately jump back to the beginning, rather than executing the remainder of the loop and then jumping back to the beginning. Like the BREAK command, the CONTINUE command is often used along with an IF statement to check for some condition and then force an action.

Example 13.10

```
#1> declare @COUNT int
2> select @COUNT = 1
3> while (@COUNT < 10)
4> begin
5>    select @COUNT = @COUNT + 1
6>    if (@COUNT = 8)
7>    begin
8>       continue
9>    end
10>   else
11>   begin
12>      print "LOOP AGAIN!"
13>   end
14> end
15> print "LOOP FINISHED!"
```

As you can see, Example 13.10 is identical to Example 13.9 except for the fact that we replaced the BREAK command with the CONTINUE command. Now instead of exiting the loop when @COUNT = 8, we simply jump back up to the top of the WHILE statement and continue.

13

Using the WHILE Loop to Scroll Through a Table

It may have already occurred to you that it would be very useful to scroll through a table's records one record at a time. In fact, SQL Server and many other database systems have a special type of object used to do this. This object is called a cursor and is discussed in detail in the chapter on advanced topics (Bonus Day 15). However, some database systems do not support the use of scrollable cursors (including SQL Server pre-System 10). Unfortunately, this does not mean that you will never need this functionality. Therefore, Example 13.11 is supplied to give you an idea of how to implement a rough cursor-type functionality when that functionality is not automatically supplied.

Example 13.11

The WHILE loop can be used to scroll through tables one record at a time. Transact-SQL stores a variable that can be set to tell SQL Server to return only one row at a time during a query. This variable is the rowcount variable. If you are using a different database product, determine whether your product has a similar setting. By setting this to 1 (its default is zero, which means unlimited), SQL Server returns only one record at a time from a SELECT query. You can use this one record to perform whatever operations you need to perform. By selecting the contents of a table into a temporary table that is deleted at the end of the operation, you can select out one row at a time, deleting that row when you are finished. When all the rows have been selected out of the table, you have gone through every row in the table. (As we said, this is a very rough cursor functionality!) Let's run the example now.

```
1> set rowcount 1
2> declare @PLAYER char(30)
3> create table temp_BATTERS (
4> NAME char(30),
5> TEAM int,
6> AVERAGE float,
7> HOMERUNS int,
8> RBIS int)
9> insert temp_BATTERS
10> select * from BATTERS
11> while exists (select * from temp_BATTERS)
12> begin
13>   select @PLAYER = NAME from temp_BATTERS
14>   print @PLAYER
15>   delete from temp_BATTERS where NAME = @PLAYER
16> end
17> print "LOOP IS DONE!"
```

Note that by setting the rowcount variable, you are simply modifying the number of rows returned from a SELECT. If the WHERE clause of the DELETE command returned 5 rows, 5 rows would be deleted! Also note that the rowcount variable can be reset repeatedly. Therefore, if, while within the loop, the programmer would like to query the database for some additional information, he or she could simply set rowcount back to 1 before continuing with the loop.

Summary

Today we introduced a number of topics that add some teeth to your SQL programming expertise. Until today, we had spent a great deal of time covering the many intricacies of the query and the strategies behind database design. These topics are extremely important and will provide the foundation for all database programming work you undertake. However, these topics are just that: a foundation. Think of it as learning the syntax to Visual Basic or C programming. Once you have read through the syntactical rules in the manual, you are probably not qualified to go out and produce a professional application. But, it certainly is an important start!

We briefly introduced the concepts of Static and Dynamic SQL. Dynamic SQL is discussed in much greater detail on Day 14. Static SQL was briefly mentioned because it is in use today. However, the trend is in the direction of the more flexible Dynamic SQL. After this topic, the basic tools necessary for programming with SQL were introduced.

The examples in this chapter were shown using the Transact-SQL syntax included with the Microsoft and Sybase SQL Server database products. This language provides many of the popular programming constructs found in popular third- and fourth-generation (3GL and 4GL) languages. Included in its capabilities are the IF statement, the WHILE loop, and the capability to declare and use local and global variables. On Day 15 (a bonus day used to introduce advanced SQL topics), we discuss how to combine these statements into a stored procedure that can be called from within other applications or procedures. These procedures can return values and offer many advantages, such as improved execution speed and reduced network traffic.

Q&A

Q Is there a FOR loop provided by SQL?

A Programming constructs such as the FOR loop, the WHILE loop, and the CASE statement are extensions to ANSI SQL. Therefore, the use of these items varies widely among different database systems. For instance, Oracle provides the FOR loop, while Transact SQL (SQL Server) does not. Of course, a WHILE loop can increment a variable within the loop. Doing this effectively simulates the FOR loop.

Q I am developing a Windows (or Macintosh) application whose user interface consists only of Windows GUI elements, such as windows and dialog boxes. Can the PRINT statement be used to issue messages to the user?

A SQL is entirely platform-independent. Therefore, issuing the PRINT statement will not pop up a message box. Actually, the PRINT command is most useful when debugging, because a PRINT statement executed within a stored procedure will

13

not be output to the screen anyway. To output messages to the user, your SQL procedures could return a pre-determined value that indicates success or failure. Based on these return values, the user could be notified of the status of the queries.

Workshop

The Workshop provides quiz questions to help you solidify your understanding of the material covered and exercises to provide you with experience in using what you've learned. Try to answer the quiz and exercise questions before checking the answers in Appendix F, and make sure you understand the answers before continuing to the next chapter.

Quiz

1. Decide whether the following statements are true or false:

   The use of the word SQL in Oracle's PL-SQL and Microsoft/Sybase's Transact-SQL implies that these products are fully compliant with the ANSI standard.

   Static SQL is less flexible than Dynamic SQL although its performance can be better.

Exercises

1. If your database of choice is not Sybase/Microsoft SQL Server, compare its extensions to ANSI SQL to those extensions mentioned in this chapter.

2. Write a brief set of statements that will check for the existence of some condition. If this condition is true, perform some operation. Otherwise, perform another operation.

14

Advanced SQL Topics

Introduction

By today, the fourteenth day of this book, you have received an excellent overview of Structured Query Language (SQL) and its use in developing professional database applications. We have covered every major topic used to write powerful queries to retrieve data from a database. We also touched on database design and database security. The purpose of this chapter is to cover advanced SQL topics. Included in these topics are several concepts that will be useful to you after you have truly mastered the first 14 days of this book.

The topics covered today include the following:

- ☐ Temporary tables
- ☐ Cursors
- ☐ Stored procedures
- ☐ Triggers
- ☐ Tuning databases and queries (for performance improvements)

As with much of the material covered throughout this book, examples are given using Oracle7's PL/SQL and Microsoft/Sybase SQL Server's Transact-SQL dialects. An effort was made to give examples using both flavors of SQL wherever possible. As with the rest of the examples in this book, it is not necessary to own a copy of either the Oracle7 or SQL Server database products. Feel free to choose your own database product based on your own set of requirements. (Chances are, if you are reading this to gain enough knowledge to begin a project for your job, that product has already been chosen for you.)

> **Note:** Although the vast majority of the examples within this book can be applied to any popular database management system, this does not hold true for all the material within this chapter. Concepts such as temporary tables, stored procedures, and triggers are more modern database concepts and are not supported by many manufacturers. Check your documentation to determine which of these features are included with your favorite database system.

Temporary Tables

The first advanced topic we discuss is the use of temporary tables. (Don't be intimidated by the word *advanced*—this is still database programming, not neurosurgery or rocket science.)

Temporary tables are exactly what the name implies. They are simply tables that exist temporarily within a database and are automatically dropped when the user logs out or their database connection ends. Transact-SQL creates these temporary tables in the tempdb database. This database is created upon installation of an SQL Server. There are two types of syntax used to create a temporary table.

```
SYNTAX #1:
create table #table_name (
field1 datatype,
.
.
.
fieldn datatype)
```

Syntax #1 is used to create a table in the tempdb database. This table is created with a unique name consisting of a combination of the tablename used in the CREATE TABLE command and a date-time stamp. This means that when a user creates a temporary table, this table is available only to that user. Fifty users could simultaneously issue the following commands:

```
1> create table #albums (
2> artist char(30),
3> album_name char(50),
4> media_type int)
5> go
```

Note the pound sign (#) before the table's name. This is the identifier used by SQL Server to flag a temporary table. Each of the fifty users would essentially receive their own private table for their own use. They could update, insert, and delete records from this table without worrying about other users invalidating their table's data. This table could be dropped as usual by issuing the following command:

```
1> drop table #albums
2> go
```

The table could also be dropped automatically when the user that created it logged out of the SQL Server. If this table was created using some type of dynamic SQL connection (such as SQL Server's DB-Library), the table would be deleted when that dynamic SQL connection was closed.

Syntax #2 shows another way to create a temporary table on an SQL Server. This syntax produces a different result than the syntax used in Syntax #1, so pay careful attention to the syntactical differences.

```
SYNTAX #2:
create table tempdb..tablename (
field1 datatype,
.
.
.
fieldn datatype)
```

14

Creating a temporary table using the format of Syntax #2 still results in a table being created in the tempdb database. This table's name has the same format as the name for the table created using Syntax #1. The difference is that this table is not dropped when the user's connection to the database ends. Instead, the user must actually issue a DROP TABLE command to remove this table from the tempdb database.

> **Note:** There is another way to get rid of a table that was created using the `create table tempdb..tablename` syntax. This is by shutting down and restarting the SQL Server. This causes all temporary tables to be removed from the tempdb database.

Examples 14.1 and 14.2 are used to illustrate the fact that temporary tables are indeed temporary, using the two different forms of syntax. Following these two examples, Example 14.3 illustrates a common usage of temporary tables: using temporary tables to temporarily store data returned from a query. This data can then be used with other queries.

As with all other examples in this book, you need to create a database to be used throughout the rest of this chapter. The database MUSIC is created with the following tables:

- ☐ ARTISTS
- ☐ MEDIA
- ☐ RECORDINGS

Use the following SQL statements to create these tables:

```
1> create table ARTISTS (
2> name char(30),
3> homebase char(40),
4> style char(20),
5> artist_id int)
6> go
1> create table MEDIA (
2> media_type int,
3> description char(30),
4> price float)
5> go
1> create table RECORDINGS (
2> artist_id int,
3> media_type int,
4> title char(50),
5> year int)
6> go
```

Tables 14.1, 14.2, and 14.3 show some sample data for these tables. (These are some of our favorites. Feel free to enter your own.)

Table 14.1. The ARTISTS table.

Name	Homebase	Style	Artist_ID
Soul Asylum	Minneapolis	Rock	1
Maurice Ravel	France	Classical	2
Dave Matthews Band	Charlottesville	Rock	3
Vince Gill	Nashville	Country	4
Oingo Boingo	Los Angeles	Pop	5
Crowded House	New Zealand	Pop	6
Mary Chapin-Carpenter	Nashville	Country	7
Edward MacDowell	U.S.A.	Classical	8

Table 14.2. The MEDIA table.

Media_Type	Description	Price
1	Record	4.99
2	Tape	9.99
3	CD	13.99
4	CD-ROM	29.99
5	DAT	19.99

Table 14.3. The RECORDINGS table.

Artist_Id	Media_Type	Title	Year
1	2	Hang Time	1988
1	3	Made to Be Broken	1986
2	3	Bolero	1990
3	5	Under the Table and Dreaming	1994
4	3	When Love Finds You	1994
5	2	Boingo	1987
5	1	Dead Man's Party	1984
6	2	Woodface	1990
6	3	Together Alone	1993

14

continues

Table 14.3. continued

Artist_Id	Media_Type	Title	Year
7	5	Come On, Come On	1992
7	3	Stones in the Road	1994
8	5	Second Piano Concerto	1985

Example 14.1

You can create a temporary table in the tempdb database. After inserting a dummy record into this table, log out. After logging back into the SQL Server, try to select the dummy record out of the temporary table. Note the results:

```
1> create table #albums (
2> artist char(30),
3> album_name char(50),
4> media_type int)
5> go
1> insert #albums values ("The Replacements", "Pleased To Meet Me", 1)
2> go
```

Now log out of the SQL Server connection using the EXIT (or QUIT) command. After logging back in (using isql -Uuser_name -Ppassword) and switching to the database you last used, try the following command:

```
1> select * from #albums
2> go
```

You are told that this table does not exist in the current database.

Example 14.2

Now create the table with the syntax used in Syntax #2:

```
1> create table tempdb..albums (
2> artist char(30),
3> album_name char(50),
4> media_type int)
5> go
1> insert #albums values ("The Replacements", "Pleased To Meet Me", 1)
2> go
```

After logging out and logging back in, switch to the database you were using when create table tempdb..albums() was issued, then issue the following command:

```
1> select * from #albums
2> go
```

This time, you get the following results:

artist	album_name	media_type
The Replacements	Pleased To Meet Me	1

Example 14.3

This example shows a common usage of temporary tables: storing the results of complex queries to be used for later queries.

```
1> create table #temp_info (
2> name char(30),
3> homebase char(40),
4> style char(20),
5> artist_id int)
6> insert #temp_info
7> select * from ARTISTS where homebase = "Nashville"
8> select RECORDINGS.* from RECORDINGS, ARTISTS
9> where RECORDINGS.artist_id = #temp_info.artist_id
10> go
```

The preceding batch of commands selects out the recording information for all the artists whose homebase is Nashville.

Let's review another way to write the set of SQL statements used in Example 14.3. Execute the following command and you end up with the same results:

```
1> select ARTISTS.* from ARTISTS, RECORDINGS where ARTISTS.homebase =
   "Nashville"
2> go
```

Cursors

The next topic is cursors. Cursors can best be visualized by thinking of a cursor on a word processor screen. As you press the Down Arrow key, the cursor scrolls down through the text one line at a time. Pressing the Up Arrow key scrolls your cursor up one line at a time. Hitting other keys such as Page Up and Page Down results in a leap of several lines in either direction. Database cursors operate in this same manner.

Database cursors enable the programmer to select a group of data, then scroll through the group of records (often called a recordset), examining each individual line of data as the cursor points to it. We have already examined how to use local variables to store an individual field's data. Using a combination of local variables and a cursor enables the programmer to individually examine each record and perform any external operation needed before moving on to the next record.

14

One other common use of cursors is to save a query's results for later use. A cursor's result set is created from the result set of a SELECT query. If your application or procedure requires the repeated use of a set of records, it is faster to create a cursor once and reuse it several times than to continually requery the database. (Plus, there is the added advantage of being able to scroll through the query's result set with a cursor.)

Several steps are involved in using a cursor. Listed here are the common steps required to create, use, and close a database cursor:

1. Create the cursor.

2. Open the cursor for use within the procedure or application.

3. Fetch a record's data one row at a time until you have reached the end of the cursor's records.

4. When finished with the cursor, close it.

5. Deallocate the cursor to completely discard it.

Creating a Cursor

To create a cursor, the following command must be issued (using Transact-SQL):

```
declare cursor_name cursor
    for select_statement
    [for {read only ¦ update [of column_name_list]}]
```

The Oracle7 SQL syntax used to create a cursor looks like this:

```
DECLARE cursor_name CURSOR
    FOR {SELECT command ¦ statement_name ¦ block_name}
```

By executing the `declare cursor_name cursor` statement, you have defined the cursor result set that will be used for all your cursor operations. A cursor is actually made up of two important parts: the cursor result set and the cursor position.

The following statement creates a cursor based on the ARTISTS table:

```
1> create Artists_Cursor cursor
2> for select * from ARTISTS
3> go
```

You now have a simple cursor object named Artists_Cursor that contains all the records in the ARTISTS table. Before it can actually be used, however, it must be opened.

Opening a Cursor

The command to open a cursor for use is extremely simple:

```
open cursor_name
```

Executing the following statement opens Artists_Cursor for use:

```
1> open Artists_Cursor
2> go
```

Now that the cursor has been created and opened, it can be used for scrolling through the recordset.

Scrolling a Cursor

To scroll through the cursor's result set, Transact-SQL provides the FETCH command. It looks like this:

```
fetch cursor_name [into fetch_target_list]
```

Oracle SQL provides the following syntax:

```
FETCH cursor_name {INTO : host_variable
    [[INDICATOR] : indicator_variable]
    [,      : host_variable
    [[INDICATOR] : indicator_variable] ]...
    ¦ USING DESCRIPTOR descriptor }
```

Each time the FETCH command is executed, the cursor pointer advances through the result set one row at a time. If desired, data from each row can be fetched into the fetch_target_list variables.

> **Note:** Transact-SQL enables the programmer to advance more than one row at a time. This can be accomplished by using the following command: `set cursor rows number for cursor_name`. This command cannot be used in conjunction with the INTO clause, however. It is useful only to jump forward a known number of rows instead of repeatedly executing the FETCH statement.

The following statements fetch the data from the Artists_Cursor result set and return the data to the program variables:

14

```
1> declare @name char(30)
2> declare @homebase char(40)
3> declare @style char(20)
4> declare @artist_id int
5> fetch Artists_Cursor into @name, @homebase, @style, @artist_id
6> print @name
7> print @homebase
8> print @style
9> print char(@artist_id)
10> go
```

Looking back to material covered on Day 13, you can see the value of the WHILE loop when using cursors. The WHILE loop can be used to simply loop through the entire contents of the cursor's result set until the end of the records is reached. This brings up a timely topic. That is, how do you know when you have reached the end of the records?

Testing a Cursor's Status

Transact-SQL enables the programmer to check the status of the cursor at any time. It does this through the maintenance of two global variables: @@sqlstatus and @@rowcount.

The @@sqlstatus variable is used to return status information concerning the last executed FETCH statement. (The Transact-SQL documentation states that no command other than the FETCH statement can modify the @@sqlstatus variable.) This variable contains one of three values. The following table can be found in the Transact-SQL reference manuals:

Status	Meaning
0	Successful completion of the FETCH statement
1	The FETCH statement resulted in an error
2	There is no more data in the result set

The @@rowcount variable contains the number of rows returned from the cursor's result set up to the previous fetch. This number can be used to determine the number of records in a cursor's result set.

The following code expands on the statements executed during the discussion of the FETCH statement. You now use the WHILE loop, in combination with the @@sqlstatus variable, to scroll the cursor:

```
1> declare @name char(30)
2> declare @homebase char(40)
3> declare @style char(20)
4> declare @artist_id int
5> fetch Artists_Cursor into @name, @homebase, @style, @artist_id
6> while (@@sqlstatus = 0)
7> begin
8>      print @name
9>      print @homebase
10>     print @style
11>     print char(@artist_id)
12>     fetch Artists_Cursor into @name, @homebase, @style, @artist_id
13> end
14> go
```

Now you have a fully functioning cursor! The only step left is to close this cursor when you are finished with it.

Closing a Cursor

Closing a cursor is a very simple matter. The statement to close a cursor is as follows:

```
close cursor_name
```

This cursor still exists; however, it must be reopened. Closing a cursor essentially closes out its result set, not its entire existence. When you are completely finished with a cursor, the DEALLOCATE command frees the memory associated with a cursor and frees the cursor name for use in creating other cursors. The DEALLOCATE statement syntax is as follows:

```
deallocate cursor cursor_name
```

Example 14.4 illustrates the complete process of creating a cursor, using it, and then closing it, using Transact-SQL.

Example 14.4

```
1> declare @name char(30)
2> declare @homebase char(40)
3> declare @style char(20)
4> declare @artist_id int
5> create Artists_Cursor cursor
6> for select * from ARTISTS
7> open Artists_Cursor
8> fetch Artists_Cursor into @name, @homebase, @style, @artist_id
9> while (@@sqlstatus = 0)
10> begin
11>      print @name
12>       print @homebase
13>      print @style
14>      print char(@artist_id)
15>      fetch Artists_Cursor into @name, @homebase, @style, @artist_id
16> end
17> close Artists_Cursor
18> deallocate cursor Artists_Cursor
19> go
```

```
Soul Asylum            Minneapolis       Rock        1
Maurice Ravel          France            Classical   2
Dave Matthews Band     Charlottesville   Rock        3
Vince Gill             Nashville         Country     4
Oingo Boingo           Los Angeles       Pop         5
Crowded House          New Zealand       Pop         6
Mary Chapin-Carpenter  Nashville         Country     7
Edward MacDowell       U.S.A.            Classical   8
```

The Scope of Cursors

Unlike tables, indexes, and other objects such as triggers and stored procedures, cursors do not exist as database objects once they are created. Instead, cursors have only a limited scope of use. Outside that scope, the cursor_name no longer exists.

> **Warning:** Remember, however, that memory is still allocated for the cursor even though its name may no longer exist. Before going outside the cursor's scope, it should always be closed and deallocated.

There are three regions in which a cursor can be created:

☐ **Session:** A session begins when a user logs on. If the user logged on to an SQL Server then created a cursor, this cursor_name would be existent until the user logged off. This name could not be reused during this time span by the user.

☐ **Stored Procedure:** A cursor created inside a stored procedure is good only during the execution of the stored procedure. Once the stored procedure exits, the cursor name is no longer valid.

☐ **Trigger:** Cursor creation inside a trigger has the same restrictions as one created inside a stored procedure.

Creating and Using Stored Procedures

The concept of stored procedures is an important one for the professional database programmer to master. Stored procedures are functions that contain potentially large groupings of SQL statements. These functions are called and executed just as a C, FORTRAN, or Visual Basic function would be called. A stored procedure should encapsulate a logical set of commands that are often executed (such as a complex set of queries, updates, or inserts). This enables the programmer to simply call the stored procedure as a function instead of repeatedly executing the statements inside the stored procedure. This is not the only advantage of using stored procedures, however.

Stored procedures were pioneered by Sybase, Inc. with their SQL Server product in the late 1980s. These procedures are created and then stored as part of a database, just as tables and indexes are stored inside a database. Transact SQL enables both input and output parameters to stored procedure calls. This enables the stored procedures to be created in a more generic fashion in the sense that variables can be passed in to them.

One of the biggest advantages to stored procedures lies in the design of their execution. When executing a large batch of SQL statements to a database server over a network, your application is in constant communication back and forth with this server. (For single-user applications this probably will not be a problem, but then again, for single-user applications you probably are not using a database server in the first place.) This constant communication can create an extremely heavy load on the network very quickly. As multiple users become

engaged in this communication, the performance of the network and the database server becomes increasingly slower.

By using stored procedures, the programmer can greatly reduce this communication. After the stored procedure is executed, the SQL statements run sequentially on the database server. Only when the procedure is actually finished is some message or data returned to the user's computer. This results in a performance improvement. There are other benefits to this method as well. Stored procedures are actually compiled by database engines the first time they are used. This compiled map is stored on the server with the procedure. Therefore, the SQL statements do not have to be continually re-optimized each time they are executed. This also results in a performance improvement.

To create a stored procedure using Transact-SQL, the following syntax is used:

```
create procedure procedure_name
    [[(|]@parameter_name
        datatype [(length) ¦ (precision [, scale])
        [= default][output]
    [, @parameter_name
        datatype [(length) ¦ (precision [, scale])
        [= default][output]]...[)]]
    [with recompile]
    as SQL_statements
```

After being created, the procedure can be executed using the EXECUTE command:

```
execute [@return_status = ]
    procedure_name
    [[@parameter_name =] value ¦
        [@parameter_name =] @variable [output]...]]
    [with recompile]
```

To boost your confidence, let's create a simple procedure using the contents of Example 14.4.

Example 14.5

```
1> create procedure Print_Artists_Name
2> as
3> declare @name char(30)
4> declare @homebase char(40)
5> declare @style char(20)
6> declare @artist_id int
7> create Artists_Cursor cursor
8> for select * from ARTISTS
9> open Artists_Cursor
10> fetch Artists_Cursor into @name, @homebase, @style, @artist_id
11> while (@@sqlstatus = 0)
12> begin
13>     print @name
14>     fetch Artists_Cursor into @name, @homebase, @style, @artist_id
15> end
16> close Artists_Cursor
17> deallocate cursor Artists_Cursor
18> go
```

You can now execute the Print_Artists_Name procedure using the EXECUTE statement:

```
1> execute Print_Artists_Name
2> go
```

```
Soul Asylum
Maurice Ravel
Dave Matthews Band
Vince Gill
Oingo Boingo
Crowded House
Mary Chapin-Carpenter
Edward MacDowell
```

Using Stored Procedure Parameters

Example 14.5 was an important first step because it showed the use of the simplest CREATE PROCEDURE statement. However, by looking at the syntax given here, you can see that there is more to the CREATE PROCEDURE statement than was demonstrated in Example 14.5. Stored procedures also accept parameters as input to their SQL statements. In addition, data can be returned from a stored procedure through the use of output parameters.

Input parameter names must begin with the @ symbol, and these parameters must be a valid Transact-SQL datatype. Output parameter names must also begin with the @ symbol. In addition, output parameter names must be followed by the OUTPUT keyword. (This OUTPUT keyword must be given when executing the stored procedure as well.)

Example 14.6 demonstrates the use of input parameters to a stored procedure.

Example 14.6

The following stored procedure is used to select the names of all artists whose media type is a CD:

```
1> create procedure Match_Names_To_Media @description char(30)
2> as
3>     select ARTISTS.name from ARTISTS, MEDIA, RECORDINGS
4>     where MEDIA.description = @description and
5>     MEDIA.media_type = RECORDINGS.media_type and
6>     RECORDINGS.artist_id = ARTISTS.artist_id
7> go
1> execute Match_Names_To_Media "CD"
2> go
```

Executing this statement would result in the following set of records being returned:

```
NAME
Soul Asylum
Maurice Ravel
Vince Gill
Crowded House
Mary Chapin-Carpenter
```

Example 14.7

This example demonstrates the use of output parameters. This function takes the artist's homebase as input and returns the artist's name as output:

```
1> create procedure Match_Homebase_To_Name @homebase char(40), @name
char(30) output
2> as
3>      select @name = name from ARTISTS where homebase = @homebase
4> go
1> declare @return_name char(30)
2> execute Match_Homebase_To_Name "Los Angeles", @return_name = @name
output
3> print @name
4> go
```

```
Oingo Boingo
```

Removing a Stored Procedure

By now, you can probably make an educated guess as to how to get rid of a stored procedure. If you guessed the DROP command, you are absolutely correct. The following statement removes a stored procedure from a database:

```
drop procedure procedure_name
```

This command is actually used quite often. This is because before a stored procedure can be re-created, the old procedure with its name must be dropped. From personal experience, there are few instances in which a procedure is created and then never modified. Many times, in fact, there are errors somewhere within the statements that make up the procedure. It is highly recommended that you create your stored procedures using an SQL script file containing all of your statements. This script file can then be run through your database server to execute your desired statements and rebuild your procedures. This enables you to use common text editors such as vi or Windows Notepad to create and save your SQL scripts. When running these scripts, however, you need to remember to always drop the procedure, table, and so forth from the database before creating a new one. If this is not done, errors will result.

14

The following syntax is often used in SQL Server script files before creating a database object:

```
if exists (select * from sysobjects where name = "procedure_name")
begin
     drop procedure procedure_name
end
go
create procedure procedure_name
as
.
.
.
```

These commands check the sysobjects table (where database object information is stored in SQL Server) to see if the object exists. If it does, it is dropped before the new one is created. Creating script files and following the preceding steps saves you a large amount of time (and many potential errors) in the long run.

Nesting Stored Procedures

Stored procedure calls can also be nested for increased programming modularity. This means that a stored procedure can call another stored procedure, which can then call another stored procedure, and so on. Nesting stored procedures is an excellent idea for several reasons.

The first reason is that it reduces your most complex queries down to a functional level. (Instead of executing twelve queries in a row, you could perhaps reduce these twelve queries to three stored procedure calls, depending on the situation.)

Another excellent reason for nesting stored procedures is performance. The query optimizer optimizes smaller, more concise groups of queries more effectively than one large group of statements.

When nesting stored procedures, any variables or database objects created in one stored procedure are visible to all the stored procedures it calls. Any local variables or temporary objects (such as temporary tables) are deleted at the end of the stored procedure that created these elements.

When preparing large SQL script files, the beginning programmer might run into table or database object referencing problems. When nesting stored procedures, the procedures that are called must be created before they can be called. However, the calling procedure may have created temporary tables or cursors that are then used in the called stored procedures. These called stored procedures do not know of the existence of these temporary tables or cursors, because they are created further on in the script file. The easiest way around this problem is to create the temporary objects before all the stored procedures are created. Then, drop the temporary items (in the script file) before they are created again in the stored procedure. Are you confused yet? Example 14.8 should clear up this explanation.

Example 14.8

```
1> create procedure Example14_8b
2> as
3>     select * from #temp_table
4> go
1> create procedure Example14_8a
2> as
3>     create #temp_table (
4>     data char(20),
5>     numbers int)
6>     execute Example14_8b
7>     drop table #temp_table
8> go
```

As you can see, procedure Example14_8b uses the #temp_table. However, the #temp_table is not created until later (in procedure Example14_8a). This results in a procedure creation error. In fact, because Example14_8b was not created (due to the missing table #temp_table), procedure Example14_8a is not created either (due to the non-creation of Example14_8b).

The following code fixes this problem by creating the #temp_table before the first procedure is created. This table is then dropped before the creation of the second procedure:

```
1> create #temp_table (
2> data char(20),
3> numbers int)
4> go
1> create procedure Example14_8b
2> as
3>     select * from #temp_table
4> go
1> drop table #temp_table
2> go
1> create procedure Example14_8a
2> as
3>     create #temp_table (
4>     data char(20),
5>     numbers int)
6>     execute Example14_8b
7>     drop table #temp_table
8> go
```

Designing and Using Triggers

14

Of all the terms used in this book thus far, you may be most mystified by the term *trigger*. All sorts of images may have filled your mind while you tried to determine just what we were referring to with this word. You may be disappointed, because no audible bang goes off inside your database. Triggers are extremely useful, special-purpose stored procedures. A trigger is essentially a special type of stored procedure that the programmer can create to be executed when one of three conditions occurs:

☐ An update

☐ An insert

☐ A delete

The Transact-SQL syntax to create a trigger looks like this:

```
create trigger trigger_name
  on table_name
  for {insert, update, delete}
  as SQL_Statements
```

The following is the Oracle7 SQL syntax used to create a trigger:

```
CREATE [OR REPLACE] TRIGGER [schema.]trigger_name
  {BEFORE ¦ AFTER}
  {DELETE ¦ INSERT ¦ UPDATE [OF column[, column]...]}
[OR {DELETE ¦ INSERT ¦ UPDATE [OF column [, column] ...]}]...
  ON [schema.]table
[[REFERENCING { OLD [AS] old [NEW [AS] new]
        ¦ NEW [AS] new [OLD [AS] old]}]
FOR EACH ROW
[WHEN (condition)] ]
pl/sql statements...
```

Triggers are most useful to enforce referential integrity. We discussed this concept earlier when you learned how to create tables. Referential integrity enforces rules used to ensure that data remains valid across multiple tables. Suppose a user entered the following command:

```
1> insert RECORDINGS values (12, "The Cross of Changes", 3, 1994)
2> go
```

This is a perfectly valid SQL statement and results in a new record being inserted in the RECORDINGS table. However, a quick check of the ARTISTS table shows that there is no Artist_ID = 12. A user needs only INSERT privileges in the RECORDINGS table to completely destroy your referential integrity.

> **Note:** Although it is true that many database systems can enforce referential integrity through the use of constraints in the CREATE TABLE statement, triggers provide a great deal more flexibility. They can print error messages, call other stored procedures, or try to rectify a problem, if necessary. Using constraints results in a system error message being returned to the user. (As you probably know by now, these error messages are not always helpful.)

Triggers and Transactions

The actions executed within a trigger are implicitly executed as part of a transaction. Think of this as follows:

1. A BEGIN TRANSACTION statement is implicitly issued (for tables with triggers)
2. The insert, update, or delete operation occurs
3. The trigger is called and its statements are executed
4. The trigger either rolls back the transaction, or the transaction is implicitly committed

Example 14.9

This example illustrates the solution to the RECORDINGS table update problem mentioned earlier:

```
1> create trigger check_artists
2> on RECORDINGS
3> for insert, update as
4>      if not exists (select * from ARTISTS, RECORDINGS
5>      where ARTISTS.artist_id = RECORDINGS.artist_id)
6>      begin
7>          print "Illegal Artist_ID!"
8>          rollback transaction
9>      end
10> go
```

A similar problem could exist for deletes from the RECORDINGS table also. Let's say that if a record deleted from the RECORDINGS table resulted in no recordings from an artist, you would delete the artist from the ARTISTS table. If the records have already been deleted when the trigger is fired, how do you know which Artist_ID should be deleted? There are two methods to solve this problem:

☐ Delete all the artists from the ARTISTS table who no longer have any recordings in the RECORDINGS table. (See Example 14.10a.)

☐ Examine the deleted logical table. Transact-SQL maintains two tables: one called Deleted and another called Inserted. These tables look identical in structure to the table on which the trigger is created. They are used to maintain the most recent changes to the actual table itself. Therefore, you could retrieve the artist IDs from the Deleted table, then delete these IDs from the ARTISTS table. (See Example 14.10b.)

14

Example 14.10a

```
1> create trigger delete_artists
2> on RECORDINGS
3> for delete as
4> begin
5>      delete from ARTISTS where artist_id not in
6>      (select artist_id from RECORDINGS)
7> end
8> go
```

Example 14.10b

```
1> create trigger delete_artists
2> on RECORDINGS
3> for delete as
4> begin
5>      delete ARTISTS from ARTISTS, deleted
6>      where ARTIST.artist_id  = deleted.artist_id
7> end
8> go
```

Restrictions on Using Triggers

The use of triggers brings with it a few restrictions:

☐ Triggers cannot be created on temporary tables.

☐ Triggers must be created on tables in the current database.

☐ Triggers cannot be created on views.

☐ When a table is dropped, all triggers associated with that table are automatically dropped with it.

Nested Triggers

Triggers can also be nested. Say that you have created a trigger to fire on a delete, for instance. If this trigger itself then deletes a record, the database server can be set to fire another trigger. Obviously, this would result in a loop, ending only when all the records in the table were deleted (or some internal trigger conditions were met). This nesting behavior is not the default, however. The environment must be set to enable this type of functionality. Consult your database server's documentation for more information on this topic.

Tuning Databases and SQL Queries

Tuning a database is the process of fine-tuning the database server's performance. Tuning a query is the process of fine-tuning a query for improved performance. These are actually two different topics. Tuning a database involves many database management tasks, such as

planning disk space, memory usage, and process priorities. A query can be tuned by carefully selecting indexes or experimenting with a variety of statements to examine which method returns the best results.

Tuning a Database

Tuning a database is heavily dependent on the specific database system you have chosen for your task. Listed here are some common tasks that together comprise the art of database tuning:

- ☐ Minimize the size required for the database.
- ☐ Experiment with the user process's time slice variable. This time slice controls the amount of time the database server's scheduler allocates to each user's process.
- ☐ Optimize the network packet size used by applications. The larger the amount of data sent over the network, the larger the network packet size should be. (Consult your database and network documentation for more details on this matter.)
- ☐ Store transaction logs on separate hard disks to improve database read/write performance.
- ☐ Split extremely large tables across multiple disks to improve database read/write performance.

Obviously, there is much more to tuning databases than preparing queries and letting them fly. Professionals who do this for a living often specialize on one database product and learn as much as they possibly can about its features and idiosyncracies. Although it is often looked upon as a painful task, tuning can be very lucrative for the people who truly understand it.

Tuning SQL Queries

Tuning SQL queries, on the other hand, is a task that every database developer should understand and practice. Tuning queries is often done after the actual queries and programming logic have been satisfactorily developed and tested.

Although each system has its own peculiarities, the following list describes several tasks often performed to improve query performance:

- ☐ Convert all large queries that are executed often to stored procedures. This reduces network traffic and results in a precompiled procedure stored in the database instead of a large query that must be re-optimized each time it is executed.
- ☐ Create indexes that improve the performance of queries, especially joins.
- ☐ Indexes should be created for queries that return less than 5 percent of a table's rows.
- ☐ Index columns that are used in WHERE clauses.

14

☐ Index columns that are commonly used in JOIN clauses.

☐ Do not index columns with a small number of distinct values. This does not result in much of a performance improvement. (In fact, a poor choice of index can often slow a query down.)

GROUP BY clauses and subqueries notoriously perform more slowly than joins. In situations where two indexed columns could be joined together, this is almost always faster than using subqueries to return data.

Summary

This chapter was intended to be a bonus day for users who have found themselves increasingly involved with database programming. Many database programmers today have a variety of tools at their fingertips, especially with the popularity of programming environments such as Visual Basic, Delphi, and PowerBuilder. These tools are great for executing queries and updating data with a database. However, as you become increasingly involved with databases, you will learn that there are significant advantages to using the various tools and topics discussed in this chapter. Unfortunately, concepts such as cursors, triggers, and stored procedures are recent database innovations and have a low degree of standardization across products. However, the basic theory of usage behind all these features remains the same regardless of the database management system.

Temporary tables are tables that exist temporarily during a user's session. These tables typically exist in a special database (named tempdb under SQL Server) and are often given a special date-time stamp along with their name so that they can be uniquely identified. Temporary tables can be used to store a result set from a query for later usage by other queries. Performance can erode, however, if many users are creating and using temporary tables all at once, due to the large amount of activity occurring in the tempdb database.

Cursors are commonly used to store a result set in order to scroll through this result set one record at a time (or several records at a time, if desired). The FETCH statement is used in conjunction with a cursor to retrieve an individual record's data and also to scroll the cursor to the next record. Various system variables can be monitored to determine whether the end of the records has been reached.

Stored procedures are database objects that can be used to combine many different SQL statements into one function. Stored procedures can accept and return parameter values as well as call other stored procedures. These procedures are executed on the database server and are stored in compiled form in the database. This results in a performance improvement (compared to executing stand-alone queries).

Triggers are a special case of stored procedures that are executed when a table undergoes an insert, a delete, or an update operation. These triggers are often used to enforce referential integrity, and can themselves be used to call other stored procedures.

Databases can be tuned to improve the performance of the individual applications that access them. This process often requires an in-depth knowledge of the database management system itself. Various parts of the system can be fine-tuned to maximize the performance of the database server. In addition, individual queries can be tuned through the use of indexes.

Workshop

The workshop provides quiz questions to help solidify your understanding of the material covered, as well as exercises to provide you with experience in using what you have learned. Try to answer the quiz and exercise questions before checking the answers in Appendix F, and make sure you understand the answers before continuing to the next chapter.

Quiz

1. Answer the following questions, true or false.

    Microsoft Visual C++ allows the programmer to call the ODBC API directly.

    The ODBC API can be called directly only from a C program.

    Dynamic SQL requires the use of a pre-compiler.

Exercises

1. Write down on a piece of paper a sample database application you can envision. (This chapter used a music collection to illustrate its points.) Break this application into logical data groupings.

2. After this sample application has been envisioned, write down the various queries you think will be required to complete this application.

3. Following this step, try to imagine the various rules you would like maintained in the database.

4. Create a database schema for the various groups of data you came up with in Step 1.

5. Convert the various queries you wrote down in Step 2 to stored procedures.

6. Convert the various rules you wrote down in Step 3 to triggers.

7. Combine Steps 4, 5, and 6 into a large script file that can be used to build the database and all its associated procedures.

8. Insert some sample data (this can also be a part of the script file in Step 7).

9. Execute the procedures you have created to test out their functionality.

14

Dynamic Uses
of SQL

Introduction

As you can see, the title of this book is *Teach Yourself SQL in 14 Days*. We still stand by this title although this is the fifteenth day. This is because, by now, you have taught yourself SQL. We have covered every major topic used to write powerful queries to retrieve data from a database. We also touched on database design and database security. The purpose of this chapter is to show you where to start to apply what you have learned so far. This chapter covers, in very broad strokes, practical applications of SQL. We focus on applications in the Microsoft Windows environment, but the principles involved are just as applicable to other software platforms. This chapter covers the following:

☐ Overviews of Personal Oracle7, ODBC (Open Database Connectivity), InterBase ISQL, Microsoft's Visual C++, and Borland's Delphi

☐ Setting up your environment for SQL

☐ Creating the database using Oracle7, Microsoft Query, and InterBase ISQL

☐ Using SQL inside applications written in Visual C++ and Delphi

After reading this chapter, you will know where to start applying your new SQL skills. This is your next step into a larger world.

A Quick Trip

In this section we look at several commercial products. The purpose of this section is to provide a general understanding of these products and how they relate to SQL. We look at these products in the context of the Microsoft Windows operating system, but, as we mentioned in the introduction, the principles, if not the products themselves, apply across various software platforms.

ODBC

One of the underlying technologies in the Windows operating system is Open Database Connectivity (ODBC). This enables Windows-based programs to access a database through a driver. Rather than having a custom interface to each database, something you might very well have to write yourself, you can connect to the database of your choice through a driver. This is very much like the concept of Windows' printer drivers, where you write your program without regard for the printer. Individual differences, which in DOS programming you were responsible for writing directly to various printers, are handled by the printer driver. The end result is that you spend your programming time on the tasks peculiar to your program, not writing your own printer drivers.

ODBC takes this same concept and applies it to databases. The visual part of ODBC resides in the Control Panel in Windows 3.1 and 3.11, as shown in Figure 15.1, and in its own program group in Windows NT.

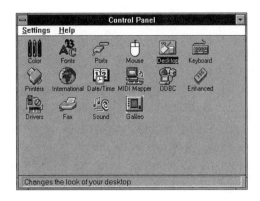

Figure 15.1.
ODBC in the midst of the Control Panel.

We cover ODBC in more detail in the next section.

Personal Oracle7

Personal Oracle7 is the popular database's latest incursion into the personal PC market. We used Oracle7 to do the SQL examples in the first several chapters. The Oracle7 installation leaves you with a number of programs.

Don't be put off by sheer numbers—you need to use only a few of these programs to perform basic SQL functions. We built all the examples used in the first several chapters using only the Oracle Database Manager and SQL*Plus 3.1. These are both shown in Figure 15.2.

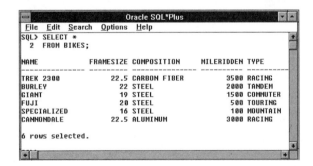

Figure 15.2.
*Oracle7's SQL*Plus.*

ISQL

The tool used in the other examples is Borland's ISQL. It is essentially the same as Oracle7, except that Oracle7 is character-oriented and ISQL is more Windows-like.

An ISQL screen is shown in Figure 15.3. You type your query in the top edit box, and the result appears in the lower box. The Previous and Next buttons scroll you through the list of all the queries you have made during your session.

Figure 15.3.
InterBase's Interactive SQL.

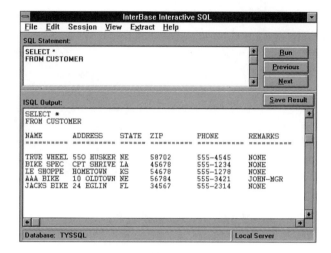

Visual C++

Dozens of books have been written about Visual C++. For the examples in this book, we used Version 1.52. The procedures we used are applicable to the 32-bit version, C++ 2.0. It is used here because of its simple interface with ODBC. It is not the only compiler with the capability to connect to ODBC. If you use a different compiler, this section provides a good point of departure.

Visual C++ installs quite a few tools. We use only two: the compiler and the resource editor.

Delphi

The last tool we examine is Borland's Delphi. The subject of the latest crop of books, Delphi is designed to provide a scalable interface to various databases.

Delphi has two programs that we use: the InterBase Server (Ibmgr) and the Windows ISQL (Wisql), which you have already seen.

Setting Up

Enough with the introductions—let's get to work. After you install your SQL engine or your ODBC-compatible compiler, you must do a certain amount of stage setting before the stars can do their stuff. With both Oracle7 and InterBase, you need to log on and create an account for yourself. The procedures are essentially the same. The hardest part we found was sorting through the hardcopy and on-line documentation for the default passwords. Both of these systems come with a default system administrator account. (See Figure 15.4.)

After logging in and creating an account, you are ready to create your database.

Figure 15.4.
*InterBase Security
manager screen.*

Creating the Database

This is where all your SQL training starts to pay off. First, you have to fire up the database you want to use. Oracle7 uses a stop light visual metaphor, shown in Figure 15.5.

Figure 15.5.
*Oracle7 Database
Manager.*

After you get the green light, you can open up the SQL*Plus 3.1 tool shown in Figure 15.6.

Figure 15.6.
*Oracle SQL*Plus.*

At this point, you can create your tables and enter your data using the CREATE and INSERT keywords you have learned. Another common way of doing this is with a script file. A script file is usually a text file with the SQL commands typed out in the proper order. Look at this excerpt from a script file delivered with Oracle7:

```
-----------------------------------------------------------
-- Script to build seed database for Personal Oracle
-----------------------------------------------------------
-- NTES
    Called from buildall.sql
-- MODIFICATIONS
--  rs  12/04/94 - Comment, clean up, resize, for production

-----------------------------------------------------------
startup nomount pfile=%rdbms71%\init.ora
--  Create database for Windows RDBMS
create database oracle
    controlfile reuse
    logfile '%oracle_home%\dbs\wdblog1.ora' size 400K reuse,
            '%oracle_home%\dbs\wdblog2.ora' size 400K reuse
    datafile '%oracle_home%\dbs\wdbsys.ora' size 10M reuse
    character set WE8ISO8859P1;
```

The details here are not important. The syntax varies slightly with the implementation of SQL and the database you are using. You load this script into your SQL engine through Open option in the File menu. (See Figure 15.7 for the Script Open dialog box.)

Figure 15.7.

Script Open dialog box from Oracle7.

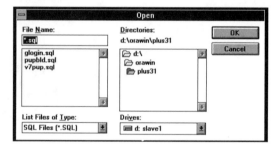

Borland's InterBase handles this in a similar way. This is an excerpt from one of those files:

```
/*
 *  Add countries.
 */
INSERT INTO country (country, currency) VALUES ('USA',         'Dollar');
INSERT INTO country (country, currency) VALUES ('England',     'Pound');
INSERT INTO country (country, currency) VALUES ('Canada',      'CdnDlr');
INSERT INTO country (country, currency) VALUES ('Switzerland', 'SFranc');
INSERT INTO country (country, currency) VALUES ('Japan',       'Yen');
INSERT INTO country (country, currency) VALUES ('Italy',       'Lira');
INSERT INTO country (country, currency) VALUES ('France',      'FFranc');
INSERT INTO country (country, currency) VALUES ('Germany',     'D-Mark');
INSERT INTO country (country, currency) VALUES ('Australia',   'ADollar');
INSERT INTO country (country, currency) VALUES ('Hong Kong',   'HKDollar');
INSERT INTO country (country, currency) VALUES ('Netherlands', 'Guilder');
INSERT INTO country (country, currency) VALUES ('Belgium',     'BFranc');
INSERT INTO country (country, currency) VALUES ('Austria',     'Schilling');
INSERT INTO country (country, currency) VALUES ('Fiji',        'fdollar');
```

There is nothing magic here. Over time, programmers always find ways of saving keystrokes. If you are playing along at home, enter the following tables:

```
/* Table: CUSTOMER, Owner: PERKINS */
CREATE TABLE CUSTOMER (NAME CHAR(10),
        ADDRESS CHAR(10),
        STATE CHAR(2),
        ZIP CHAR(10),
        PHONE CHAR(11),
        REMARKS CHAR(10));

/* Table: ORDERS, Owner: PERKINS */
CREATE TABLE ORDERS (ORDEREDON DATE,
        NAME CHAR(10),
        PARTNUM INTEGER,
        QUANTITY INTEGER,
        REMARKS CHAR(10));

/* Table: PART, Owner: PERKINS */
CREATE TABLE PART (PARTNUM INTEGER,
        DESCRIPTION CHAR(20),
        PRICE NUMERIC(9, 2));
```

Now fill these tables with the following data:

SELECT * FROM CUSTOMER

NAME	ADDRESS	STATE	ZIP	PHONE	REMARKS
TRUE WHEEL	550 HUSKER	NE	58702	555-4545	NONE
BIKE SPEC	CPT SHRIVE	LA	45678	555-1234	NONE
LE SHOPPE	HOMETOWN	KS	54678	555-1278	NONE
AAA BIKE	10 OLDTOWN	NE	56784	555-3421	JOHN-MGR
JACKS BIKE	24 EGLIN	FL	34567	555-2314	NONE

SELECT * FROM ORDERS

ORDEREDON	NAME	PARTNUM	QUANTITY	REMARKS
15-MAY-1996	TRUE WHEEL	23	6	PAID
19-MAY-1996	TRUE WHEEL	76	3	PAID
2-SEP-1996	TRUE WHEEL	10	1	PAID
30-JUN-1996	TRUE WHEEL	42	8	PAID
30-JUN-1996	BIKE SPEC	54	10	PAID
30-MAY-1996	BIKE SPEC	10	2	PAID
30-MAY-1996	BIKE SPEC	23	8	PAID
17-JAN-1996	BIKE SPEC	76	11	PAID
17-JAN-1996	LE SHOPPE	76	5	PAID
1-JUN-1996	LE SHOPPE	10	3	PAID
1-JUN-1996	AAA BIKE	10	1	PAID
1-JUL-1996	AAA BIKE	76	4	PAID
1-JUL-1996	AAA BIKE	46	14	PAID
11-JUL-1996	JACKS BIKE	76	14	PAID

SELECT * FROM PART

PARTNUM	DESCRIPTION	PRICE
54	PEDALS	54.25

```
42 SEATS                       24.50
46 TIRES                       15.25
23 MOUNTAIN BIKE              350.45
76 ROAD BIKE                  530.00
10 TANDEM                    1200.00
```

Once you have entered this data, the next step is to create an ODBC connection. To do this, open the control panel (if you are in Win 3.1 or 3.11) and double-click the ODBC icon.

Note: Several flavors of SQL engines load ODBC. Visual C++, Delphi, and Oracle7 load ODBC as part of their setup. Fortunately, ODBC is becoming as common as printer drivers.

The initial ODBC screen comes up, as shown in Figure 15.8.

Figure 15.8.

ODBC's Data Sources selection.

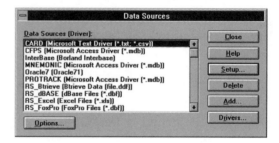

This screen shows the current ODBC connections. You want to create a new connection. Assuming you used InterBase and called the new database TYSSQL (give yourself 10 bonus points if you know what TYSSQL stands for), press the Add button and select the InterBase Driver. This is shown in Figure 15.9.

From this selection you move to the setup screen. Fill it in as shown in Figure 15.10.

Of course you can use your own name, depending on the account you set up for yourself. The only tricky bit here, at least for us, was figuring out what InterBase wanted as a database name. Those of you coming from a PC or small database background will have to get used to some odd-looking pathnames. These pathnames tell the SQL engine where to look for the database in the galaxy of computers that could be connected via LANs.

Figure 15.9.
Driver selection.

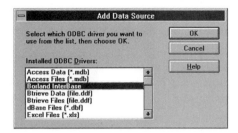

Figure 15.10.
Driver setup.

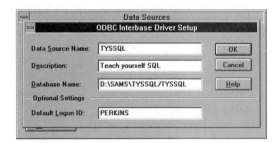

Using Microsoft Query to Perform a Join

Now that you have made an ODBC connection, we need to make a slight detour to a rather useful tool called Microsoft Query. This program is loaded along with Visual C++. We have used it to solve enough database and coding problems to pay for the cost of the compiler several times over. Query normally installs itself in its own program group. Find it and open it. It should look like Figure 15.11.

Figure 15.11.
Microsoft Query.

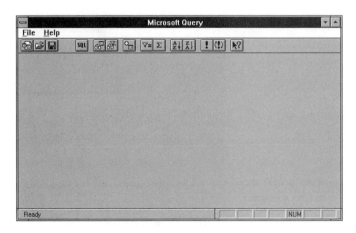

Select File/New Query. Your TYSSQL ODBC link does not appear, so press the Other button to bring up the Data Sources dialog box, shown in Figure 15.12, and select TYSSQL.

Figure 15.12.
Data Sources dialog box.

Press OK, which returns you to the Select Data Source dialog box. Select TYSSQL and press Use, as shown in Figure 15.13.

Figure 15.13.
Select Data Source dialog box.

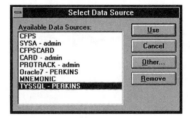

Again, small database users aren't used to logging in, but you get used to it. Type your password to move though the screen shown in Figure 15.14.

Figure 15.14.
Logging in to an InterBase database.

This next screen, shown in Figure 15.15, presents you with the tables associated with the database you have connected to. Select PART, ORDERS, and CUSTOMER, and press Close.

Your screen should look like Figure 15.16. Double-click ADDRESS and NAME from the CUSTOMER table. Then double-click ORDEREDON and PARTNUM from ORDERS.

Now for some magic! Press the button marked SQL. Your screen should now look like Figure 15.17.

Figure 15.15.
Table selection in Query.

15

Figure 15.16.
Visual representation of a table in Query.

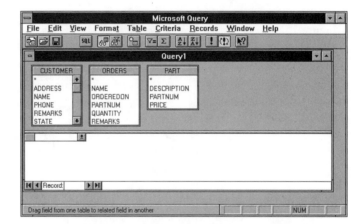

Figure 15.17.
The query that Query built.

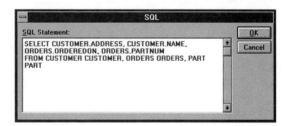

What's this? This program created the query that generated the table. This is one of the two things you use this tool for. The first is to check the ODBC connection. If it works here, it should work in the program. This can help you determine whether a problem is in the database or in the program. The other thing you use Query for is to generate and check queries. Add this line:

```
WHERE CUSTOMER.NAME = ORDERS.NAME AND PART.PARTNUM = ORDERS.PARTNUM
```

in the SQL box and press OK. Figure 15.18 shows the remarkable result.

You have just performed a join! Not only that, but the fields you joined on have been graphically connected in the table diagrams (note the zigzag lines between NAME and PARTNUM).

Query is an important tool to have in your SQL arsenal on the Windows software platform. It lets you examine and manipulate tables and queries. You can also use it to create tables and manipulate data. If you work in Windows with ODBC and SQL, get this tool, or have your company or client buy it for you. It is not as interesting as a network version of DOOM, but it will save you time and money. Now that you have established an ODBC link, let's use it in a program.

Figure 15.18.

Graphic representation in Query of a join.

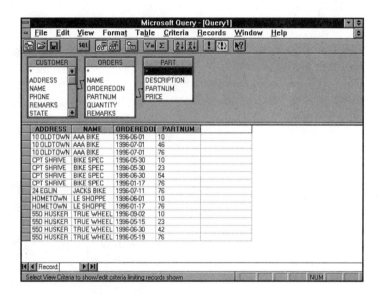

Using Visual C++ and SQL

Let's get right to work. Call up Visual C++ and select AppWizard, as shown in Figure 15.19. The name and subdirectory for your project do not have to be identical.

> **Note:** The source code for this example is located in Appendix B.

Press the Options button and fill out the screen, as shown in Figure 15.20.

Press OK, then choose Database Options. Make the choices shown in Figure 15.21.

This last choice brings up a Data Source button. Press it, and make the choices shown in Figure 15.22.

Figure 15.19.
Initial project setup.

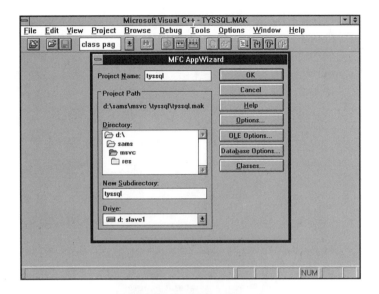

Figure 15.20.
The Options dialog box.

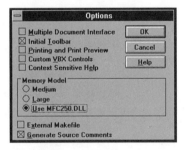

Figure 15.21.
The Database Options dialog box.

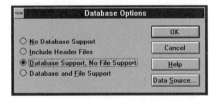

Figure 15.22.
Data source selection.

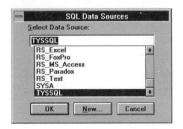

Then select the CUSTOMER table from the Select a Table dialog box, shown in Figure 15.23.

Figure 15.23.
Table selection.

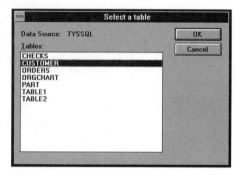

Now you have selected the CUSTOMER table from the TYSSQL database. Go back to the AppWizard basic screen by pressing OK twice. Once there, pressing OK again brings you to Figure 15.24, showing what the program generates for you.

Figure 15.24.
AppWizard's new application information.

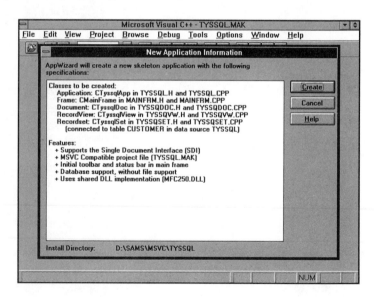

After the program is generated, you need to use the resource editor to design your main screen. Select App Studio from the Tools menu. This launches App Studio. The form you design will be simple—just enough to show some of the columns in your table as you scroll through the rows. Your finished form should look something like Figure 15.25.

Figure 15.25.
Finished form in App Studio.

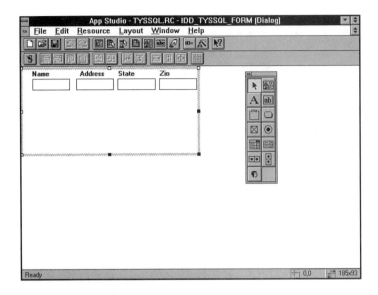

For simplicity we named the Edit Boxes IDC_NAME, IDC_ADDRESS, IDC_STATE, and IDC_ZIP. It really doesn't matter what you name them. Press Ctrl+W to launch the Class Wizard page to the Member Variables, and set them up according to Figure 15.26.

Figure 15.26.
Adding member variables in Class Wizard.

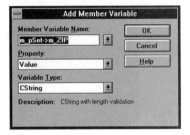

> **Note:** Note that the program was nice enough to provide links to the table you are connected to. This is one of the benefits of working through Microsoft's Wizards or Borland's Experts.

Save your work: Press Alt+Tab to get back to the compiler and compile the program. If all went well, your output should look like Figure 15.27. If it doesn't, retrace your steps and try again.

Now run your program. It should appear, after that pesky login screen, and look like Figure 15.28.

This is an impressive program, considering you have written zero lines of code so far. Use the arrow keys on the toolbar to move back and forth in the database. Notice that the order of the data is the same as its input order. It is not alphabetical (unless you typed it in that way). How can you change this?

Figure 15.27.

A clean compile for the test program.

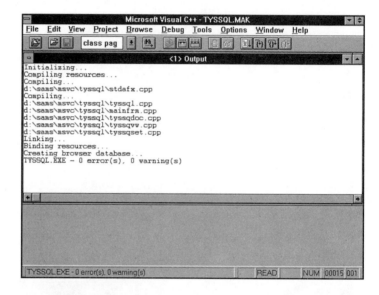

Figure 15.28.

The test program.

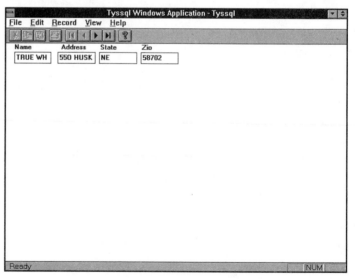

Your connection to the database is encapsulated in a class called Ctyssqlset, which the AppWizard created for you. Look at the header file (tyssqlset.h):

```
// tyssqset.h : interface of the CTyssqlSet class
//
////////////////////////////////////////////////////////////////////////////
class CTyssqlSet : public CRecordset
{
DECLARE_DYNAMIC(CTyssqlSet)
public:
CTyssqlSet(CDatabase* pDatabase = NULL);
// Field/Param Data
//{{AFX_FIELD(CTyssqlSet, CRecordset)
Cstring     m_NAME;
Cstring     m_ADDRESS;
Cstring     m_STATE;
Cstring     m_ZIP;
Cstring     m_PHONE;
Cstring     m_REMARKS;
//}}AFX_FIELD
// Implementation
protected:
virtual CString GetDefaultConnect();// Default connection string
virtual CString GetDefaultSQL();// default SQL for Recordset
virtual void DoFieldExchange(CFieldExchange* pFX);// RFX support
};
```

There are a couple of notable things here. First, member variables have been constructed for all the columns in the table. Second, there are two interesting functions: GetDefaultConnect and GetDefaultSQL. Look at their implementations from tyssqlset.cpp:

```
CString CTyssqlSet::GetDefaultConnect()
{
return "ODBC;DSN=TYSSQL;";
}
CString CTyssqlSet::GetDefaultSQL()
{
return "CUSTOMER";
}
```

GetDefaultConnect is used to make the ODBC connection. You shouldn't change it. However, the second function, GetDefaultSQL, enables you to do some interesting things. Change it to this:

```
return "SELECT * FROM CUSTOMER ORDER BY NAME";
```

Recompile and, like magic, your table is sorted by name, as shown in Figure 15.29.

Without going into a tutorial on the Microsoft Foundation Class (MFC), let us just say that you can manipulate CRecordSet and Cdatabase objects, join and drop tables, update and insert rows, and generally have all the fun possible in SQL. You have looked as far over the edge as you can, and we have pointed the way to integrate SQL into C++ applications. Topics suggested for further study are CRecordSet and Cdatabase (both in the C++ books on-line), ODBC API (the subject of several books), and the APIs provided by Oracle and Sybase (which are both similar to the ODBC API).

Figure 15.29.

Database order changed by SQL.

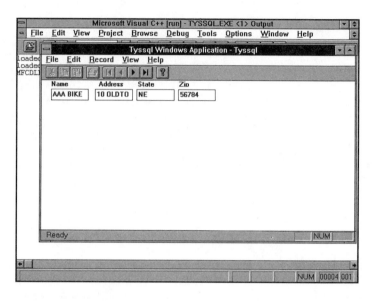

Using Delphi and SQL

Another important database tool on the Windows software platform is Delphi. The splash that comes up as the program is loading has a picture of the Oracle at Delphi, with the letters *SQL* wrapped around them. In the previous example, using C++, you rewrote one line of code. Using Delphi, you will join two tables without writing a single line of code! Let's get started.

Note: The code for this program is located in Appendix C.

Double-click Delphi's icon to get it started. At rest, it looks like Figure 15.30.

Delphi requires that you register any ODBC connections you are going to use in your programming. Select BDE (Borland Database Environment) from the Tools menu, and then fill out the dialog box shown in Figure 15.31.

Figure 15.30.
The Delphi program-ming environment.

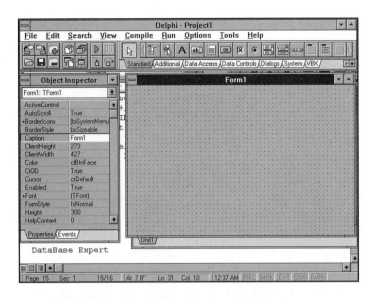

Figure 15.31.
Registering your connections.

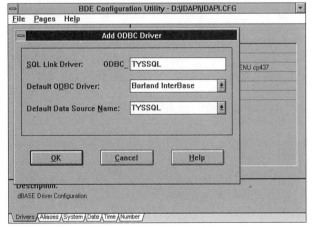

Flip over the Aliases property page and assign the name TYSSQL, as shown in Figure 15.32.

Select File/New Form to make the following selections. First, choose the Database Form from the Experts tab page, shown in Figure 15.33.

Figure 15.32.
Adding a new alias.

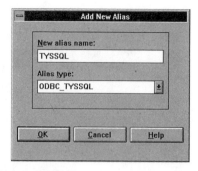

Figure 15.33.
The Experts page in the Browse gallery.

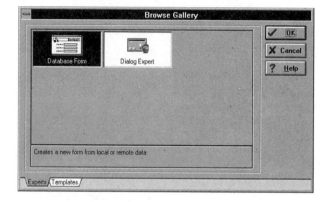

Then choose the master/detail form and TQuery objects, as shown in Figure 15.34.

> **Note:** Delphi enables you to work with either a query or a table. If you need flexibility, we recommend the TQuery object. If you need the whole table without modification, use the TTable object.

Now select the TYSSQL data source you set up earlier, as shown in Figure 15.35.

Choose the PART table as the master, as shown in Figure 15.36.

Choose all its fields, as shown in Figure 15.37.

Pick the Horizontal display mode, as shown in Figure 15.38.

Figure 15.34.
The Database Form Expert dialog box.

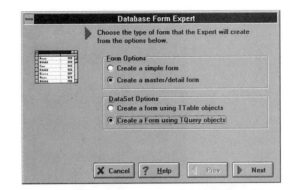

Figure 15.35.
Choosing a data source.

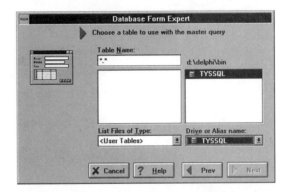

Figure 15.36.
Choosing a table.

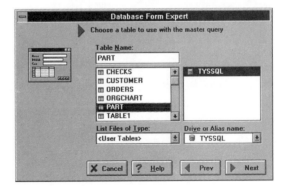

Dynamic Uses of SQL

Figure 15.37.
Adding all the fields.

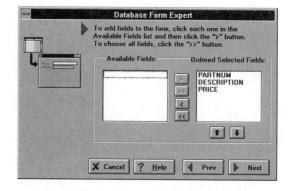

Figure 15.38.
Display mode selection.

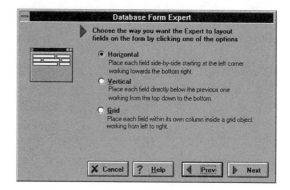

Then choose ORDERS, select all its fields, and select Grid for its display mode, as shown in Figures 15.39, 15.40, and 15.41.

Figure 15.39.
Choosing the table for the detail part of the form.

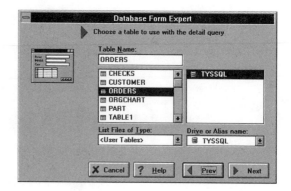

Figure 15.40.
Selecting all the fields.

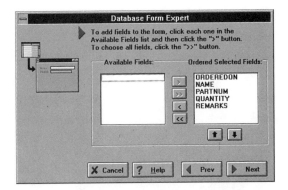

Figure 15.41.
Selecting the orientation.

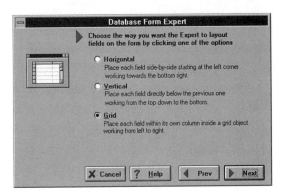

Now the software enables you to make a join. Let's join on PARTNUM, as shown in Figure 15.42.

Figure 15.42.
Making the join.

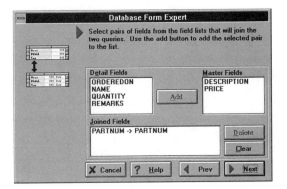

Now go ahead and generate the form. Your end result looks like Figure 15.43.

Figure 15.43.
The finished form.

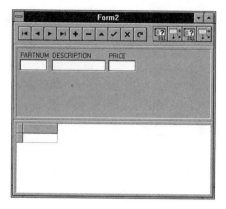

Compile and run the program. As you select different parts, the order for them should appear in the lower table, as shown in Figure 15.44.

Figure 15.44.
The finished program.

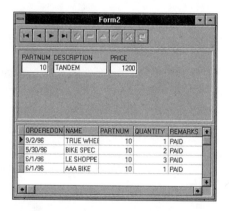

Close the project and click one or both of the query objects on the form. When you click an object, the Object Inspector to the left of the screen in Figure 15.45 shows the various properties.

Clicking the SQL property on the Object Inspector raises the dialog box shown in Figure 15.45. Try playing with the query to see what happens. Just think what you might do if you started writing code!

Figure 15.45.
The query in the TQuery object.

Summary

Finally, you have reached the end of your trip through SQL. You have covered a lot of ground. In this chapter we showed you where to start applying SQL using ordinary, everyday stuff you find lying about your hard drive. The best way to build on what you have learned is to go out and query. Query as much as you can. If you aren't using SQL now, chances are you will be using it soon. Good luck!

Q&A

Q What is the difference between the ODBC API and the APIs provided by Oracle and Sybase?

A On a function-by-function level, they are remarkably similar. This is not a coincidence. Different corporate teamings and divorces have led to libraries that were derived from somewhat of a common base. ODBC's API is more general because it is not specific to any database. If you need to do something specific to a database or tune the performance of a specific database, you might consider using its own API library in your code.

Workshop

The workshop provides quiz questions to help solidify your understanding of the material covered, as well as exercises to provide you with experience in using what you have learned. Try to answer the quiz and exercise questions before checking the answers in Appendix F, and make sure you understand the answers before continuing to the next chapter.

Quiz

1. In which object does Microsoft Visual C++ place its SQL?
2. In which object does Delphi place its SQL?

Exercises

1. Change the sort order on the C++ example from ascending to descending on the State field.
2. Go out, find an application that needs SQL, and use it.

Week 1 spent a great deal of time introducing a very important topic: The SELECT Query. Week 2 branched out into a variety of topics, all of which combine to form a thorough introduction to the Structured Query Language.

On Day 8, data manipulation language (DML) statements were introduced. These are SQL statements that can be used to modify the data within a database. The three commands most used are the following: INSERT, DELETE, and UP-DATE. On Day 9, we discussed how to actually design and build a database. The commands used to do this are CREATE DATABASE and CREATE TABLE. A table can be created with any number of fields, each of which can be a database-vendor defined datatype. You can use the ALTER DATA-BASE command to change the physical size or location of a database. To remove a database or a table within a database, use the DROP DATABASE and DROP TABLE statements.

On Day 10, we discussed two concepts that can be used to present a different view of data to the user than what physically exists on the disk. The view is a virtual table created from the output of a SELECT statement. Indexes are used to order the records within a table based on the contents of a field or fields.

Following this introduction to database design, on Day 11 we discussed transaction management. This was our first introduction to actually programming with SQL. Transactions are started with the BEGIN TRANSACTION statement. To save the work of a transaction, use the COMMIT TRANSACTION statement. Issuing the ROLLBACK TRANSACTION command cancels the work of a transaction.

Day 12 focused on database security. Although the implementation of database security varies widely among database products, several commands are commonly found. The GRANT command grants permissions to a user. The REVOKE command can be used to remove these permissions.

The final two days, Days 13 and 14, focused on developing application programs using SQL. This can be done using several techniques. Static SQL typically involves the use of a precompiler and is static at run-time. Dynamic SQL has become very popular over the last few years because of its flexibility. Sample programs were given using Dynamic SQL in combination with the Visual C++ and Delphi development toolkits.

On Day 15, we discussed advanced usages of SQL. Cursors can be used to scroll through a set of records. Stored Procedures are database objects used to execute several SQL statements in a row. Typically, stored procedures can accept and return values. Triggers are a special type of stored procedure that are executed when records are inserted, updated, or deleted within a table.

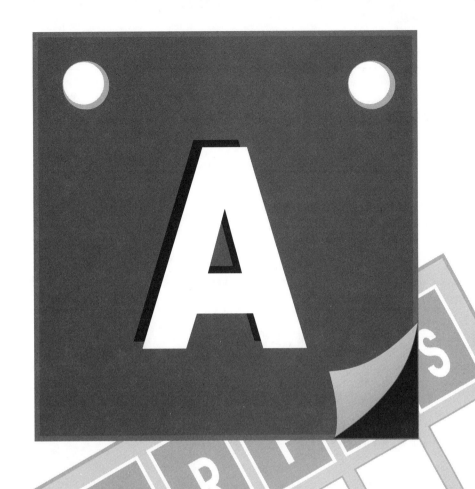

Glossary of Common SQL Statements

ALTER DATABASE

```
ALTER DATABASE database_name;
```

The ALTER DATABASE command is used to change the size or settings of a database. Its syntax varies widely among different database systems.

ALTER USER

```
ALTER USER user
```

The ALTER USER statement is provided to change a user's system settings such as passwords.

BEGIN TRANSACTION

The BEGIN TRANSACTION statement signifies the beginning of a user transaction. A transaction ends when it is either committed (see COMMIT TRANSACTION) or canceled (see ROLLBACK TRANSACTION). A transaction is a logical unit of work.

CLOSE CURSOR

```
close cursor_name
```

The CLOSE cursor_name statement closes the cursor and clears it of data. To completely remove the cursor, use the DEALLOCATE CURSOR statement.

COMMIT TRANSACTION

The COMMIT TRANSACTION statement saves all work begun since the beginning of the transaction (since the BEGIN TRANSACTION statement was executed).

CREATE DATABASE

CREATE DATABASE database_name is used to create a new database. Many different options can be supplied, such as what device to create the database on and what size the initial database should be

CREATE INDEX

```
CREATE INDEX index_name
ON table_name(column_name1, [column_name2], ...);
```

An index can be created to order the contents of a table based on the contents of the indexed field(s).

CREATE PROCEDURE

```
create procedure procedure_name
   [[(]@parameter_name
     datatype [(length) ¦ (precision [, scale])
     [= default][output]
   [, @parameter_name
     datatype [(length) ¦ (precision [, scale])
     [= default][output]]...[)]]
   [with recompile]
   as SQL_statements
```

The CREATE PROCEDURE statement creates a new stored procedure in the database. This stored procedure can consist of SQL statements and can then be executed using the EXECUTE command. Stored procedures support passing input and output parameters, and can return an integer value for status checking.

CREATE TABLE

```
CREATE TABLE table_name
(   field1 datatype [ NOT NULL ],
    field2 datatype [ NOT NULL ],
    field3 datatype [ NOT NULL ]...)
```

This statement is used to create a new table within a database. Each optional field is provided with a name and datatype for creation within that table.

CREATE TRIGGER

```
create trigger trigger_name
   on table_name
   for {insert, update, delete}
   as SQL_Statements
```

The CREATE TRIGGER statement creates a trigger object in the database that will execute its SQL statements when its corresponding table is modified through an INSERT, UPDATE, or DELETE. Triggers can also call stored procedures to execute complex tasks.

CREATE USER

```
CREATE USER user
```

The CREATE USER statement is used to create a new user account complete with user_id and password.

CREATE VIEW

```
CREATE VIEW <view_name> [(column1, column2...)] AS
SELECT <table_name column_names>
FROM <table_name>
```

A view is often described as a virtual table. Views are created from the output of a select statement. Once these views are created, they can be queried, and data within the view can be modified under certain conditions.

DEALLOCATE CURSOR

```
deallocate cursor cursor_name
```

The DEALLOCATE CURSOR statement completely removes the cursor from memory and frees the name for use by another cursor. The cursor should be closed using the CLOSE CURSOR statement before deallocating it.

DECLARE CURSOR

```
declare cursor_name cursor
    for select_statement
```

The DECLARE CURSOR statement creates a new cursor from the select_statement query. The FETCH statement is used to scroll the cursor through the data until the end of the data has been reached.

DROP DATABASE

```
DROP DATABASE database_name;
```

The DROP DATABASE statement completely deletes a database, including all data and the database's physical structure on disk.

DROP INDEX

```
DROP INDEX index_name;
```

The DROP INDEX statement removes an index from a table.

DROP PROCEDURE

```
drop procedure procedure_name
```

This statement drops a stored procedure from the database similar to the function of the DROP TABLE and DROP INDEX statements.

DROP TABLE

```
DROP TABLE table_name;
```

The DROP TABLE statement drops a table from a database.

DROP TRIGGER

```
DROP TRIGGER trigger_name
```

The DROP TRIGGER statement removes a trigger from a database.

DROP VIEW

```
DROP VIEW view_name;
```

The DROP VIEW statement removes a view from a database.

EXECUTE

```
execute [@return_status = ]
   procedure_name
   [[@parameter_name =] value ¦
     [@parameter_name =] @variable [output]...]]
```

The EXECUTE command runs a stored procedure and its associated SQL statements. Parameters can be passed to the stored procedure, and data can be returned in these parameters if the output keyword is used.

FETCH

```
fetch cursor_name [into fetch_target_list]
```

The FETCH command loads the contents of the cursor's data into the provided program variables. After the variables have been loaded, the cursor scrolls to the next record.

FROM

```
FROM <tableref> [, <tableref> ...]
```

This specifies which TABLES are used and/or JOINed.

GRANT

```
GRANT role TO user
```

or

```
GRANT system_privilege TO {user_name ¦ role ¦ PUBLIC}
```

The GRANT command is used to grant a privilege or role to a user who has been created using the CREATE USER command.

GROUP BY

```
GROUP BY <col> [, <col> ...]
```

This groups all the rows with the same column value.

HAVING

```
HAVING <search_cond>
```

This is valid only with GROUP BY and limits the selection of groups to those satisfying the search condition.

INTERSECT

```
INTERSECT
```

Returns all the common elements of two select statements.

ORDER BY

```
ORDER BY <order_list>
```

This orders the returned values by the specified column(s).

ROLLBACK TRANSACTION

The ROLLBACK TRANSACTION statement effectively cancels all work done within a transaction (since the BEGIN TRANSACTION statement was executed).

REVOKE

```
REVOKE role FROM user;
```

or

```
REVOKE {object_priv ¦ ALL [PRIVILEGES]}
[, {object_priv ¦ ALL [PRIVILEGES]} ] ...
ON [schema.]object
FROM {user ¦ role ¦ PUBLIC} [, {user ¦ role ¦ PUBLIC}] ...
```

The REVOKE command removes a database privilege from a user whether it be a system privilege or a role.

SELECT

```
SELECT [DISTINCT ¦ ALL]
```

This is the beginning of each data retrieval statement. The modifier DISTINCT specifies unique values and prevents duplicates. ALL is the default and allows duplicates.

UNION

```
UNION
```

This returns all the elements of two select statements.

WHERE

```
WHERE <search_cond>
```

This limits the rows retrieved to those meeting the search condition.

Source Code Listings for the C++ Program Used on Day 15

```cpp
// tyssqvw.h : interface of the CTyssqlView class
//
///////////////////////////////////////////////////////////////////////

class CTyssqlSet;

class CTyssqlView : public CRecordView
{
protected: // create from serialization only
    CTyssqlView();
    DECLARE_DYNCREATE(CTyssqlView)

public:
    //{{AFX_DATA(CTyssqlView)
    enum { IDD = IDD_TYSSQL_FORM };
    CTyssqlSet* m_pSet;
    //}}AFX_DATA

// Attributes
public:
    CTyssqlDoc* GetDocument();

// Operations
public:
    virtual CRecordset* OnGetRecordset();

// Implementation
public:
    virtual ~CTyssqlView();
#ifdef _DEBUG
    virtual void AssertValid() const;
    virtual void Dump(CDumpContext& dc) const;
#endif

protected:
    virtual void DoDataExchange(CDataExchange* pDX);// DDX/DDV support
    virtual void OnInitialUpdate(); // called first time after construct

// Generated message map functions
protected:
    //{{AFX_MSG(CTyssqlView)
        // NOTE - the ClassWizard will add and remove member functions here.
        //      DO NOT EDIT what you see in these blocks of generated code !
    //}}AFX_MSG
    DECLARE_MESSAGE_MAP()
};

#ifndef _DEBUG  // debug version in tyssqvw.cpp
inline CTyssqlDoc* CTyssqlView::GetDocument()
   { return (CTyssqlDoc*)m_pDocument; }
#endif


///////////////////////////////////////////////////////////////////////

// tyssql.h : main header file for the TYSSQL application
```

```
//

#ifndef __AFXWIN_H__
    #error include 'stdafx.h' before including this file for PCH
#endif

#include "resource.h"        // main symbols

/////////////////////////////////////////////////////////////////////////////
// CTyssqlApp:
// See tyssql.cpp for the implementation of this class
//

class CTyssqlApp : public CWinApp
{
public:
    CTyssqlApp();

// Overrides
    virtual BOOL InitInstance();

// Implementation

    //{{AFX_MSG(CTyssqlApp)
    afx_msg void OnAppAbout();
        // NOTE - the ClassWizard will add and remove member functions here.
        //     DO NOT EDIT what you see in these blocks of generated code !
    //}}AFX_MSG
    DECLARE_MESSAGE_MAP()
};


/////////////////////////////////////////////////////////////////////////////
// tyssqset.h : interface of the CTyssqlSet class
//
/////////////////////////////////////////////////////////////////////////////

class CTyssqlSet : public CRecordset
{
DECLARE_DYNAMIC(CTyssqlSet)

public:
    CTyssqlSet(CDatabase* pDatabase = NULL);

// Field/Param Data
    //{{AFX_FIELD(CTyssqlSet, CRecordset)
    CString     m_NAME;
    CString     m_ADDRESS;
    CString     m_STATE;
    CString     m_ZIP;
    CString     m_PHONE;
    CString     m_REMARKS;
    //}}AFX_FIELD

// Implementation
```

```cpp
protected:
    virtual CString GetDefaultConnect();     // Default connection string
    virtual CString GetDefaultSQL();      // default SQL for Recordset
    virtual void DoFieldExchange(CFieldExchange* pFX);    // RFX support
};

// tyssqdoc.h : interface of the CTyssqlDoc class
//
/////////////////////////////////////////////////////////////////////////////

class CTyssqlDoc : public CDocument
{
protected: // create from serialization only
    CTyssqlDoc();
    DECLARE_DYNCREATE(CTyssqlDoc)

// Attributes
public:
    CTyssqlSet m_tyssqlSet;

// Operations
public:

// Implementation
public:
    virtual ~CTyssqlDoc();
#ifdef _DEBUG
    virtual void AssertValid() const;
    virtual void Dump(CDumpContext& dc) const;
#endif

protected:
    virtual BOOL OnNewDocument();

// Generated message map functions
protected:
    //{{AFX_MSG(CTyssqlDoc)
        // NOTE - the ClassWizard will add and remove member functions here.
        //    DO NOT EDIT what you see in these blocks of generated code !
    //}}AFX_MSG
    DECLARE_MESSAGE_MAP()
};

/////////////////////////////////////////////////////////////////////////////
// stdafx.h : include file for standard system include files,
//   or project specific include files that are used frequently, but
//      are changed infrequently
//

#include <afxwin.h>          // MFC core and standard components
#include <afxext.h>          // MFC extensions (including VB)
#include <afxdb.h>           // MFC database classes


///////////////////////////////////////////////////////////////////

//{{NO_DEPENDENCIES}}
```

```
// App Studio generated include file.
// Used by TYSSQL.RC
//
#define IDR_MAINFRAME                   2
#define IDD_ABOUTBOX                    100
#define IDD_TYSSQL_FORM                 101
#define IDP_FAILED_OPEN_DATABASE        103
#define IDC_NAME                        1000
#define IDC_ADDRESS                     1001
#define IDC_STATE                       1002
#define IDC_ZIP                         1003

// Next default values for new objects
//
#ifdef APSTUDIO_INVOKED
#ifndef APSTUDIO_READONLY_SYMBOLS

#define _APS_NEXT_RESOURCE_VALUE        102
#define _APS_NEXT_COMMAND_VALUE         32771
#define _APS_NEXT_CONTROL_VALUE         1004
#define _APS_NEXT_SYMED_VALUE           101
#endif
#endif


/////////////////////////////////////////////////////

// mainfrm.h : interface of the CMainFrame class
//
/////////////////////////////////////////////////////////////////////////////

class CMainFrame : public CFrameWnd
{
protected: // create from serialization only
    CMainFrame();
    DECLARE_DYNCREATE(CMainFrame)

// Attributes
public:

// Operations
public:

// Implementation
public:
    virtual ~CMainFrame();
#ifdef _DEBUG
    virtual void AssertValid() const;
    virtual void Dump(CDumpContext& dc) const;
#endif

protected:  // control bar embedded members
    CStatusBar   m_wndStatusBar;
    CToolBar     m_wndToolBar;

// Generated message map functions
protected:
```

```
    //{{AFX_MSG(CMainFrame)
    afx_msg int OnCreate(LPCREATESTRUCT lpCreateStruct);
        // NOTE - the ClassWizard will add and remove member functions here.
        //    DO NOT EDIT what you see in these blocks of generated code!
    //}}AFX_MSG
    DECLARE_MESSAGE_MAP()
};

/////////////////////////////////////////////////////////////////////////////

// tyssqvw.cpp : implementation of the CTyssqlView class
//

#include "stdafx.h"
#include "tyssql.h"

#include "tyssqset.h"
#include "tyssqdoc.h"
#include "tyssqvw.h"

#ifdef _DEBUG
#undef THIS_FILE
static char BASED_CODE THIS_FILE[] = __FILE__;
#endif

/////////////////////////////////////////////////////////////////////////////

// CTyssqlView

IMPLEMENT_DYNCREATE(CTyssqlView, CRecordView)

BEGIN_MESSAGE_MAP(CTyssqlView, CRecordView)
    //{{AFX_MSG_MAP(CTyssqlView)
        // NOTE - the ClassWizard will add and remove mapping macros here.
        //    DO NOT EDIT what you see in these blocks of generated code!
    //}}AFX_MSG_MAP
END_MESSAGE_MAP()

/////////////////////////////////////////////////////////////////////////////
// CTyssqlView construction/destruction

CTyssqlView::CTyssqlView()
    : CRecordView(CTyssqlView::IDD)
{
    //{{AFX_DATA_INIT(CTyssqlView)
    m_pSet = NULL;
    //}}AFX_DATA_INIT
    // TODO: add construction code here
}

CTyssqlView::~CTyssqlView()
{
}

void CTyssqlView::DoDataExchange(CDataExchange* pDX)
```

```
{
    CRecordView::DoDataExchange(pDX);
    //{{AFX_DATA_MAP(CTyssqlView)
    DDX_FieldText(pDX, IDC_ADDRESS, m_pSet->m_ADDRESS, m_pSet);
    DDX_FieldText(pDX, IDC_NAME, m_pSet->m_NAME, m_pSet);
    DDX_FieldText(pDX, IDC_STATE, m_pSet->m_STATE, m_pSet);
    DDX_FieldText(pDX, IDC_ZIP, m_pSet->m_ZIP, m_pSet);
    //}}AFX_DATA_MAP
}

void CTyssqlView::OnInitialUpdate()
{
    m_pSet = &GetDocument()->m_tyssqlSet;
    CRecordView::OnInitialUpdate();

}

/////////////////////////////////////////////////////////////////////////////
// CTyssqlView diagnostics

#ifdef _DEBUG
void CTyssqlView::AssertValid() const
{
    CRecordView::AssertValid();
}

void CTyssqlView::Dump(CDumpContext& dc) const
{
    CRecordView::Dump(dc);
}

CTyssqlDoc* CTyssqlView::GetDocument() // non-debug version is inline
{
    ASSERT(m_pDocument->IsKindOf(RUNTIME_CLASS(CTyssqlDoc)));
    return (CTyssqlDoc*)m_pDocument;
}
#endif //_DEBUG

/////////////////////////////////////////////////////////////////////////////
// CTyssqlView database support

CRecordset* CTyssqlView::OnGetRecordset()
{
    return m_pSet;
}


/////////////////////////////////////////////////////////////////////////////
// CTyssqlView message handlers


// tyssqset.cpp : implementation of the CTyssqlSet class
//

#include "stdafx.h"
```

```cpp
#include "tyssql.h"
#include "tyssqset.h"

//////////////////////////////////////////////////////////////////////////
// CTyssqlSet implementation

IMPLEMENT_DYNAMIC(CTyssqlSet, CRecordset)

CTyssqlSet::CTyssqlSet(CDatabase* pdb)
    : CRecordset(pdb)
{
    //{{AFX_FIELD_INIT(CTyssqlSet)
    m_NAME = "";
    m_ADDRESS = "";
    m_STATE = "";
    m_ZIP = "";
    m_PHONE = "";
    m_REMARKS = "";
    m_nFields = 6;
    //}}AFX_FIELD_INIT
}

CString CTyssqlSet::GetDefaultConnect()
{
    return "ODBC;DSN=TYSSQL;";
}

CString CTyssqlSet::GetDefaultSQL()
{
    return "SELECT * FROM CUSTOMER ORDER BY NAME";
}

void CTyssqlSet::DoFieldExchange(CFieldExchange* pFX)
{
    //{{AFX_FIELD_MAP(CTyssqlSet)
    pFX->SetFieldType(CFieldExchange::outputColumn);
    RFX_Text(pFX, "NAME", m_NAME);
    RFX_Text(pFX, "ADDRESS", m_ADDRESS);
    RFX_Text(pFX, "STATE", m_STATE);
    RFX_Text(pFX, "ZIP", m_ZIP);
    RFX_Text(pFX, "PHONE", m_PHONE);
    RFX_Text(pFX, "REMARKS", m_REMARKS);
    //}}AFX_FIELD_MAP
}

// tyssql.cpp : Defines the class behaviors for the application.
//

#include "stdafx.h"
#include "tyssql.h"

#include "mainfrm.h"
#include "tyssqset.h"
#include "tyssqdoc.h"
#include "tyssqvw.h"
```

```
#ifdef _DEBUG
#undef THIS_FILE
static char BASED_CODE THIS_FILE[] = __FILE__;
#endif

/////////////////////////////////////////////////////////////////////////
// CTyssqlApp

BEGIN_MESSAGE_MAP(CTyssqlApp, CWinApp)
    //{{AFX_MSG_MAP(CTyssqlApp)
    ON_COMMAND(ID_APP_ABOUT, OnAppAbout)
        // NOTE - the ClassWizard will add and remove mapping macros here.
        //    DO NOT EDIT what you see in these blocks of generated code!
    //}}AFX_MSG_MAP
END_MESSAGE_MAP()

/////////////////////////////////////////////////////////////////////////
// CTyssqlApp construction

CTyssqlApp::CTyssqlApp()
{
    // TODO: add construction code here,
    // Place all significant initialization in InitInstance
}

/////////////////////////////////////////////////////////////////////////
// The one and only CTyssqlApp object

CTyssqlApp NEAR theApp;

/////////////////////////////////////////////////////////////////////////
// CTyssqlApp initialization

BOOL CTyssqlApp::InitInstance()
{
    // Standard initialization
    // If you are not using these features and wish to reduce the size
    //  of your final executable, you should remove from the following
    //  the specific initialization routines you do not need.

    SetDialogBkColor();         // Set dialog background color to gray
    LoadStdProfileSettings();   // Load standard INI file options (including MRU)

    // Register the application's document templates.  Document templates
    //  serve as the connection between documents, frame windows and views.

    CSingleDocTemplate* pDocTemplate;
    pDocTemplate = new CSingleDocTemplate(
        IDR_MAINFRAME,
        RUNTIME_CLASS(CTyssqlDoc),
        RUNTIME_CLASS(CMainFrame),      // main SDI frame window
        RUNTIME_CLASS(CTyssqlView));
    AddDocTemplate(pDocTemplate);

    // create a new (empty) document
```

```
    OnFileNew();

    if (m_lpCmdLine[0] != '\0')
    {
        // TODO: add command line processing here
    }


    return TRUE;
}

/////////////////////////////////////////////////////////////////////////////
// CAboutDlg dialog used for App About

class CAboutDlg : public CDialog
{
public:
    CAboutDlg();

// Dialog Data
    //{{AFX_DATA(CAboutDlg)
    enum { IDD = IDD_ABOUTBOX };
    //}}AFX_DATA

// Implementation
protected:
    virtual void DoDataExchange(CDataExchange* pDX);      // DDX/DDV support
    //{{AFX_MSG(CAboutDlg)
        // No message handlers
    //}}AFX_MSG
    DECLARE_MESSAGE_MAP()
};

CAboutDlg::CAboutDlg() : CDialog(CAboutDlg::IDD)
{
    //{{AFX_DATA_INIT(CAboutDlg)
    //}}AFX_DATA_INIT
}

void CAboutDlg::DoDataExchange(CDataExchange* pDX)
{
    CDialog::DoDataExchange(pDX);
    //{{AFX_DATA_MAP(CAboutDlg)
    //}}AFX_DATA_MAP
}

BEGIN_MESSAGE_MAP(CAboutDlg, CDialog)
    //{{AFX_MSG_MAP(CAboutDlg)
        // No message handlers
    //}}AFX_MSG_MAP
END_MESSAGE_MAP()

// App command to run the dialog
void CTyssqlApp::OnAppAbout()
{
```

```
    CAboutDlg aboutDlg;
    aboutDlg.DoModal();
}

////////////////////////////////////////////////////////////////////////
// CTyssqlApp commands
// tyssqdoc.cpp : implementation of the CTyssqlDoc class
//

#include "stdafx.h"
#include "tyssql.h"

#include "tyssqset.h"
#include "tyssqdoc.h"

#ifdef _DEBUG
#undef THIS_FILE
static char BASED_CODE THIS_FILE[] = __FILE__;
#endif

////////////////////////////////////////////////////////////////////////
// CTyssqlDoc

IMPLEMENT_DYNCREATE(CTyssqlDoc, CDocument)

BEGIN_MESSAGE_MAP(CTyssqlDoc, CDocument)
    //{{AFX_MSG_MAP(CTyssqlDoc)
        // NOTE - the ClassWizard will add and remove mapping macros here.
        //    DO NOT EDIT what you see in these blocks of generated code!
    //}}AFX_MSG_MAP
END_MESSAGE_MAP()

////////////////////////////////////////////////////////////////////////
// CTyssqlDoc construction/destruction

CTyssqlDoc::CTyssqlDoc()
{
    // TODO: add one-time construction code here
}

CTyssqlDoc::~CTyssqlDoc()
{
}

BOOL CTyssqlDoc::OnNewDocument()
{
    if (!CDocument::OnNewDocument())
        return FALSE;

    // TODO: add reinitialization code here
    // (SDI documents will reuse this document)

    return TRUE;
}
```

```cpp
/////////////////////////////////////////////////////////////////////////
// CTyssqlDoc diagnostics

#ifdef _DEBUG
void CTyssqlDoc::AssertValid() const
{
    CDocument::AssertValid();
}

void CTyssqlDoc::Dump(CDumpContext& dc) const
{
    CDocument::Dump(dc);
}
#endif //_DEBUG

/////////////////////////////////////////////////////////////////////////
// CTyssqlDoc commands

// stdafx.cpp : source file that includes just the standard includes
//   stdafx.pch will be the pre-compiled header
//   stdafx.obj will contain the pre-compiled type information

#include "stdafx.h"

// mainfrm.cpp : implementation of the CMainFrame class
//

#include "stdafx.h"
#include "tyssql.h"

#include "mainfrm.h"

#ifdef _DEBUG
#undef THIS_FILE
static char BASED_CODE THIS_FILE[] = __FILE__;
#endif

/////////////////////////////////////////////////////////////////////////
// CMainFrame

IMPLEMENT_DYNCREATE(CMainFrame, CFrameWnd)

BEGIN_MESSAGE_MAP(CMainFrame, CFrameWnd)
    //{{AFX_MSG_MAP(CMainFrame)
        // NOTE - the ClassWizard will add and remove mapping macros here.
        //     DO NOT EDIT what you see in these blocks of generated code !
    ON_WM_CREATE()
    //}}AFX_MSG_MAP
END_MESSAGE_MAP()

/////////////////////////////////////////////////////////////////////////
// arrays of IDs used to initialize control bars

// toolbar buttons - IDs are command buttons
static UINT BASED_CODE buttons[] =
```

```
{
    // same order as in the bitmap 'toolbar.bmp'
    ID_EDIT_CUT,
    ID_EDIT_COPY,
    ID_EDIT_PASTE,
        ID_SEPARATOR,
    ID_FILE_PRINT,
        ID_SEPARATOR,
    ID_RECORD_FIRST,
    ID_RECORD_PREV,
    ID_RECORD_NEXT,
    ID_RECORD_LAST,
        ID_SEPARATOR,
    ID_APP_ABOUT,
};

static UINT BASED_CODE indicators[] =
{
    ID_SEPARATOR,              // status line indicator
    ID_INDICATOR_CAPS,
    ID_INDICATOR_NUM,
    ID_INDICATOR_SCRL,
};

/////////////////////////////////////////////////////////////////////////////
// CMainFrame construction/destruction

CMainFrame::CMainFrame()
{
    // TODO: add member initialization code here
}

CMainFrame::~CMainFrame()
{
}

int CMainFrame::OnCreate(LPCREATESTRUCT lpCreateStruct)
{
    if (CFrameWnd::OnCreate(lpCreateStruct) == -1)
        return -1;

    if (!m_wndToolBar.Create(this) ||
        !m_wndToolBar.LoadBitmap(IDR_MAINFRAME) ||
        !m_wndToolBar.SetButtons(buttons,
          sizeof(buttons)/sizeof(UINT)))
    {
        TRACE("Failed to create toolbar\n");
        return -1;       // fail to create
    }

    if (!m_wndStatusBar.Create(this) ||
        !m_wndStatusBar.SetIndicators(indicators,
          sizeof(indicators)/sizeof(UINT)))
    {
        TRACE("Failed to create status bar\n");
```

```
        return -1;       // fail to create
    }

    return 0;
}

//////////////////////////////////////////////////////////////////////
// CMainFrame diagnostics

#ifdef _DEBUG
void CMainFrame::AssertValid() const
{
    CFrameWnd::AssertValid();
}

void CMainFrame::Dump(CDumpContext& dc) const
{
    CFrameWnd::Dump(dc);
}

#endif //_DEBUG

//////////////////////////////////////////////////////////////////////
// CMainFrame message handlers
```

Source Code
Listings for the
Delphi Program
Used on Day 15

```
program Tyssql;

uses
  Forms,
  Unit1 in 'UNIT1.PAS' {Form1},
  Unit2 in 'UNIT2.PAS' {Form2};

{$R *.RES}

begin
  Application.CreateForm(TForm2, Form2);
  Application.CreateForm(TForm1, Form1);
  Application.Run;
end.
unit Unit1;

interface

uses
  SysUtils, WinTypes, WinProcs, Messages, Classes, Graphics, Controls,
  Forms, Dialogs;

type
  TForm1 = class(TForm)
  private
    { Private declarations }
  public
    { Public declarations }
  end;

var
  Form1: TForm1;

implementation

{$R *.DFM}

end.

unit Unit2;

interface

uses
  SysUtils, WinTypes, WinProcs, Messages, Classes, Graphics, Controls,
  StdCtrls, Forms, DBCtrls, DB, DBGrids, DBTables, Grids, Mask, ExtCtrls;

type
  TForm2 = class(TForm)
    ScrollBox: TScrollBox;
    Label1: TLabel;
    EditPARTNUM: TDBEdit;
    Label2: TLabel;
    EditDESCRIPTION: TDBEdit;
    Label3: TLabel;
```

```
      EditPRICE: TDBEdit;
      DBGrid1: TDBGrid;
      DBNavigator: TDBNavigator;
      Panel1: TPanel;
      DataSource1: TDataSource;
      Panel2: TPanel;
      Panel3: TPanel;
      Query1: TQuery;
      Query2: TQuery;
      DataSource2: TDataSource;
      procedure FormCreate(Sender: TObject);
    private
      { private declarations }
    public
      { public declarations }
    end;

var
  Form2: TForm2;

implementation

{$R *.DFM}

procedure TForm2.FormCreate(Sender: TObject);
begin
  Query1.Open;
  Query2.Open;
end;

end.
```

D

Resources

Books

☐ *Developing Sybase Applications*
Imprint: Sams
Author: Daniel J. Worden
ISBN: 0-672-30700-6

☐ *Sybase Developer's Guide*
Imprint: Sams
Author: Daniel J. Worden
ISBN: 0-672-30467-8

☐ *Teach Yourself Delphi in 21 Days*
Imprint: Sams
Author: Andrew Wozniewicz
ISBN: 0-672-30470-8

☐ *Delphi Developer's Guide*
Imprint: Sams
Authors: Steve Teixeira and Xavier Pacheco
ISBN: 0-672-30704-9

☐ *Delphi Programming Unleashed*
Imprint: Sams
Author: Charlie Calvert
ISBN: 0-672-30499-6

☐ *Essential Oracle 7.2*
Imprint: Sams
Author: Tom Luers
ISBN: 0-672-30873-8

☐ *Developing Personal Oracle7 Applications*
Imprint: Sams
Author: David Lockman
ISBN: 0-672-30757-X

☐ *Teach Yourself C++ Programming in 21 Days*
Imprint: Sams
Author: Jesse Liberty
ISBN: 0-672-30541-0

Magazines

- [ ] DBMS: Database and client/server solutions

  DBMS
  P.O Box 469039
  Escondido, CA 92046-9039
  800-334-8152

- [ ] *Oracle Magazine*
  500 Oracle Parkway
  Box 659510
  Redwood Shores, CA 94065-1600
  415-506-5304

Internet URLs for the Keyword SQL

- [ ] `http://www.aslaninc.com/`

  Aslan Computing Inc.: Specializes in SQL databases, Windows development tools, Windows NT networking, and World Wide Web services.

- [ ] `http://www.radix.net/~ablaze/`

  Ablaze Business Systems, Inc.: A leading Microsoft Solution Provider specializing in Visual Basic, MS Server, PowerBuilder, and the Internet.

- [ ] `http://www.fourgen.com/`

  FourGen: Open systems software supporting Windows, 4GL, UNIX, SQL, and OLE standards.

- [ ] `http://www.indirect.com/www/steelep4/ddi.html`

  Digital Dreamshop: Providers of innovative client/server applications, computer graphics services, and commercial software programming in Visual Basic, Access, Transact-SQL, C++, and Delphi.

- [ ] `http://www.novalink.com/bachman/index.html`

  Bachman Information Systems: Vendor of database design tools for Sybase and Microsoft SQL Server databases and other development tools.

- [ ] `http://www.datatools.com/`

  DataTools, Inc.: Develops client/server database administrative tools, including SQL-BackTrack, a comprehensive database backup and recovery tool.

- [ ] `http://www.everyware.com/`

  EveryWare Development Corp.: Developers of Butler SQL, the SQL database server for Macintosh.

http://www.edb.com/nb/index.html

Netbase: Netbase provides a low-cost client/server SQL database for UNIX.

http://unisql.www.nttdata.jp/

NTT Data Communications Systems: UniSQL. The UniSQL home page is in Japanese.

http://www.quadbase.com/quadbase.htm

Quadbase: Quadbase-SQL is a high-performance, full-featured, industrial-strength SQL relational DBMS.

http://bbs.andyne.on.ca/gql/gql.html

GQL (Andyne Computing): An ad hoc query tool designed to provide easy access to SQL databases in a client-server environment.

http://www.sagus.com/

Software AG of North America (SAGNA): Develops and markets open, multi-platform product solutions in the areas of distributed computing (ENTIRE), application engineering (NATURAL), SQL query and reporting (ESPERANT), database management (ADABAS), and data warehousing.

http://www.nis.net/sqlpower/

Sql Power Tools: Second-generation tools for SQL developers and database administrators.

http://world.std.com/~engwiz/

English Wizard: English Wizard translates plain English into SQL for access to your database.

http://www.microsoft.com/SQL/

Microsoft.

http://www.jcc.com/sql_stnd.html

SQL Standards: The central source of information about the SQL standards process and its current state.

http://www.sybase.com/WWW/

Connecting to Sybase SQL Server via WWW.

http://www.ncsa.uiuc.edu/SDG/People/jason/pub/gsql/starthere.html

GSQL: A Mosaic-SQL gateway.

FTP Sites

☐ `ftp://ftp.cc.gatech.edu/pub/gvu/www/pitkow/gsql-oracle/oracle-backend.html`
GSQL: Oracle Backend.

Newsgroups

☐ `news:comp.databases.oracle`
Usenet: The SQL database products of the Oracle Corporation.

☐ `news:comp.databases.sybase`
Usenet: Implementations of the SQL Server.

☐ `bit.databases.mssql-l`

☐ `bit.listserv.sqlinfo`

ASCII Table

Dec X_{10}	Hex X_{16}	Binary X_2	ASCII	Dec X_{10}	Hex X_{16}	Binary X_2	ASCII
000	00	0000 0000	null	027	1B	0001 1011	←
001	01	0000 0001	☺	028	1C	0001 1100	∟
002	02	0000 0010	☻	029	1D	0001 1101	↔
003	03	0000 0011	♥	030	1E	0001 1110	▲
004	04	0000 0100	♦	031	1F	0001 1111	▼
005	05	0000 0101	♣	032	20	0010 0000	space
006	06	0000 0110	♠	033	21	0010 0001	!
007	07	0000 0111	•	034	22	0010 0010	"
008	08	0000 1000	◘	035	23	0010 0011	#
009	09	0000 1001	○	036	24	0010 0100	$
010	0A	0000 1010	◙	037	25	0010 0101	%
011	0B	0000 1011	♂	038	26	0010 0110	&
012	0C	0000 1100	♀	039	27	0010 0111	'
013	0D	0000 1101	♪	040	28	0010 1000	(
014	0E	0000 1110	♫	041	29	0010 1001	)
015	0F	0000 1111	☼	042	2A	0010 1010	*
016	10	0001 0000	►	043	2B	0010 1011	+
017	11	0001 0001	◄	044	2C	0010 1100	,
018	12	0001 0010	↕	045	2D	0010 1101	-
019	13	0001 0011	‼	046	2E	0010 1110	.
020	14	0001 0100	¶	047	2F	0010 1111	/
021	15	0001 0101	§	048	30	0011 0000	0
022	16	0001 0110	▬	049	31	0011 0001	1
023	17	0001 0111	↨	050	32	0011 0010	2
024	18	0001 1000	↑	051	33	0011 0011	3
025	19	0001 1001	↓	052	34	0011 0100	4
026	1A	0001 1010	→	053	35	0011 0101	5

Dec X_{10}	Hex X_{16}	Binary X_2	ASCII	Dec X_{10}	Hex X_{16}	Binary X_2	ASCII
054	36	0011 0110	6	081	51	0101 0001	Q
055	37	0011 0111	7	082	52	0101 0010	R
056	38	0011 1000	8	083	53	0101 0011	S
057	39	0011 1001	9	084	54	0101 0100	T
058	3A	0011 1010	:	085	55	0101 0101	U
059	3B	0011 1011	;	086	56	0101 0110	V
060	3C	0011 1100	<	087	57	0101 0111	W
061	3D	0011 1101	=	088	58	0101 1000	X
062	3E	0011 1110	>	089	59	0101 1001	Y
063	3F	0011 1111	?	090	5A	0101 1010	Z
064	40	0100 0000	@	091	5B	0101 1011	[
065	41	0100 0001	A	092	5C	0101 1100	\
066	42	0100 0010	B	093	5D	0101 1101	]
067	43	0100 0011	C	094	5E	0101 1110	^
068	44	0100 0100	D	095	5F	0101 1111	–
069	45	0100 0101	E	096	60	0110 0000	`
070	46	0100 0110	F	097	61	0110 0001	a
071	47	0100 0111	G	098	62	0110 0010	b
072	48	0100 1000	H	099	63	0110 0011	c
073	49	0100 1001	I	100	64	0110 0100	d
074	4A	0100 1010	J	101	65	0110 0101	e
075	4B	0100 1011	K	102	66	0110 0110	f
076	4C	0100 1100	L	103	67	0110 0111	g
077	4D	0100 1101	M	104	68	0110 1000	h
078	4E	0100 1110	N	105	69	0110 1001	i
079	4F	0100 1111	O	106	6A	0110 1010	j
080	50	0101 0000	P	107	6B	0110 1011	k

E

Dec X_{10}	Hex X_{16}	Binary X_2	ASCII	Dec X_{10}	Hex X_{16}	Binary X_2	ASCII
108	6C	0110 1100	l	135	87	1000 0111	ç
109	6D	0110 1101	m	136	88	1000 1000	ê
110	6E	0110 1110	n	137	89	1000 1001	ë
111	6F	0110 1111	o	138	8A	1000 1010	è
112	70	0111 0000	p	139	8B	1000 1011	ï
113	71	0111 0001	q	140	8C	1000 1100	î
114	72	0111 0010	r	141	8D	1000 1101	ì
115	73	0111 0011	s	142	8E	1000 1110	Ä
116	74	0111 0100	t	143	8F	1000 1111	Å
117	75	0111 0101	u	144	90	1001 0000	É
118	76	0111 0110	v	145	91	1001 0001	æ
119	77	0111 0111	w	146	92	1001 0010	Æ
120	78	0111 1000	x	147	93	1001 0011	ô
121	79	0111 1001	y	148	94	1001 0100	ö
122	7A	0111 1010	z	149	95	1001 0101	ò
123	7B	0111 1011	{	150	96	1001 0110	û
124	7C	0111 1100	¦	151	97	1001 0111	ù
125	7D	0111 1101	}	152	98	1001 1000	ÿ
126	7E	0111 1110	˜	153	99	1001 1001	Ö
127	7F	0111 1111	Δ	154	9A	1001 1010	Ü
128	80	1000 0000	Ç	155	9B	1001 1011	¢
129	81	1000 0001	ü	156	9C	1001 1100	£
130	82	1000 0010	é	157	9D	1001 1101	¥
131	83	1000 0011	â	158	9E	1001 1110	₧
132	84	1000 0100	ä	159	9F	1001 1111	ƒ
133	85	1000 0101	à	160	A0	1010 0000	á
134	86	1000 0110	å	161	A1	1010 0001	í

Dec X_{10}	Hex X_{16}	Binary X_2	ASCII	Dec X_{10}	Hex X_{16}	Binary X_2	ASCII
162	A2	1010 0010	ó	189	BD	1011 1101	╜
163	A3	1010 0011	ú	190	BE	1011 1110	╛
164	A4	1010 0100	ñ	191	BF	1011 1111	┐
165	A5	1010 0101	Ñ	192	C0	1100 0000	└
166	A6	1010 0110	ª	193	C1	1100 0001	┴
167	A7	1010 0111	º	194	C2	1100 0010	┬
168	A8	1010 1000	¿	195	C3	1100 0011	├
169	A9	1010 1001	⌐	196	C4	1100 0100	─
170	AA	1010 1010	¬	197	C5	1100 0101	┼
171	AB	1010 1011	½	198	C6	1100 0110	╞
172	AC	1010 1100	¼	199	C7	1100 0111	╟
173	AD	1010 1101	¡	200	C8	1100 1000	╚
174	AE	1010 1110	«	201	C9	1100 1001	╔
175	AF	1010 1111	»	202	CA	1100 1010	╩
176	B0	1011 0000	░	203	CB	1100 1011	╦
177	B1	1011 0001	▒	204	CC	1100 1100	╠
178	B2	1011 0010	▓	205	CD	1100 1101	═
179	B3	1011 0011	│	206	CE	1100 1110	╬
180	B4	1011 0100	┤	207	CF	1100 1111	╧
181	B5	1011 0101	╡	208	D0	1101 0000	╨
182	B6	1011 0110	╢	209	D1	1101 0001	╤
183	B7	1011 0111	╖	210	D2	1101 0010	╥
184	B8	1011 1000	╕	211	D3	1101 0011	╙
185	B9	1011 1001	╣	212	D4	1101 0100	╘
186	BA	1011 1010	║	213	D5	1101 0101	╒
187	BB	1011 1011	╗	214	D6	1101 0110	╓
188	BC	1011 1100	╝	215	D7	1101 0111	╫

Dec X_{10}	Hex X_{16}	Binary X_2	ASCII	Dec X_{10}	Hex X_{16}	Binary X_2	ASCII
216	D8	1101 1000	÷	243	F3	1111 0011	≤
217	D9	1101 1001	⌐	244	F4	1111 0100	⌠
218	DA	1101 1010	⌐	245	F5	1111 0101	⌡
219	DB	1101 1011	■	246	F6	1111 0110	÷
220	DC	1101 1100	■	247	F7	1111 0111	≈
221	DD	1101 1101	▌	248	F8	1111 1000	°
222	DE	1101 1110	▐	249	F9	1111 1001	•
223	DF	1101 1111	▬	250	FA	1111 1010	·
224	E0	1110 0000	α	251	FB	1111 1011	√
225	E1	1110 0001	β	252	FC	1111 1100	ⁿ
226	E2	1110 0010	Γ	253	FD	1111 1101	²
227	E3	1110 0011	π	254	FE	1111 1110	■
228	E4	1110 0100	Σ	255	FF	1111 1111	
229	E5	1110 0101	σ				
230	E6	1110 0110	µ				
231	E7	1110 0111	γ				
232	E8	1110 1000	Φ				
233	E9	1110 1001	θ				
234	EA	1110 1010	Ω				
235	EB	1110 1011	δ				
236	EC	1110 1100	∞				
237	ED	1110 1101	ø				
238	EE	1110 1110	∈				
239	EF	1110 1111	∩				
240	F0	1110 0000	≡				
241	F1	1111 0001	±				
242	F2	1111 0010	≥				

Answers

Day 1

Quiz Answers

1. What makes SQL a nonprocedural language?

   It only determines what should be done, not how it should be done. It is up to the database to implement the SQL request. This is a big plus in cross-platform, cross-language development.

2. How can you tell if a database is truly relational?

   Apply Dr. Codd's 12 (we know there are 13) rules. They represent an excellent definition of a relational database.

3. What can you do with SQL?

   Select, insert, modify, and delete the information in a database. Perform system security functions and set user's permissions on tables and databases. Handle online transaction processing within an application. Create stored procedures and triggers to reduce application coding. Transfer data between different databases.

Day 2

Quiz Answers

1. Is there a difference it what 'SELECT * FROM CHECKS;' and 'select * from checks;' return?

   Answer: No, capitalization will not affect the results of the query on most implementations of SQL.

2. None of the following queries work. Why?

   A. Select *

   Answer: Needs a FROM clause

   B. Select * from checks

   Answer: Needs a ; at the end to signify we are done with the query.

   C. Select amount name FROM checks;

   There needs to be a comma between amount and name. The interpreter will expect another keyword after amount without it.

Exercise Answers

1. SELECT CHECK#, REMARKS FROM CHECKS;
2. SELECT DISTINCT REMARKS FROM CHECKS;

Day 3

Quiz Answers

1. Write a query that returns everyone in the database whose last name begins with 'M'.

   SELECT * FROM FRIENDS WHERE LASTNAME LIKE 'M%';

2. Write a query that returns everyone who lives in Illinois with a first name of 'AL'.

   SELECT * FROM FRIENDS

   WHERE STATE = 'IL'

   AND FIRSTNAME = 'AL';

3. Given two tables(PART1 and PART2) containing columns named PARTNO how would you find out which parts numbers are in both tables? How would you write the query.

   Use the INTERSECT. Remember this returns rows common to both queries.

   SELECT PARTNO FROM PART1

   INTERSECT

   SELECT PARTNO FROM PART2;

4. What shorthand could you use instead of WHERE a > 10 AND a < 30?

   WHERE a BETWEEN 10 AND 30;

Exercise Answers

```
SQL> SELECT (FIRSTNAME || 'FROM') NAME, STATE
  2 FROM FRIENDS
  3 WHERE STATE = 'IL'
  4 AND
  5 LASTNAME = 'BUNDY';
```

```
NAME                 ST
-----------------    --
AL                   FROM IL
```

Day 4

Quiz Answers

1. What function capitalizes the first letter of a character string and makes the rest lowercase?

   `INITCAP.`

2. What functions are also known by the name Group functions?

   `Aggregate Functions`

Exercise Answers

1. Using the TEAMSTATS TABLE in the section on aggregate functions, write a query to determine who is batting under .25 (for the baseball challenged average is hits/ab).

```
SQL> SELECT NAME FROM TEAMSTATS
  2 WHERE (HITS/AB) < .25;
```

```
NAME
-----------------
HAMHOCKER
CASEY
```

Day 5

Quiz Answers

1. Which clause works just like LIKE(<exp>%)?

   `STARTING WITH.`

2. Why won't the SQL engine let me SELECT several columns to display when I am only using a few (or one) of them in the GROUP BY clause?

   Because the SQL engine doesn't know what to do with the unique values in the additional columns when it groups the results by the columns specified in the ORDER BY clause.

Exercise Answers

1. Using the ORG CHART TABLE used in many of the preceding examples, find how many people in each TEAM have 30 days or more of sick leave.

```
SELECT TEAM, COUNT(TEAM)
FROM ORGCHART
GROUP BY TEAM
```

```
TEAM             COUNT
===============  ===========

COLLECTIONS          2
MARKETING            3
PR               1
RESEARCH             2
```

Which represents the number of people on each TEAM.

```
SELECT TEAM, COUNT(TEAM)
FROM ORGCHART
WHERE SICKLEAVE >=30
GROUP BY TEAM
```

```
TEAM             COUNT
===============  ===========

COLLECTIONS          1
MARKETING            1
RESEARCH             1
```

This is the number of people on each team with a SICKLEAVE balance of 30 days or more.

Day 6

Quiz Answers

1. How many rows would a two table JOIN produce if one table had 50,000 rows and the other had 100,000?

   A lot of rows, more specifically, 5,000,000,000.

2. Can you JOIN more than one table?

   Yes, you can join many tables.

Exercise Answers

1. In the section on joining tables to themselves, the last example returned two combinations. Rewrite the query so only one entry comes up for each redundant part number.

```
SELECT F.PARTNUM, F.DESCRIPTION,
S.PARTNUM,S.DESCRIPTION
FROM PART F, PART S
WHERE F.PARTNUM = S.PARTNUM
AND F.DESCRIPTION <> S.DESCRIPTION
AND F.DESCRIPTION > S.DESCRIPTION
```

Output

```
PARTNUM     DESCRIPTION      PARTNUM      DESCRIPTION
==========  ===============  ===========  ====================
76          ROAD BIKE        76           CLIPPLESS SHOE
```

This solves the problems by imposing an order on the QUERY. You will only return the result where one Description outranks the other alphabetically.

Day 7

Quiz Answers

1. In the section on nesting subqueries, the subquery used returned several values:

   ```
   LE SHOPPE
   BIKE SPEC
   LE SHOPPE
   BIKE SPEC
   JACKS BIKE
   ```

   Some of these are duplicates. Why aren't these duplicates in the final result set?

   The result set has no duplicates because the query that called the subquery:

   ```
   SELECT ALL C.NAME, C.ADDRESS, C.STATE,C.ZIP
   FROM CUSTOMER C
   WHERE C.NAME IN
   ```

   returned only its rows, where NAME was in the list examined by the statement IN. Don't confuse this simple IN with the more complex JOIN.

Exercise Answers

1. Write a query, using the Table ORDERS, to return all the NAMES and ORDEREDON dates for every store that comes after 'JACKS BIKES' in the alphabet.

Input

```
SELECT NAME, ORDEREDON
FROM ORDERS
WHERE NAME > ALL
(SELECT NAME
FROM ORDERS
WHERE NAME ='JACKS BIKE')
```

Output

```
NAME        ORDEREDON
==========  ===========
TRUE WHEEL  15-MAY-1996
TRUE WHEEL  19-MAY-1996
TRUE WHEEL  2-SEP-1996
TRUE WHEEL  30-JUN-1996
LE SHOPPE   17-JAN-1996
LE SHOPPE   1-JUN-1996
```

Day 8

Quiz Answers

1. What is wrong with the following statements:

   A. `DELETE COLLECTIONS;`

      If you would like to delete all of the records from the COLLECTIONS table, you must use the following syntax:

      `DELETE FROM COLLECTIONS;`

      Keep in mind that this will delete all records. You can qualify which records you would like deleted using the following syntax:

      ```
      DELETE FROM COLLECTIONS
      WHERE VALUE = 125
      ```

      This would delete all records with a value of 125.

   B. `INSERT INTO COLLECTIONS`
      `SELECT * FROM TABLE_2`

      This statement was designed to take all of the records from TABLE_2 and insert them into the COLLECTIONS table. The main problem here is that we used the INTO keyword with the INSERT statement. When copying data from one table into another table, you must use the following syntax:

      ```
      INSERT COLLECTIONS
      SELECT * FROM TABLE_2;
      ```

      Also, remember that the data types of the fields selected from TABLE_2 must exactly match the data types and order of the fields within the COLLECTIONS table.

   C. `UPDATE COLLECTIONS ("HONUS WAGNER CARD", 25000, "FOUND IT");`

      Here, we confused the UPDATE function with the INSERT function. To UPDATE values into the COLLECTIONS table, use the following syntax:

      ```
      UPDATE COLLECTIONS
      SET NAME = "HONUS WAGNER CARD",
      VALUE = 25000,
      REMARKS = "FOUND IT";
      ```

Day 9

Quiz Answers

1. Answer the following questions (true or false):

   The ALTER DATABASE statement is often used to modify an existing table's structure.

False. On most systems, there is no such thing as an ALTER DATABASE command. If there were, this is still an incorrect statement. The ALTER TABLE
command is used to modify an existing table's structure.

The DROP TABLE command is functionally equivalent to the DELETE FROM
<table_name> command.

False. The DROP TABLE command is not equivalent to the DELETE FROM
<table_name> command. The DROP TABLE command will completely delete the
table along with its structure from the database. The DELETE FROM... command
will only remove records from a table. The table's structure will still be left in the
database.

To add a new table to a database, use the CREATE TABLE command.

True.

2. What is wrong with the following statements?

```
CREATE TABLE new_table (
ID NUMBER,
FIELD1 char(40),
FIELD2 char(80),
ID char(40);
```

There are two problems with this statement. First, the name ID is repeated within
the table. Even though the data types are different, it is still illegal to reuse a field
name within a table. Second, the closing parenthesis was left off the end of the
statement. It should look like this:

```
CREATE TABLE new_table (
ID NUMBER,
FIELD1 char(40),
FIELD2 char(80));
ALTER DATABASE BILLS (
COMPANY char(80));
```

The command to modify a field's datatype or length is the ALTER TABLE
command, not the ALTER DATABASE command.

Day 10

Quiz Answers

1. What will happen if a unique index is created on a non-unique field?

Depending on which database you are using, you will receive some type of error
and no index at all will be created. Unique indexes require that the field (or fields)
that make them up combine to form a unique value.

Exercise Answers

1. Examine the database system you are using. Does it support views? What options are you allowed to use when creating a view? Write a simple SQL statement that will create a view using the appropriate syntax. Perform some traditional operations such as SELECT, DELETE, etc. then DROP the view.

2. Examine the database system you are using to determine how it supports indexes. You will undoubtedly have a wide range of options such as were discussed in this chapter. Try out some of these options on a table that exists within your database. In particular, determine if you are allowed to create UNIQUE or CLUSTERED indexes on a table within your database.

   Indexes can be created using a variety of methods. Microsoft Access allows the developer to use graphical tools to add indexes to a table. These indexes can combine multiple fields, and the sort order can also be set graphically. Other systems require that the CREATE INDEX statement be typed in at a command line.

3. If possible, locate a table that has several thousand records. Use a stopwatch or clock to time a variety of operations against the database. Add some indexes and see if you can notice a performance improvement. Try to follow the tips given to you within this chapter.

   Indexes improve performance when a small subset of records is returned. As queries return larger portions of a table's records, the performance improvement gained by using indexes becomes negligible. In fact, there are situations where using indexes can actually slow queries down.

Day 11

Quiz Answers

1. When nesting transactions, issuing a ROLLBACK TRANSACTION command will cancel the current transaction and roll the batch of statements back into the upper-level transaction. True or false?

   When nesting transactions, any rollback of a transaction cancels all of the transactions currently in progress. The effect of all of the transactions will not truly be saved until the outer transaction has been committed.

2. Savepoints can be used to "save off" portions of a transaction (true or false).

   True. Savepoints enable the programmer to "save off" statements within a transaction. If desired, the transaction can then be rolled back to this save_point instead of to the beginning of the transaction.

Day 12

Quiz Answers

1. What is wrong with the following statement:

   `SQL> GRANT CONNECTION TO DAVID;`

   There is no CONNECTION role. The proper syntax would be

   `SQL> GRANT CONNECT TO DAVID;`

2. True or False: Dropping a user will cause all objects owned by that user to be dropped as well.

   This is true only if the DROP USER user_name CASCADE statement is executed. The CASCADE option tells the system to drop all objects owned by the user as well as that user.

Exercise Answers

1. Experiment with your database system's security by creating a table and by creating a user. Experiment with this user by giving it different privileges and then taking them away.

   This is the best way to learn the intricacies of the GRANT, REVOKE, CREATE USER, and DROP USER command. If you own a new version of your product, it might have a graphical interface to its security features. These graphical interfaces greatly improve the system security process. Instead of you having to type in command after command, all of the information required can be found within a dialog box or simple windowing application.

Day 13

Quiz Answers

1. Decide whether the following statements are true or false:

   a. The use of the word SQL in Oracle's PL-SQL and Microsoft/Sybase's Transact SQL implies that these products are fully compliant with the ANSI standard.
   False. The word SQL is not copyright-protected. The products mentioned do comply with much of the ANSI standard, but they, by no means, fully comply with everything in that standard.

   b. Static SQL is less flexible than Dynamic SQL, although its performance can be better.

True. Static SQL requires the use of a precompiler, and its queries cannot be prepared at runtime. This is less flexible, but because the query is already processed, the performance can be better.

Exercise Answers

1. If your database of choice is not Sybase/Microsoft SQL Server, compare its extensions to ANSI SQL to those extensions mentioned in this chapter.

   Because nearly all of this chapter dealt with Transact SQL, we did not explore the many other extensions to ANSI SQL. Most documentation that accompanies database products makes some effort to point out any SQL extensions provided. Keep in mind that using these extensions will make porting your queries to other databases more difficult.

2. Write a brief set of statements that will check for the existence of some condition. If this condition is true, perform some operation. Otherwise, perform another operation.

   This operation require the use of an IF statement. If the IF statement is not available to you, this programming logic may need to be written *up* in your application's code.

Day 14

Quiz Answers

1. Answer the following questions, true or false:

   a. Microsoft Visual C++ enables the programmer to call the ODBC API directly.

   False. Microsoft Visual C++ encapsulates the ODBC library within a set of C++ classes. These classes provide a higher-level interface to the ODBC functions. This results in an easier-to-use set of functions, but the overall functionality is somewhat limited. If the ODBC Software Development Kit (SDK) is purchased (it can be obtained by joining the Microsoft Developer's Network), the API can be called directly from within a Visual C++ application.

   b. The ODBC API can only be called directly from a C program.

   False. The ODBC API resides within DLLs that can be bound by a number of languages, including Visual Basic and Borland's Object Pascal.

   c. Dynamic SQL requires the use of a precompiler.

   False. Static SQL requires a precompiler. Dynamic SQL is just that: dynamic. The SQL statements used with Dynamic SQL can be prepared and executed at runtime unlike Static SQL.

Index

Symbols

A

B

bcp (bulk copy) tool, 163
BEGIN statement, 255
BEGIN TRANSACTION
  statement, 213, 316
beginning transactions,
  212-215
BETWEEN operator,
  54-55
BLOBs (Binary Large
  Objects), 174
books, 342
BREAK statement
  (WHILE loop),
  258-259

C

C++ source code for day
  15, 324-336
call level interfaces, 15
canceling transactions,
  217-221
capitalization
  INITCAP function, 77
  LOWER function,
    77-78
  queries, 18
  UPPER function,
    77-78
case-insensitivity
  (queries), 18
CEIL function, 70
character functions,
  76-84
  CHR, 76
  CONCAT, 77
  INITCAP, 77
  INSTR, 83
  LENGTH, 83-84
  LOWER, 77-78

LPAD, 78-79
LTRIM, 79-80
REPLACE, 80-81
RPAD, 78-79
RTRIM, 79-80
SUBSTR, 81-82
TRANSLATE, 82-83
UPPER, 77-78
character operators,
  44-48
  concatonation symbol
    (||), 47-48
  LIKE statement, 44-45
  underscore (_), 45-47
CHR function, 76
clauses, 90-110
  combining, 105-109
  GROUP BY, 97-102
  HAVING, 102-105
  ORDER BY, 93-97
  STARTING WITH,
    92-93
  WHERE, 29-30, 91-92
client/server computing,
  9-10
CLOSE CURSOR
  statement, 316
closing cursors, 273
clustered indexes, 205
Codd, E. F., 5
columns
  fields, 6
  INSERT statement,
    152
  NULL values, 152-153
  ordering, 21-22
  renaming, 32-33
    views, 187-188
  selecting, 22-23
  UNIQUE attribute,
    153

combining clauses,
  105-109
commas, 22
COMMIT statement
  (transactions), 215-217
COMMIT TRANSAC-
  TION statement, 316
communications (stored
  procedures), 274
comparison operators,
  38-44
  equal sign (=), 40-41
  greater than operator
    (>), 41-42
  greater than or equal to
    operator (>=), 41-42
  inequalities (< > or !=),
    43-44
  less than operator (<),
    42-43
  less than or equal to
    operator (<=), 42-43
  null values, 39-40
composite indexes,
  201-202
  UNIQUE keyword,
    202-204
CONCAT function, 77
concatonation symbol
  (||), 47-48
conditions, 28-30
  WHERE clause, 29-30
Connect role (security),
  232
CONTINUE statement
  (WHILE loop), 259
conversion functions,
  84-85
  TO_CHAR, 84-85
  TO_NUMBER, 85
converting units (views),
  195

Add to Your Sams Library Today with the Best Books for Programming, Operating Systems, and New Technologies

The easiest way to order is to pick up the phone and call
1-800-428-5331
between 9:00 a.m. and 5:00 p.m. EST.
For faster service please have your credit card available.

ISBN	Quantity	Description of Item	Unit Cost	Total Cost
0-672-30757-X		Developing Personal Oracle7 Applications	$45.00	
0-672-30873-8		Essential Oracle7	$25.00	
0-672-30474-0		Windows 95 Unleashed (Book/CD-ROM)	$35.00	
0-672-30602-6		Programming Windows 95 Unleashed (Book/CD)	$49.99	
0-672-30717-0		Tricks of the DOOM Programming Gurus (Book/CD-ROM)	$39.99	
0-672-30714-6		Internet Unleashed, 2E (Book/3 CD-ROMs)	$45.00	
0-672-30737-5		World Wide Web Unleashed (Book/CD)	$39.99	
0-672-30669-7		Plug-n-Play Internet (Book/Disk)	$35.00	
0-672-30676-X		Teach Yourself PowerBuilder 4.0 in 14 Days	$29.99	
0-672-30695-6		Developing PowerBuilder 4 Applications, 3E (Book/CD-ROM)	$45.00	
0-672-30685-9		Windows NT 3.5 Unleashed, 2E	$39.99	
0-672-30561-5		C Progamming: Just the FAQs	$25.00	
0-672-30705-7		Linux Unleashed (Book/CD-ROM)	$49.99	

❏ 3 ½" Disk

❏ 5 ¼" Disk

		Shipping and Handling: See information below.		
		TOTAL		

Shipping and Handling: $4.00 for the first book, and $1.75 for each additional book. Floppy disk: add $1.75 for shipping and handling. If you need to have it NOW, we can ship product to you in 24 hours for an additional charge of approximately $18.00, and you will receive your item overnight or in two days. Overseas shipping and handling adds $2.00 per book and $8.00 for up to three disks. Prices subject to change. Call for availability and pricing information on latest editions.

201 W. 103rd Street, Indianapolis, Indiana 46290

1-800-428-5331 — Orders   1-800-835-3202 — FAX   1-800-858-7674 — Customer Service

Book ISBN 0-672-30855-X

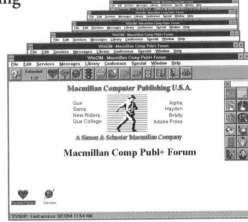